The Study of Religion and its Meaning

Religion and Reason 12

*Method and Theory
in the Study and Interpretation of Religion*

GENERAL EDITOR
Jacques Waardenburg, *University of Utrecht*

BOARD OF ADVISERS
Th. P. van Baaren, *Groningen*
R. N. Bellah, *Berkeley*
E. Benz, *Marburg*
U. Bianchi, *Rome*
H. J. W. Drijvers, *Groningen*
W. Dupré, *Nijmegen*
S. N. Eisenstadt, *Jerusalem*
M. Eliade, *Chicago*
C. Geertz, *Princeton*
K. Goldammer, *Marburg*
P. Ricœur, *Paris*
M. Rodinson, *Paris*
N. Smart, *Lancaster*
G. Widengren, *Stockholm*

MOUTON · THE HAGUE · PARIS · NEW YORK

The Study of Religion and its Meaning

*New Explorations in Light of
Karl Popper and Emile Durkheim*

by

J. E. BARNHART

North Texas State University

MOUTON · THE HAGUE · PARIS · NEW YORK

ISBN: 90-279-7762-3

© 1977, Mouton Publishers, The Hague, The Netherlands
Jacket design by Jurriaan Schrofer

Printed in Great Britain

For Jack and Betty

Preface

When Alasdair MacIntyre and Antony Flew wrote the Preface to *New Essays in Philosophical Theology* (1955) over twenty years ago, they asked not to be identified with the logical positivists and the Vienna Circle, which had stamped the scarlet letter *M* across metaphysics, especially religious metaphysics. I wish to go further than many of the contributors to *New Essays* by arguing the indefensibility of both the Vienna Circle's verification principle and Wittgenstein's attempts to give religious language a kind of diplomatic immunity from outside criticism. With Karl Popper I believe that metaphysics can sometimes be meaningful even when it is not scientifically testable. At the same time, I do not accept the neo-Wittgensteinians' claim that religious language has its own special epistemological rules and criteria of meaning and truth. Positivists repressed the disciplines of philosophical theology and philosophy of religion by declaring them meaningless. But neo-Wittgensteinians have equally repressed these two disciplines by restricting their cognitive meaningfulness to the circle of believers only.

A third school of philosophy that has had much to say about religion is phenomenology. In this book I do not so much do direct battle with this school as regard it has having run out of gas. The quest for the 'essence of religion' – like the quest for the Holy Grail – has nevertheless led to many interesting and fruitful adventures off the main trail. But today talk of finding the essence of religion is regarded as quaint at best. By contrast, neo-phenomenologists, speaking of 'structures' rather than essences, are eager to make use of social and behavioral sciences in exploring these structures. In so doing, they advance far beyond the purist Edmund Husserl.

But there is no return either to Husserl or to the Vienna Circle. In this book I work from the assumption that the study of religion is a joint endeavor to be carried on by theologians, anthropologists, philosophers, linguists, psychologists, sociologists, and many others. This is no outrageous thesis; for even before the attempts of positivists and phenomenologists to take epistemological shortcuts, various disciplines had begun fruitful inquiries into religious structures, beliefs, and behaviors. It is easy to see how astronomy and biology have affected religious beliefs. It is to be expected that in the years to come the social and behavioral sciences, as well as the life sciences, will continue both to challenge and to enrich our understanding of religion. Professionally I am a philosopher; but I join many other contemporary students of religion in holding that philosophy of religion cannot thrive in isolation from the study of religion by other disciplines. When someone offers insight and understanding to us as students of religion, we are now more likely to consider it without demanding that our benefactor present his pedigree. Indeed, the old debate regarding who 'truly understands' religion – the insiders or the outsiders – seems pointless inasmuch as it is obvious that we who study religion today are able to enrich our understanding by consulting both insiders and outsiders, both believers and unbelievers.

Denton, Texas
J. E. BARNHART

Contents

PREFACE VII

CHAPTER 1: PROBLEMS IN DEFINING 'RELIGION' 1
  A. Expecting too much from one definition 1
  B. The problem of an evaluative definition 3
  C. The problem of a diluted definition 3
  D. The problem of an expanded definition 4
  E. The problem of the true religion 4
  F. The preliminary definition of 'religion' 6
  G. Explicating core-concern with finitude 8
  H. Religion and magic 10
  I. Dimensions of religion 11

CHAPTER 2: RESPONSES TO THE CONCERN WITH FINITUDE 13
  A. The response definition of 'religion' 13
  B. Reductionism 15
  C. Rational thinking develops its own problems 15
  D. The issue of objectivity 16
  E. Empirical testing 18
  F. The question of consistency 19
  G. What to do with contradiction 20
  H. On seeing contradictions 21
  I. On protecting one's central beliefs 24
  J. Seeking out threatening challenges to belief 26
  K. Hypocrisy and contradiction 28

CHAPTER 3: THE EMOTIONAL DIMENSION OF RELIGIOUS RESPONSES ... 31
 A. Response to loss and defeat ... 31
 B. Frustration and anger ... 32
 C. The study of covert and overt behaviors ... 34
 D. Preventive religion ... 35
 E. The religion of the insiders ... 36
 F. Religion and separation ... 38
 G. Balancing the need for unity and separateness ... 41

CHAPTER 4: THE MORAL DIMENSION OF RELIGION ... 43
 A. The impact of Positivism ... 43
 B. The problem of moral conventionalism ... 44
 C. The procedure of moral appeal and inquiry ... 45
 D. On transcending convention ... 46
 E. Moral authority ... 48
 F. The interchange between communities ... 49
 G. The gift of nature ... 50
 H. The animal and primitive roots of society ... 51
 I. Sources of social and moral transcendence ... 52
 J. Religious commitment to the society perceived as protector ... 53
 K. Born again ... 53
 L. Theological ethics ... 54
 M. From involvement to moral commitment ... 55
 N. The quest for a rock-bottom ethical foundation ... 57
 O. The risk of involvement ... 60

CHAPTER 5: RELIGIOUS EDUCATION ... 63
 A. The myth of the neutral point of view ... 63
 B. Required courses – A Church-State problem? ... 64
 C. Presenting a variety of viewpoints ... 65
 D. The Religion of the Republic and its 'Sunday School' ... 67
 E. A serious threat to the plan ... 68
 F. Christianity and the Religion of the Republic ... 68
 G. The influence of the Religion of the Republic ... 70

H.	The secular outlook and the Religion of the Republic	71
I.	Conclusion	73

CHAPTER 6: THE MYSTIC AND GOD   75
- A. Mysticism and oneness   75
- B. Mysticism and ineffability   77
- C. Observing the 'inner' world   78
- D. The social construction of reality   81
- E. More than eliminating external stimuli   84
- F. The mystic's 'knowledge' of God   87

CHAPTER 7: CORE-DEPRIVATION AND THE PROMISE OF FULFILLMENT   91
- A. Theology: problem or solution?   91
- B. Perfect being as perfect solution   92
- C. Core-concern and universal reconciliation   94
- D. Reconciliation of desires   94
- E. 'Original' conflict and 'ultimate' solution   95
- F. All perfections are finite states   97
- G. Pride and guilt   97
- H. Rising expectation in religion   99
- I. Teaching people to fall into despair   103
- J. The right to life after death   104
- K. Naturalism and Christian *hybris*   105
- L. Freeing imagination from conviction   107
- M. The sin of desiring to be *infinitely* sinful   108

CHAPTER 8: IS GOD VERIFIABLE?   111
- A. The verification criterion   111
- B. Confusion regarding God-talk   114
- C. Social tolerance does not entail loss of epistemological rigor   116
- D. Eschatological verification   117
- E. Indefinite postponement of verification   119
- F. Infinite regress and empty conclusion   121
- G. Hell – The Achilles' heel of Hick's argument   121
- H. The problem of induction   123

Contents

CHAPTER 9: RELATIVISM AND CONTRADICTION   125
  A. What epistemological relativism entails   125
  B. No universal criterion of truth   125
  C. The method of internal criticism   126
  D. God-talk without theism   129
  E. Contradiction as a test of falsity   129
  F. An example of embarrassment over contradiction   130
  G. The role of dogmatism   132
  H. The pressure of contradiction   134
  I. Expansion of the belief-system   136
  J. Summary   138

CHAPTER 10: DAVID HUME'S THREAT TO FAITH   141
  A. Karl Popper – Opponent of verificationism   141
  B. Hume's position   141
  C. The radical implications of Hume's argument   143
  D. New conjectures and inspiration   145
  E. Doubt and belief   146
  F. Science and religion – Some differences and similarities   148
  G. Faith in rational inquiry   149
  H. Two meanings of 'Rational'   151
  I. From faith to faith   152
  J. From conjecture to conjecture   154

CHAPTER 11: MEANING IN THEOLOGY   157
  A. Careful about procedures   157
  B. The question of meaning   159
  C. Do theological statements have cognitive meaning?   161
  D. Extending the boundaries of theological meaning   163
  E. Theology as a distinct reality   165
  F. Theology and transcendent objective reference   167
  G. The problem of translating from one language game to another   169
  H. Transforming one language game into another   171
  I. Will God-talk talk itself to death?   173
  J. Tillich's transitional linguistics   175

K.	What does God-talk talk itself into?	177
L.	Who are the opponents of God-talk?	178

CHAPTER 12: THE-MEANING-OF-LIFE QUESTION ... 183
- A. More than cognitive meaning — 183
- B. Meaning through a cosmic goal — 184
- C. Meaning through finite sources of enjoyment — 187
- D. Meaning through belonging to a significant group — 188
- E. Meaning through recognition — 190
- F. Meaning through satisfaction of strong expectations — 191
- G. Meaning through a sense of control and personal wholeness — 192
- H. Meaning through a sense of aesthetic completeness — 193
- I. Meaning through orientation — 194
- J. Meaning through service to others — 195
- K. Conclusion — 195

BIBLIOGRAPHY — 197

INDEX OF NAMES — 209

SUBJECT INDEX — 213

1

Problems in Defining 'Religion'

A. EXPECTING TOO MUCH FROM ONE DEFINITION

It is a notorious fact that the attempt merely to define RELIGION has sustained a heated controversy among theologians, philosophers, and social scientists interested in studying religion. Many disputants believe that the issue regarding which of the religions is the ideal and true one is settled by the definition of RELIGION that one agrees to accept. Other disputants, defining RELIGION in such a way as to rule out some of what have been traditionally regarded as historical religions, seem to be oblivious to the fact that they have tried to do with a single definition what their opponents would insist can be done only by sustained and complex argument if it can be done at all.

On the one hand, one writer says that we can avoid confusion about the definition of RELIGION by defining it as Calvinistic Christianity of the Westminster Confession (cf. Clark, 1963: 25, 30-32; 1961: 23-25, 27). On the other hand, another writer speaks of 'the absurdity of trying to pin RELIGION down to a single theology or a single institutional form' (cf. Cohen, 1959). The philosopher Harold Höffding, contending that 'that which expresses the innermost tendency of all religions is the axiom of the conservation of values' (1906: 215), is saying that an individual may be genuinely religious without believing in a supernatural being, whereas social scientist M. E. Spiro (1966: 96) defines RELIGION in such a way as to include necessarily the belief in gods, God, or at least 'superhuman' beings (cf. Goody, 1961; Horton, 1960). Anthony Wallace goes so far as to insist on the following:

It is the premise of every religion – and this premise is religion's defining characteristic – that souls, supernatural beings, and supernatural forces exist. Furthermore, ... certain minimal categories of behaviors, in the context of the supernatural premise, are always found in association with one another and ... are the substance of religion itself (1966: 52).

Still another anthropologist noted for his work in the field of religion – Ward E. Goodenough – is willing to study Marxism as a religion despite its official atheism. He writes:

If concern with salvation is a religious concern, then I cannot dismiss Marxist definitions of it [i.e. salvation] from the domain of religion because they eschew references to spirits. In other respects, I often find it hard to distinguish behaviorally between those of my acquaintances who are ardent Marxists and those who are ardent Fundamentalists (1974: 168).

There seems, then, to be an unresolved problem as to whether the definition of RELIGION is necessarily to include reference to supernatural (or at least superhuman) being(s).

Clifford Geertz, another anthropologist, in his significant book *Islam Observed* seems to use the phrase 'inherent structure of reality' instead of 'everlasting supernatural Being'. Religion, for Geertz, entails 'the conviction that the values one holds are grounded in the inherent structure of reality' (1968: 97). This definition is something of a compromise between the two extremes in this controversy. The one extreme insists on including in the definition of RELIGION a reference to supernatural being(s); the other extreme puts aside the issue of the supernatural in order to insist on 'fundamental concern with values' as the core of religion. Geertz says that religion is the conviction that the fundamental values are rooted in the 'inherent structure of things', which is general enough to include various views of the supernatural or perhaps the views of those Marxists who believe that 'History' (or some other cosmic *Lebensmacht*) is on their side. But this definition excludes some forms of atheistic Buddhism as well as religious humanists. Also it seems to rule out rather arbitrarily people who, while having profound religious concerns, are nevertheless unable to believe that their dearest values are rooted in eternity (or the inherent structure of reality).[1]

B. THE PROBLEM OF AN EVALUATIVE DEFINITION

There is also the problem of the 'evaluative' definition of religion. Freud and anthropologist Weston La Barre (1972) think that religion is a universal malady that ought to be cured. Whereas many others think that religion gives 'meaning' to life, cures 'soul sickness', and renders life worth living (cf. Chalmers and Irving, 1965), Ludwig Feuerbach, defining RELIGION in such a way as to load it heavily with evaluations, insists that the belief in and worship of a transcendent, supernatural God, far from giving 'meaning' to human existence, does in fact both devalue it and subvert human creativity.

Some Tillichians might wish to say that Feuerbach's protest presupposes an 'ultimate concern' that passes judgment on theism. But H. J. W. Drijvers (1973: 57) rejects Tillich's famous notion of 'ultimate concern' just *because* 'ultimacy' is clearly a value term. Despite the existence of 'a bewildering variety of contradictory definitions of religion', philosopher E. S. Brightman (1940: 17) insists that 'religion differs from science in being concerned about values'. This, unfortunately, overlooks the fact that, as J. Bronowski and R. B. Lindsay note, science is passionately concerned with a value or ideal called truth. And some critics have complained that religion has not shown sufficient 'concern' for this value (Lindsay, 1963: Chap. 2).

C. THE PROBLEM OF A DILUTED DEFINITION

What is 'common to all . . . who experience what they regard as

1. The debate regarding the definition of RELIGION probably helped in changing the Selective Service Law in the United States. The following quotations from the journal entitled *Religious Humanism* (4:1 [Winter 1970], 33) are worthy of note: 'Another case helping to establish the precedent that a humanistic conscience is equivalent to a religion has been won'. 'We bear witness to the presence in America of a Religions Humanist faith which includes many young people who are not formally affiliated with any Humanist Church or religious fellowship.' In response to an article entitled 'The Vanity of Humanism', a humanist wrote: 'Faithful humanists are challenged by these assaults to speak and write in defense of the humanist faith' (ibid.).

religion?' (Brightman, 1940:15) A definition of RELIGION which does not exclude any tradition that is already within the general assortment of religious phenomena (Geertz) is a diluted definition pleasing no one. Many who are recognized as strongly religious will protest that a lowest common denominator definition cannot capture the 'essence' of religion. But even the phenomenological quest for 'essence' has had to give way to the new search for religious 'structures'.

D. THE PROBLEM OF AN EXPANDED DEFINITION

Any attempt to expand the definition of religion in order to save it from remaining the diluted lowest common denominator will run into the problem of exclusiveness. To be sure, all definitions exclude. That is what we require of them. But *what* shall we exclude and include? The general assortment of religious phenomena is variegated, rich, complex, and often ambiguous. Shall we charge in with a linguist ax and lop off all religious phenomena that contradict our own religion? The problem here becomes a kind of paradox. If we try to gain depth in our definition of RELIGION, we lose scope and breadth. But if we seek breadth, we lose depth. No matter which way we turn, our definition seems to displease a great number of those who insist that they are religious. Indeed, it has frequently been contended that many people who do *not* claim to be religious are, nevertheless, very religious. This might very well be the case. A person can have an excellent digestive system without even knowing what a digestive system is. Or a person can have cancer without his knowing it. So, it is at least conceivable that a person may be religious without his having learned to so classify himself.

E. THE PROBLEM OF THE TRUE RELIGION

Evangelical Christians claim to know what the true religion is. One such evangelical explains that the origin of religion began, not with the ghost dance or any other pathological state, but with a 'special revelation' given to Adam, who was created in God's image.

The religions of today therefore are descendants of the one original religion, and because of this common origin they are colloquially called religion. If the divergence is not so great as to obscure this religion, people do not scruple to call the phenomena religious. Thus Islam is always called a religion because of its inheritance from Judaism. When the divergence becomes greater, hesitation sets in. This is seen where people wonder whether Buddhism is a religion or merely a philosophy (Clark, 1961: 24f).

Clearly, what this evangelical Christian is doing is taking his own Calvinistic Christianity as expressed in the Westminster confession and using it as the definition of the 'true religion'. He then decides that any other phenomenon is religious to the extent that it approximates the true religion. Judaism is closer than Islam to the true religion, and Islam is closer than Buddhism.

In developing the content of this present chapter over a period of years, I have sent out a number of drafts to be criticized by various scholars and students of religion. It is of interest that many of the religious 'liberals' have protested my using the above evangelical because they regard him as too narrow and extreme. Perhaps they are right – if we accept their own implicit definition of RELIGION, which presumably they do not regard as narrow. But in gaining breadth, does this definition lose depth? Evangelical Christians would say that the liberal definition of RELIGION does lack depth. Karl Barth goes even further by stating unequivocally the following words of religious exclusiveness:

It is therefore unthinkable to set Islam and Christianity side by side, as if in monotheism at least they have something in common. In reality, nothing separates them so radically as the different ways in which they appear to say the same thing – there is only one God (1957, II, 1: 449).

Liberals may charge Barth with being extreme, but the charge is itself either extreme or hollow. The fact is that liberals strongly disagree with Barth and evangelicals regarding what true religion is. Every religious formulation is necessarily restrictive and exclusive in some sense in that it simply does not permit just any statement to count as a religious statement worthy of belief. Hinduism is restrictive to the extent that it flatly rejects the evangelical's claim to superiority or their claim that Jesus Christ is the fullest revelation of God. Hinduism is restrictive to the extent that it denies that Jesus was the virgin born, unique Son of God. Liberals are restrictive when they deny that ultimate reality is as Sankara says it is. The neo-Orthodox verbal trick of defining its own view and commitment as 'faith', while all others are classified pejoratively as 'religion', is self-consciously restrictive. Evangelical Christians certainly see Feuerbach's definition of RELIGION as restrictive, to say nothing of the definitions of Freud and La Barre.

It seems to be impossible to find a neutral definition that, while enjoying depth, will not offend great numbers of people. We seem to be forced to conclude that no single definition of RELIGION can do the job required of it. On the other hand, we cannot simply accept a variety of contradictory definitions, for that would not help the cause of better communication required if the study of religion is to progress. What I propose, therefore, is that we divide the definition of RELIGION into three *kinds* of definitions of RELIGION. No single definition can carry the burden that has been expected of it. No one definition can both set forth the defining characteristics of the true religion and at the same time set forth an acceptable definition to cover a large spectrum of religions. I suggest, therefore, the following three kinds of definitions of 'religion': (1) preliminary definition, (2) response definition, and (3) definition of the ideal religion.[2]

F. THE PRELIMINARY DEFINITION OF 'RELIGION'

Very concisely, RELIGION as defined preliminarily is *concern or pre-occupation with one's own finitude, or with the contingency of the real or imagined finite reality with which one holds himself to be identical in some fundamental sense.* Our knowledge of other cul-

2. I will not attempt to stipulate just how many words a definition must have or must be limited to. Nor will I make any distinction between the meanings of words and their uses.

tures prevents us from insisting on a single view of a person's perceived self-identity. Certain Protestants may perceive their core-concern with finitude in very individualistic terms, whereas a tribal member might not think of his self-identity apart from the tribe. The point of the *core-concern with finitude* (as I will call it) is that one's identity, however it is perceived, is taken to be thoroughly contingent and terribly finite (cf. Moore, 1938: 73f.). The old debate as to whether individuals or cultural structures antedate one another is cursed by the habit of seeing both culture and the individual as static entities over against one another.

The preliminary definition of RELIGION focuses on the core-concern, around which a variety of other concerns, rituals, words, documents, prayers, beliefs, special experiences, etc. tend to cluster. The preliminary definition does not even attempt to define the true and ideal religion. On the other hand, the door is left open for the possibility for various claims regarding the ideal and true definition to be made and defended, for the preliminary and ideal definitions are different kinds of definitions. Hence, the preliminary definition neither dilutes the ideal definition nor requires it to make this or that particular claim. Or, to be more exact, while there is some relationship between these two kinds of definitions, nevertheless the requirements that the preliminary places on the ideal will not be strongly objected to. To be sure, I certainly cannot prove that no one will ever object, but my point is that the preliminary definition can be acceptable to those who happen to be in profound and severe disagreement with one another regarding what they define as the ideal and true religion. No preliminary definition could settle profound religious disputes – which is what some definitions have been required to do. But the preliminary definition as core-concern with finitude can provide a way by which workable communications may be considerably improved and fruitful research may be carried out.

I doubt that it makes sense to talk of a wholly neutral definition, for it is unclear what a neutral definition would be. If the definition that I propose is not wholly neutral, it nevertheless does have the advantage of providing a kind of court in which various disputants can come to explore their differences without, by simply entering the court, having automatically to surrender their religious convictions from the start. However, in securing this advantage, the proposed preliminary definition does forthrightly reject the demand that any one candidate for the ideal and true religion be crowned at the start without critical debate and without gaining a hearing from the other candidates. In other words, the attempt to *cut off* the investigation of *various* candidates to the ideal and true religion must be itself cut off if the preliminary definition of RELIGION is to be genuinely preliminary. The purpose of it is, after all, to open up, not close off, discussion, debate, and research regarding a loose assortment of phenomena traditionally classified as religion.

G. EXPLICATING CORE-CONCERN WITH FINITUDE[3]

The preliminary definition of religion is the formulated problems rising out of core-concern, which is not just any concern. Gautama was not basically concerned with how deep the ocean is, how to make cheese, or how fast various birds can fly. His core-concern (like that of Schleiermacher, Theresa, Muhammad, and others) was manifested in more than verbal responses. It occupied much of his time, energy, and thoughts. It affected and changed various aspects of his life. According to William E. Hocking, 'Religion is a reaction to "our finite situation" ' (7912: 50). But the forms that the reaction or response take are bewilderingly diverse. (Later I will deal with the response definition of RELIGION.)

Rudolf Otto's influential study of religion is in many ways an attempt to explicate the core-concern, although he often fuses together the response definition and the preliminary definition. Tillich may blur them when he says that 'it is the finitude of being which drives us to the question of God' (1952, I: 166), although, to be fair, he does *not* say that concern with finitude leads necessarily to

---

3. The Quaker word 'concern' is used because of its richness. It suggests such meanings as 'involvement', 'preoccupation', 'care', and 'anxiety'. I do not regard the phrase 'concern with' to be significantly different from 'concern over' or 'concern about'. *Core*-concern is the central, predominate, and pervasive concern that characterizes religion at the preliminary level. Religion at this level is the preoccupation with the sense of one's own (or one's group's) finitude.

questions about God. Indeed, one may also entertain questions about God in an abstract way, that is, without suffering core-concern or existential concern (*Sorge*). Freud (1943: 42) is profoundly aware of this core-concern when he speaks of religion as rising out of a sense of helplessness. Schleiermacher can respond with talk of the Infinite only because he thinks of himself 'in the midst of finitude'. He may or may not be correct in saying that the feeling of absolute dependence *is* the experience of God in the self. But he is like many others traditionally regarded as religiously concerned when, in speaking of the sense of absolute dependence, he clearly reveals a core-concern with finitude (1928: 17, 126). Karl Barth, Muhammad, Gautama, or a religious humanist may each in his own way disagree with Schleiermacher's particular response to the core-concern with finitude, but they share with him this concern.

A number of things or situations can evoke core-concern with finitude. Tillich points out that a sense of temporal finitude may arise in the awareness of death, spatial finitude in the awareness that we can be displaced and removed from our roots, and finitude in terms of cause and substance when our effectiveness and identity are threatened (1952, I: 192–201; cf. Oates, 1973: 50f.). Verbally the core-concern may be expressed in such words as 'lost', 'utterly alienated', 'cut off', 'hopeless', 'undone', and 'meaningless'. In agreement with B. Malinowski, sociologist J. Milton Yinger (1970) writes, 'Death is the most difficult and serious problem with which religions attempt to deal.' He goes on to speak of 'religious responses to frustration and suffering'. But this must not be taken to mean that just any experienced frustration is core-concern with finitude, which is probably why Yinger says more precisely that 'religion is an effort to deal with the anxiety that springs from the sense of *helplessness* and frustration' (p. 126. Italics added), for frustration that seems unconquerable leads to a sense of helplessness. (Whether 'anxiety' is an additional factor beyond 'the sense of helplessness' is a debate that phenomenologists and behaviorists can carry out. There does seem to be a difference between simply being helpless and reflecting on the fact of one's helplessness.) If, as Yinger suggests, death, unresolved injustice, the haunting sense of failure, and the feeling of helplessness are universal, then it is not surprising that universally there seem to be *responses* to these concerns (p. 130). When writing of 'ultimate problems', Yinger seems to have in mind those problems that persist as 'continuing, recurrent, *permanent* problems of human existence' that are not conspicuously solved in our empirical existence. Hence, it follows that whatever would resolve all the problems would indeed be what Yinger called the 'ultimate victory' (p. 33). Various responses to the core-concern (with its apparently ineradicable and momentous problems) have promised ultimate victory, although not all have so promised.

Yinger, employing Tillich's phrase 'ultimate concern', seems not to load it with a reference to some 'ultimate reality'. Severe and prolonged deprivation and ineradicable momentous problems bring about 'ultimate concern'. Yinger writes, 'If the food supply is precarious – not occasionally but endemically – its production is an ultimate concern' (p. 35). Both Muslims and Christians respond to this concern by claiming that in heaven the supply of food and drink will be endless. Some forms of Buddhism teach that even the craving for food can be nipped in the bud. Nirvana makes heaven unnecessary. Sometimes Yinger and others use the terms 'fundamental' and 'basic', as well as 'ultimate', to refer to the conditions that seem to remind people of the utter contingency of their existence and the fact that they seem to walk on the edge of chaos and defeat. Even when science and technology produce powerful machines, the possibility of being ruined by the machines' mistakes may evoke core-concern (pp. 70f.).

H. RELIGION AND MAGIC

The debate as to whether religion is or is not magic, or whether it overlaps with magic, has gone on for years, often fruitlessly because the core-concern with finitude and the various responses to this concern were blurred together. It seems obvious that various magical practices have often developed in response to the core-concern. In *that* sense magic sometimes is colored or motivated by the religious core-concern. But when we are focusing on *a particular response* to the core-concern, then we cannot proclaim in a priori fashion that religion (as responses) is magical or is not magical in nature. This is an empirical question to be tested by carefully formulated hypotheses and critical observations. One response may be magic-laden, while another may be relatively free of it. Being overwhelmed with confusion, disorder, a sense of chaos, images of destruction, incurable boredom, or a sense of overwhelming guilt, meaninglessness, or ignorance – these are possible situations and experiences of core-concern. While they are perhaps universal – or nearly so – nevertheless the ways of responding to them are incredibly diverse and numerous, and it should be no surprise to us that many adults and children have resorted to magical beliefs and practices in trying to cope with the core-concern. Indeed, some of the verbal and non-verbal behaviors that may be classified as core-concern with finitude seem in varying degrees to be expressed in the idiom of magic.

I. DIMENSIONS OF RELIGION

Is religion essentially moral, emotional, or cognitive? Is it simply doing one's moral duty, or a feeling or emotion, or the intellectual love of God? Empirical observations reveal that the core-concern with finitude may be expressed in any or all of these dimensions. For example, a severe conflict in one's values (or in the values of one's identity group) may involve a moral crisis, disturbed emotional behavior, and cognitive disorientation. Indeed, the cognitive dimension will invariably be an essential ingredient in the other dimensions, for one must *understand* in at least a minimal way that a conflict has come about. For a cerebral species such as human beings, the emotional and moral forms of existence are mediated by cognition. Those who speak of religion as pure emotion ignore the complexity of human existence even at a relatively primitive level.

In summary, we may observe that the core-concern and the responses to it are emotional, cognitive, and moral (or at least evaluative). Doubtless there are also other 'dimensions' than these three. Which one of the dimensions is emphasized or slighted varies from one setting and tradition to another.

Responses to the Concern with Finitude

A. THE RESPONSE DEFINITION OF 'RELIGION'

The previous chapter distinguished three kinds of definitions of RELIGION – (1) the preliminary definition as core-concern with finitude, (2) the response definition in the sense of responses to the core-concern, and (3) the ideal definition, that is, the response that is cognitively, morally, and emotionally superior to the others. The importance of making this three-fold distinction should become clearer in this chapter and the next.

There are two important reasons for distinguishing core-concern from the responses to it. In the first place, while two or more individuals or groups may have considerable agreement regarding the manifestations of core-concern, they may have strong disagreements on how to deal with it, that is, how to respond to it. It is important to study the various responses of each in terms of his or its own structures and patterns as well as in comparison with the responses of other people and groups. In the second place, because it includes the examination of both similarities and differences among various religions, a comparative study has a direct bearing on evaluating which responses, or cluster and pattern of responses, more fully approximates the ideal religion.

The word RELIGION is often used to refer to one or more clusters (patterns, traditions, etc.) of responses to core-concern. It is here that plurality and diversity in the study of religion come to be emphasized. Two scholars, while disagreeing sharply regarding the definition of the ideal religion, may nevertheless travel a long way together in their research and inquiry into (1) numerous manifestations of the core-concern with finitude, and (2) the variety of religious responses, that is, the variety of ways of coming to terms with this core-concern.

Albert A. Ellis' work *Is Objectivism a Religion?* (1968) offers insight into how a behavioral pattern characterized as 'economic' or 'scientific' may actually function as a religion, that is, as a response to especially the cognitive dimension of core-concern. Craving the absolute assurance that their hypotheses will not be subject to the decay and uncertainty that they observe all about them, some people turn their hypotheses into untestable convictions. As a guarantee of overcoming permanent finitude (whether cognitive, emotional, or ethical), *salvation* is manifested in many styles and forms. A careful reading of Ayn Rand's defense of laissez-faire capitalism, for example, reveals it to be less an economic treatise than a theodicy. It is no theory or hypothesis from which she is willing to draw and formulate observable experiments that might falsify her claims if the experiments fail the tests. Salvation cannot be doubted! For many people, 'scientific socialism' functions as a form of sweeping salvation, and its defense often looks like an elaborate theodicy. Both capitalism and socialism have each its own Dr. Panglosses to give 'blessed assurance' that the Invisible Hand or the *Lebensmacht* will eventually be verified (eschatological verification).

This is not to say that capitalism, socialism, or any other economic movement or view is *necessarily* religious (in the sense of functioning as a response to core-concern). Furthermore, an economic, etc. viewpoint is not invalidated merely by serving also as a religious response. However, there is the possibility of a conflict of interests in that at least two interests are being served more or less. For example, an economic program can eliminate some undesirable aspects of life. But it cannot solve the problem of human death. It can only postpone death. When an economic program begins to be represented as a cure of all core-concern, then it is made to bear a load so heavy that it may cease even to function well as a limited economic program. Indeed, a movement may be more religious than economic even though it calls itself an economic view and even denounces religion.

B. REDUCTIONISM

To say that a complex symbolic system, organization, or movement is motivated or colored by core-concern with finitude is to say that it functions to some extent as a religious response. But it does not follow of necessity that either the symbolic system, the organization, or the movement is *nothing but* a religion. Copernicus, Newton, and many other scientists may have had strong religious motives underlying their cognitive ventures into astronomy, optics, and physics. Doubtless many great minds have been profoundly concerned to prove that the vast universe stretching beyond even our wildest dreams is, nevertheless, 'ultimately' harmonious and orderly. A quest can both be religious in its concern and demonstrate intellectual integrity. What divides religion (as core-concern) from disciplined rational thinking (including science and philosophy) is the latter's tendency to let the cognitive responses to core-concern be challenged by critical argument and empirical testing.

C. RATIONAL THINKING DEVELOPS ITS OWN PROBLEMS

Religion as core-concern has the problem of finding some way either to overcome the threat of permanent finitude or to come to terms with it in some other way. Science, philosophy, and other forms of rational inquiry may have religious roots; but rational inquiry cannot maintain its own integrity and character unless it generates and remains sensitive to its own distinguishing problems. Copernicus had to follow what he took to be the directions and leads of the astronomical problem at hand if he was to be true to the cognitive dimension of his own existence. While the commitment to the value that may be called 'cognitive integrity' is no categorical imperative, neither is it a purely hypothetical imperative. Rather, it involves what may be called the 'logic of commitment'. Very simply, if one is committed to R, then he must, to remain committed, follow the implications of R. Rational inquiry may have a mother and father, so to speak, which gave it birth, and which may even help sustain it. But rational inquiry can never gain its own identity unless it is guided by critical cross-examination, imaginative speculation, and empirical testing of some sort. Out of the core-concern with finitude may very well emerge a longing for reliable and stable cognitive answers to certain questions. But the answers that rational inquiry permits may or may not satisfy the emotional, moral, etc. dimensions of the questioning agent.

The key point here is that the cognitive dimension of human life has characteristics of its own that cannot be reduced to any other dimension. A father may desperately hope that his son is not addicted to heroin; but the cognitive inquiry as to whether in fact the son is on heroin, while perhaps motivated by the father's concern, cannot be controlled or swayed by the father's feelings. The *commitment* to the regulative ideal of truth is distinct from the father's commitment to his son's welfare or the pilgrim's commitment to find everlasting bliss in heaven. The same individual may manifest various kinds of commitments in his own life, but this does not mean that the commitments are themselves the same. Despite his profound psychological insight, Kierkegaard never seems to see clearly this elementary point.

D. THE ISSUE OF OBJECTIVITY

The cognitive commitment to the ideal of truth (i.e., to find the truth to specific questions) does not require the sincere inquirer to exterminate all prior beliefs pertaining to the question he is working on. An open mind must not be confused with a blank mind. Empirical inquiry need not embrace a theory of the tabula rasa but rather a commitment to engage in observations that put one's prior beliefs to the test. Furthermore, an open mind does not necessarily entail that one be either a believer or an unbeliever in X. Nor does it entail agnosticism. (Contrary to William James, agnosticism is not necessarily and completely on the side of unbelief. Indeed, it is possible to regard unbelief as positive belief in a rival claim or way of life. In some ways, unbelief is 'other-belief', which is composed of views and convictions that run contrary to one's own.)[1]

To put one's beliefs to the test is not to presuppose that they will be falsified. The Old Testament represents Elijah as putting his faith to the test just because he was confident that his rival's faith would be eliminated by the test and that his own would remain standing. Elijah is portrayed as confidently expecting a certain specifically predicted outcome. By contrast, many putative 'believers' seem quite unwilling to put their views to the test. They seem sometimes to be saying that they are not confident that their views will pass the test. It is as if they *expected* that their view would not endure the critical ordeal. This, then, raises the question as to whether we can accurately say that they do in fact believe in their position (or in what their position asserts as true).

Objectivity of inquiry is not a question of eliminating one's prior expectations (cognitive beliefs). Rather, *objectivity is the commitment to let one's expectations, beliefs, convictions, or affirmations be put to test.* Kierkegaard's thesis of passionate subjectivity obscures this point in some ways and yet emphasizes it in other ways. Looked at from one angle, his protests against the established Christendom of his time may be regarded as a protest against the failure to put the faith to test. The so-called 'proofs' for God's existence seem empty to him because they involve no 'risk of faith'.

Unfortunately, Kierkegaard is so preoccupied with the psychology of believing that he loses sight of the fact that to test one's beliefs is different from testing oneself as a believer. (To ask whether one really does believe in what he professes to believe in is one thing. To ask whether *what* one believes in deserves rational commitment is another thing.) Kierkegaard seems greatly preoccupied with 'proving'

1. See Paul W. Pruyser, 'Problems in the psychological study of religious unbelief' (1974: 185-200). In this excellent article Pruyer sometimes confuses the beliefs themselves from the psychological states of the believers. The study of the putative psychological state of unbelievers is not very useful inasmuch as everyone is an unbeliever just because he holds to views that are contrary to other views. If you do not believe the statement that I have just made, I do not think that an inquiry into your psychological states will be very informative to either you or me as they pertain to the problematic statement just made.

himself in his concern to become a Christian. Indeed, the question of whether Christian salvation, God, etc. are nothing more than human inventions is not even clearly formulated by him. In *Concluding Unscientific Postscript* (1941: 18f.) Kierkegaard states plainly that his problem is to find the right 'relationship to Christianity', which 'does not raise the question of the truth of Christianity'.

E. EMPIRICAL TESTING

Yet there is a subtlety to Kierkegaard that is not just ambiguity. In his treatment of the story of Abraham and Isaac he seems to gain a glimpse of the position that the only way to test one's belief is to do something with it. Strange as it may sound, Kierkegaard – the author of *Concluding Unscientific Postscript* – had in some ways a more profound grasp of modern scientific procedures than did many of the so-called rationalists of his day. (I will argue in a later chapter that Karl R. Popper is correct to emphasize that science develops only if it engages in test cases.) Modern science differs from ancient science in its emphasis upon experimental testing. Instead of simply classifying phenomena as they exist in their 'natural' state, modern science creates new situations and circumstances in which the phenomena's new reactions may be studied.

Kierkegaard represents Abraham as an individual who would *act on*, or *do something with*, his faith. If God is known to be God only in the act of the 'risk of faith', then as far as Kierkegaard is concerned, passive European Christendom does not know God. European Christendom's failure to act on its faith may in some ways be compared to a scientist who, while affirming a theory, will not suggest any experiments by which it may be tested. Kierkegaard portrays Abraham as the believer who will risk the outcome of his convictions and will let God be God in new and unnatural – even supernatural – situations.

It is a mistake to say that Abraham is portrayed as simply void of all expectations of the outcome of his act of taking Isaac to the mountain – as if Abraham were a zombi or a sleep-walker. However, although Kierkegaard speaks often of the risk of faith and even comes very close to grasping what modern experimentalism is about, he nevertheless pulls back at the most crucial point. He calls upon his countrymen to take the existential leap that promises to bring them into the burning presence of God. But he has not come to terms with the possibility that Jehovah's fire may not come from heaven or the possibility that the next Abraham may walk away from an altar red with the blood of his slain Isaac. In short, for all his talk of risk, Kierkegaard cannot bring himself to subscribe unequivocally to the test of falsifiability. After the drums of existential passion have died down, he stands without having taken the experimental risk of faith.

F. THE QUESTION OF CONSISTENCY

Some interpreters see Kierkegaard as so desperately concerned to receive salvation that he is simply prepared to disregard the cognitive dimension of religion altogether. Indeed, he seems to be deliberately defiant of rationality when he designates the Incarnation as the 'absolute paradox'. It is not simply Walter Kaufmann and Brand Blanshard who find fault with what they regard as Kierkegaard's anti-intellectualism, for such Christians as conservative E. J. Carnell (1960: 154) and liberal L. Harold DeWolf (1957: 187f.; 1949) have strongly criticized what they see as his brazen revolt against reason.

It is one thing to be hesitant in advocating experimental testing of one's beliefs. But when apparent contradictions in our formulated beliefs fall, as it were, in our paths and remain there with embarrassing conspicuousness, then we feel ourselves under pressure to try to do something about the contradictions. Is Kierkegaard, then, simply someone who has lost his sensitivity to contradictions? Is his emphasis upon 'paradox' an arrogant attempt to label a vice a virtue?

W. T. Stace goes so far as to argue that religion, unlike science, makes the bold assertion that 'contradiction and paradox lie at the heart of things'. In short, 'there is contradiction in the Ultimate. . . . In the self-contradictory doctrine of the Trinity they [i.e., the great theologians] threw the Mystery of God uncompromisingly in men's faces' (1952: 8).

Discovering contradictions abounding in religious talk, Stace concludes that religion not only does not feel moved to overcome these contradictions, but glorifies them, calls them mysteries and paradoxes, and asserts boldly that that which is most enduringly real does stand in self-contradiction. I wish to challenge this drastic and sweeping thesis.

G. WHAT TO DO WITH CONTRADICTION

Earlier I noted that the core-concern with finitude tends to have a cognitive dimension as well as emotional and moral dimensions, and probably other dimensions. The cognitive dimension may be stressed more in one tradition than another, but it is never wholly eliminated. This is because human beings tend to *communicate* aspects of their responses to core-concern. They verbalize at least minimal descriptive statements pertaining to core-concern. They may even develop stories that embody accounts of how core-concern has been, or is to be, dealt with.

The line between a purely descriptive use of language and the use of language for the purpose of reasoning and arguing a point is not always easy to draw. This is partly because description is already carried on against a background of beliefs. Indeed, I would argue that even primitive paintings and inscriptions are more than pure self-expression. Animals have a kind of language of self-expression and may even have some measure of descriptive powers. But humans attempt to explain and account for happenings and situations. Religious traditions are riddled with attempts to explain or account for suffering, death, or whatever. Sometimes even the ritual has to be placed in a wider setting beyond simply the local movements of human bodies and the releasing of utterances.

Religions as responses to core-concern have also set forth prescriptions, directions, instructions, commandments, imperatives, exhortations, etc. as a means of guiding people in what was regarded as the proper way of dealing with finitude. Consistency, or at least the avoidance of self-contradiction is, therefore, an everyday, practical matter of not mixing up the directions, etc. The 'logic' that is used in directing the neophyte in how to hunt the prey is the very same 'logic' used in directing the neophyte in the way of salvation. This logic at its most elementary form is simply the avoidance of self-contradicting instructions and directions in attaining the goal or in receiving the gift (of salvation or whatever).

It is not surprising that the verbal expressions of core-concern and the verbal responses to this concern would tend to develop statements that at least appear to be in some contradiction with one another. Some miscommunication at an elementary level is a fact of all human existence, religion included.

I do not think Stace has made a strong case for the view that religion (*every* cognitive response to core-concern?) is absolutely content with the conclusion that there is no final or ultimate resolution to contradictory assertions. The fact that religions harbor some contradictions does not entail that believers have no desire to see them eliminated at least 'eventually' or 'ultimately'. In referring to the doctrine of the Trinity, Stace overlooks the fact that this doctrine was not simply asserted to be a divine mystery and then left alone. Nicea and the other church councils tried their best to eliminate self-contradiction from the doctrine without emptying it of the content that they took to be essential. Most Christian theologians have been only too eager to acknowledge that their formulations of the doctrine will be superseded by a fuller understanding in the next life. Theologians even on earth have returned again and again to this doctrine to try their hand at it, so to speak. Why? Because, among other things, the existence of at least apparent contradiction in the doctrine has stood as an indication of incompleteness and imperfection, and thus has been a perpetual challenge.

H. ON SEEING CONTRADICTIONS

In almost all traditions purporting to respond to core-concern, there have been some people more sensitive than others to contradictions. This point can be broken down into two subpoints. In the first place, not all people see the same contradictions or apparent contradictions. In the second place, some people see the contradictions but are not moved to do anything about them because they think that they will be, or have been, resolved. In his article 'The problem of consistency in Thai religion' (1972), Steven Piker notes that when an anthropologist asks villagers about certain apparent contradictions in their Buddhist faith, they simply assume that '*someone* much more schooled in Buddhist doctrine surely can' provide satisfying answers. Professor Piker explains that

> all villagers and virtually all monks residing in local *wats* feel that there are enormous segments of the Buddhist religion about which they know nothing at all or next to nothing. And in this also they are in large measure correct. This is not to depreciate the villager's literal knowledge of a good deal that is fundamental to Theravada Buddhism. It is rather to affirm what villagers themselves (and rural monks as well) almost invariably affirm when we tell them we want to talk to them about Buddhism so that we can learn about the religion: Go see the truly learned monks in Bangkok, they tell us; they can answer your questions. I should note that villagers and, especially, many of the monks with whom we talked considerably underrate their own knowledge of Buddhism in this humble litany, but that isn't the point. They feel, with justification, that there is an enormous amount to Buddhism – indeed, to Tai Buddhism – which is unquestionably valid but which is simply beyond their experience and comprehension. Believing this, it is easy for many villagers to suppose (when, for example, an anthropologist asks them to reconcile their beliefs in the potential effectiveness of amulets with their belief in *Kamma*) that even though *they* are not able to provide a wholly consistent answer, *someone* much more schooled in Buddhist doctrine surely can. So, 'go to Bangkok and ask the truly learned monks. . . .' And, of course, if such an answer *does* exist, that certainly must be sufficient; it doesn't matter that they are unable to provide it (p. 225).

Professor Piker goes on to note that some of the high-ranking learned monks of national reputation and from Bangkok came to a village to participate in one of the most elaborate and expensive ceremonies, which was solely for the purpose of *amulet consecration*. The villager quite naturally inferred that if these superior monks with honorary titles could participate in such a grand ceremony, then surely the 'apparent inconsistencies [between belief in amulets and beliefs in

Kamma] *are* resolved, but in a way that he does not or cannot comprehend' (p. 226. The words in brackets added).

This way in which the lay villager handles apparent contradictions in his Buddhism is not significantly different from the way that, say, a devout Catholic layman handles apparent contradictions in his Catholicism. On many occasions I have heard lay Catholics express faith in the ability of their priests – or at least the Catholic theologians – to resolve the contradictions. Of course, the question of how far one goes up the ladder, so to speak, in settling on *someone* who can resolve the contradictions will be answered differently by different groups and individuals. The priest may say that, while he himself cannot resolve the contradictions, the theologians can. Theologians may have to turn to heaven for the final resolution.

In this connection we may return to Søren Kierkegaard, who, so it would seem, is prepared to say that no final resolution is required at all. The 'absolute paradox', so it would seem, is an affirmation of contradiction in the heart of the Ultimate. However, Kierkegaard rejects this position because he believes that in the mind of someone – namely God – all contradictions are somehow resolved. 'Reality', he insists, 'is a system – for God. . . .' He explains, 'An existential system cannot be formulated. Does this mean that no such system exists? By no means; nor is this implied in our assertions. Reality itself is a system – for God; but it cannot be a system for any [finite] existing spirit' (1941: 107. The bracketed word added).

By no means is Kierkegaard oblivious to the presence of contradictions that sometimes appear in theological treatises. Indeed, his own method of 'infinite subjectivity' may be seen as in part a response to the realization that theological systems are, after all, infected with human finitude.[2] Convinced that all theological systems begin sooner or later to develop contradictory statements, Kierkegaard chooses to use contradiction as a catapult of existential and passionate faith. I

---

2. Kierkegaard rejects the theory of the Bible as a revelation of propositions that contain no inconsistencies with one another. Even those evangelical Christians who hold to the hypothesis of the inerrancy of Scripture do not profess to extend this inerrancy to systematic theology. Evangelical theologians think of their works as 'based on', rather than simply formally 'deduced from', the Bible.

will not go further into that particular point but rather will point out here that Kierkegaard clings to the belief that the existence of contradictions in any cognitive system is a flaw within the system. Contending in *Philosophical Fragments* (1936) that God 'cannot betray himself', Kierkegaard even appeals to divine self-consistency (p. 44). He rejects one particular view of God solely on the ground that to accept it 'would be a contradiction for God' (p. 19). To those who would repudiate 'the principle of contradiction' Kierkegaard says that their repudiation itself makes use of the principle they try to overthrow (p. 91f.).

However, whether the 'new organ' of 'infinite subjectivity' is the way to deal with the ubiquitous presence of contradictions in our cognitive structures is an issue that must be postponed for later chapters in this book. One of those chapters will consider Karl Popper's thesis that our cognitive conjectures eventually suffer refutation; that is, they come to embrace statements that are in contradiction with basic statements previously included within the system.

I. ON PROTECTING ONE'S CENTRAL BELIEFS

Earlier in this chapter, I indicated that Kierkegaard is not altogether willing to run the risk of testing his basic or central beliefs about God, Christ, and salvation. It is true that he does concede that theological systems eventually grow contradictions in the way that gardens eventually grow weeds. But I am suggesting that amid all his brilliant literary devices, he makes only one rather elementary and protective epistemological move. Instead of asserting that a theological system, or even an entire sacred Scripture, is free of all contradiction, he sets forth what may be called a *capsule* of faith, which for Kierkegaard seems so compact and air tight, so to speak, that it will not let in any contradictions.

In other words, this radical existential Christian offers what he is convinced is the cognitive sine qua non of Christianity. Believing that biblical criticism makes it very difficult to propose a perfect harmony of the Gospels free of all self-contradiction, Kierkegaard nevertheless

realizes that he cannot have a faith or commitment that is absolutely void of all cognitive statements. So he sets forth what he takes to be the irreducible essence of the matter pertaining to the Christ of Christianity:
> If the disciples of Jesus had left nothing behind them but these words: 'We have believed that in such and such a year God appeared among us in the humble figure of a servant, that he lived and taught in our community, and finally died,' it would be more than enough.

Convinced that the precise historical details of the life of Jesus can never be fully secured, Kierkegaard draws his conclusion:
> The historical fact that God has existed in human form is the essence of the matter; the rest of the historical detail is not even as important as if we had to do with a human being instead of with God (1936: 87).

Needless to say, there are many traditions and individuals who do not believe that it is a historical fact at all that God existed in human form. Some deny that God exists. Others deny that Jesus ever existed except as a developed legend. Still others deny the existence of both Jesus and God. There are numerous ancient stories purporting to tell of some divine being taking on human form. In contrast to Kierkegaard, some people believe that while each of these stories – including the one about Jesus – has its own unique elements and idiom, nevertheless none carries credentials showing it to be somehow so distinct from the others as to be credible. Kierkegaard himself does not even attempt to involve himself in the question of 'the canonicity of the individual books [of the Bible], their authenticity, their integrity, the trustworthiness of their authors', etc. (1941: 26). He does not attempt to test out the hypothesis of the resurrection of Jesus by sifting through various documents of antiquity, for he is convinced that through 'infinite subjectivity', or the existential leap of faith, one encounters the contemporaneous Christ.

Yet even subjectivity requires some orientation. A leap of faith has to be in one direction rather than all directions. Hence, for all his attack on philosophy, Kierkegaard himself tries to argue philosophically that it is a better risk to go with Christianity (as he understands it) than to leap in some other direction. But suppose one takes the leap of faith – the move of infinite subjectivity – and fails to find Christ and the assurance of salvation! Kierkegaard is simply not able to entertain this as a real problem. He protects the cognitive content of his case by declining to admit that anything would falsify it. At this point he is like the evangelical Christian who holds that the Bible is an infallible or inerrant digest of God's message to humanity – except that Kierkegaard's infallible capsule is much smaller and therefore much less likely to contain statements that might stand in contradiction with the central statements of astronomy, geology, biological studies, etc.

In a later chapter the question of verification (and eschatological verification) will be examined. My own interpretation of Kierkegaard is that he is open to the possibility of his leap of faith being *verified* in some sense but is never open to the possibility of its being *falsified*. For him, there simply are no genuine test cases that could count against his Christian premises. In every case the 'fault' is said to be in the believer himself and not in the Christian claims. My contention is that in handling the problem this way Kierkegaard is not advancing a testable position but rather is attempting to argue by stipulative definition.

J. SEEKING OUT THREATENING CHALLENGES TO BELIEF

Science in its ideal manifestation is the commitment to seek out threatening and severe tests of its established positions. When true to this commitment, science actually rushes ahead in search of new ways to meet new empirical challenges instead of waiting to see whether some chance challenges will come along.[3] We can readily understand that a person would be very reluctant to have his

---

3. See Robin Horton, 'African traditional thought and Western science' (1967). In this superb article Horton is contending that science *must* – if it is to be science – be aggressive in its drive to falsify hypotheses, laws, etc. and to invent, in the process, hypotheses, etc. that hopefully will be better than the former. This aggressive and creative process goes on indefinitely.

religious beliefs or responses challenged severely, especially if the beliefs have assured him that his utter finitude is somehow not the last word. Many religious responses are words of comfort and assurance. But the aim of science qua science is not to provide either belief or disbelief that one's salvation is secure but to continue the quest for knowledge and truth. Science is first and foremost a cognitive enterprise. But religion has this and other dimensions to try to satisfy. If science happens to satisfy other human interests and concerns, that is, strictly speaking, incidental to science qua science. However, it is naïve to suppose that science has its realm, and religion its separate realm. It is in the cognitive dimension of human life that science and religion confront each other most directly.

Consider an example that Kierkegaard and Hosea could appreciate even if they would use it differently. Imagine a man who is told that his wife is a prostitute. He loves her and refuses to believe the reports. Shall we conclude that because of the husband's profound 'subjectivity' – his passionate love and commitment to his wife – the question of her prostitution cannot even be raised? Can we say that it is an illegitimate question because it is a question of 'objectivity'? Shall we instead speak of the transforming power of love?

Well, we could say that the husband may be transformed to the point where he could accept his wife's prostitution. But it is important to understand what has been transformed. The truth of the wife's activities as a prostitute has not been transformed but rather the husband's attitude and behavior. She is still a prostitute.

However, the plot thickens. The very meaning of 'prostitute' has undergone some transformation for the husband and perhaps for the wife. Previously a 'prostitute' meant, for him, someone who, if married, was unfaithful, immoral, etc. Now, however, the meaning of 'prostitute' has changed somewhat. Previously the word contained an emotive and evaluative meaning of a special kind. Now it does not. Religion tends to bring in emotive and evaluative meanings simply because its concern is more than that of cognition alone. A husband might say, 'Oh no! You are mistaken; my wife is not a prostitute. She could never do that to me!' A believer in God might say, 'You are quite mistaken, God must exist. It simply couldn't be true that he does not exist.'

But *why* could it not be true that there is no God? In a strictly *cognitive* context this question is not, 'What would happen to John if he came to believe that there is no God?' Nor is the question, 'What would happen to Henry if he should come to believe that there *is* a God?' The cognitive question of God's existence is not concerned at all with these other questions unless the cognitive issue has shifted from the question of God's existence to the other question of the consequences of *belief and disbelief* in God. Religion often tends to confuse the cognitive question with the emotional and moral implications of the question. To the extent that religion does this, it manifests a lack of discipline. To the extent that science shows no regard to emotive and evaluative concerns, then to that extent it is considerably limited. But this does not mean that it is thereby *cognitively* limited. Kierkegaard is not always clear on this point.

The cognitive commitment of science may be expressed in this way: 'If ideas are to be used as efficient tools of explanation and prediction, they must not be allowed to become tools of anything else' (Horton, 1967: 164).

K. HYPOCRISY AND CONTRADICTION

In this chapter, I have argued that whenever people endeavor to communicate effectively with one another and are concerned to set forth utterances purporting to have cognitive content, then they will tend to find contradictions to be a source of frustration and irritation. Science and rational inquiry in general actually train people to become more sensitive to contradictions.

Because they usually involve the cognitive dimension, religious responses are also sensitive to some contradictions. Those who think that religion is purely emotional or purely moral in its character fail to see that neither emotional nor moral responses can for human beings take place wholly divorced from a background of beliefs, expectations, and assumptions. There is no way to escape the fact that the human animal is a cognitive animal even in his religious responses.

While certainly more than a cognitive animal, he cannot be regarded as a human person without his cognitive depth. George Herbert Mead (1934) is correct to say that the human being would not be the social animal unless he were also a cognitive being.

Perhaps no more poignant manifestation of religion's negative reaction to contradictions can be found than in the accusation of hypocrisy. While not all cases of self-contradiction or inconsistency are cases of hypocrisy, nevertheless all cases of hypocrisy involve contradictions and inconsistencies. When hypocritical acts are described in statements, they may be seen to be in contradiction with certain other statements pertinent to the acts in question. What I am concerned to show here is that religious responses do not simply disregard contradiction or inconsistency but regard it as something less than ideal. This is not to say that people cannot live with certain contradictions in religion (and in other contexts). The point made here is that religions do show some negative reaction to contradictions.

The Emotional Dimension of Religious Responses

A. RESPONSE TO LOSS AND DEFEAT

The fact that various religions often seem to go to great length to disguise some of their contradictory statements indicates a great dissatisfaction with contradiction or cognitive inconsistency. For at least two reasons people may not simply give up their particular religious response despite its inconsistency. In the first place, the embarrassment, etc. suffered in facing the contradictions within one's religion may not be as painful as the thought of losing one's everlasting happiness or losing the effective response to finitude that their religion promises. In the second place, the believers may think that the beliefs that are alternatives to their own are also not exempted from self-contradiction or are in addition either morally corrupted or emotionally sterile.

While people seem quite reluctant to conclude that their religious views are in 'ultimate' self-contradiction, they seem more willing to accept that even in the 'ultimate' state not all *conflicts* will be resolved. Conflict and contradiction are not identical concepts. If it is more or less agreed that everyone desires happiness (or fulfillment, creative self-realization), then many religions conclude that not everyone will in fact be happy (or fulfilled) even in the envisioned ideal or ultimate state. Even universalists (of whatever variety) concede that some of the desires and interests of each individual will be excluded from the ultimate reconciliation. Not everything about each individual can be saved. To be sure, the part eliminated may be judged as unworthy of continuing, but the loss nevertheless is real.

This is another way of saying that religion serves to teach people how to accept the fact of certain defeats and losses. One of the most favored ways is that of the 'trade off', which says that if the faithful can accept the loss of X, then they will be compensated by a greater gain in Y. 'I consider', writes the Apostle Paul, 'that the sufferings of this present life are not worth comparing with the glory that is to be revealed to us' (Rom. 8:18 *RSV*).

B. FRUSTRATION AND ANGER

It is impossible to nail down one precise definition of 'emotion' that will satisfy every school of human personality. I am here concerned to show that many religious responses to finitude attempt to give direction to the body in its agitated reactions against death, sustained defeat, or other losses which are taken to be core-losses or a 'shaking of the foundations' (in contrast to trivial and peripheral losses). It is sometimes forgotten that much of religious literature is filled with every variety of protest, as well as 'emotional reactions' in the form of weeping or other 'violent' bodily manifestations (cf. Nilsson, 1954).

In addition to offering promises about the victories that can be enjoyed in the next life (when frustrations will presumably be more or less eliminated), religions have taught people various 'forms' of bodily reactions to be carried out in this life. Rituals and ceremonies serve in many traditions as a form of 'meaningful activity'. It would take books on top of books to do no more than describe the great variety of rituals and ceremonies that in one way or another manifest bodily the core-concern with finitude. Their spectrum ranges all the way from the wild and even dangerous ritual (as in the Bali spectacular theatrical performance in which the witch Rangda engages the monster Barong) to the quiet utterance of a calming chant at eventide in a monastery. Some rituals seem to transform the agitation of the glands and smooth muscles into a tranquil dance, whereas other rituals seem actually to serve to stimulate and evoke expressions of intense anxiety, dread, and even terror. In the latter case, instead of aiding the person who is frightened by death, destruction, and his own potential for evil, the ritual appears actually to create or intensify core-concern in the individual or the participating community.

Some people have reasoned that sometimes the emotions of fear and dread are latent and that the provocative ritual merely serves to bring 'out in the open' what was already 'inside'. The justification often given is that only by so bringing it out can the religious community deal with it victoriously. A similar sort of 'transference' and the like is sometimes found in psychoanalysis. Fritz Perls seems to make use of this in his Gestalt therapy, as does Thomas Stampfl's 'implosion therapy'.

> Implosion therapy serves the same purpose as desensitization, but it looks dramatically different. Instead of letting the tantrum, phobia, or whatever wear itself out, this method tries to create an internal explosion (implosion) of anxiety, frightening the patient as much as possible without letting any actual harm come to him. . . . Unlike desensitization, however, the implosive therapist starts at the top of the list, with the most frightening items; he describes them as intensively and fearsomely as he can, trying to terrify rather than sooth the patient (P. London, 1969: 61f.).

Shamans, evangelists, priests, and others have clearly utilized what has come to be designated as the 'implosion method'. They, too, have started with what many people regard as the most frightening item, namely, death or total alienation (whether in the form of hell or banishment from the tribe). I suggest that severe rites of passage, in which youths were often terrorized, served in many cases as a device to give the initiate a taste of what living would be like without the protective structures of the tribe or the community. This does not mean that those participating in such a rite could verbalize this explanation.

In any Christian groups of a fundamentalist or a holiness orientation in particular, individuals have been brought 'under conviction', which was a very terrifying 'implosion' state in which, they later confessed, they were sorely fearful that they stood on the verge of death and even eternal damnation. John Bunyan's description of his own terrified state prior to his conversion shows how various cues, stimuli, and reinforcements were employed to put him in such a state of implosion. Of course, Bunyan goes on to explain that the Holy Spirit was the underlying cause of Bunyan's state of conviction; the natural and social cues were simply, for Bunyan, tools and instruments in the hands of God.

C. THE STUDY OF COVERT AND OVERT BEHAVIORS

The former evangelist Marjoe Gortner has shown a vivid audio film of some of his own Holiness revival meetings. A careful analysis of Holiness meetings in particular suggests that various verbal and non-verbal cues and reinforcements are used both by the evangelist and his audience to bring about what may appear to be at best controlled wildness in behavior. Actually, the 'service' has very strict controls and detectable patterns, rules, and regulations. It is doubtless true that the study of religion has probably over-emphasized the examination of religious literature apart from the overt behaviors of the believers and participants. Professor A. J. Vink, arguing for 'the *methodic primacy of behavior*', says that 'religion as a cultural institution is best approached and analyzed through the behavioral aspects' (1973: 137).

What I wish to say in this connection is that (1) there are advantages to be gained in studying only the verbal behaviors of religious communities and individuals, and (2) there are other advantages to be gained in studying only the non-verbal behaviors. (3) Also special advantages can be gained in studying them in their intricate interactions and interrelationships. The aims of one's research and inquiry will to some considerable degree determine which of these three approaches will be emphasized. There is also the factor of the availability of certain observables as well as the special training of those doing the observing and research.

No dogmatic distinction needs to be drawn between covert and overt behaviors. B. F. Skinner, C. Geertz, A. J. Vink, and anthropologist M. Harris are doubtless correct to emphasize the study of overt behaviors. The research program which I am here speaking of 'directs attention to the *interaction* between behavior and environment' (Harris, 1968: 658). Of course, this interaction is mediated at least by the human organism and other contingencies. In fact, there is no philosophical reason why certain events inside the skull and skin of the human organism cannot be thought of as environment to other 'internal' events. Each internal behavior serves as partial environment to the others.

D. PREVENTIVE RELIGION

How can the intense anxiety-behavior associated with core-concern be successfully controlled? That is a major problem of religious responses. It cannot be denied that some religions seem to have a vested interest in stimulating and reinforcing at least periods of disturbing core-concern. The rationale for doing this is simply that because certain experiences like death are inevitable, people ought to face them with the proper answers and responses. Very recently in the United States an increasing number of courses and sessions have begun to spring up as a kind of naturalistic answer to especially death. What is characteristic about them is their lack of emphasis upon supernaturalistic metaphysics. For example, the entire question as to whether an individual needs to prepare for the next life is not seriously considered. The framework is basically naturalistic with a kind of let-live attitude toward whatever supernaturalistic interests the various members of the course or sessions may have. The primary purpose of the meetings is to help people to 'cope' with the threat and impact of death as it affects their human earthly existence.

Various techniques and theoretical tools are used in helping individuals to live with the fact of death. One aim is to help prevent debilitating reactions to the death of loved ones or to one's own anticipated death. The promises of supernaturalistic religions are no longer credible and effective for a number of people. It will no longer do to tell some widows that they will in only a few short years see their husbands again, in heaven, where they will enjoy bliss together forever. The loneliness, anger, depression, rage, dread, etc. often suffered at the termination of a primary human relationship (whether in death, divorce, etc.) have to be handled without recourse to the promises of supernaturalistic metaphysics. The courses and sessions on death *function* as religions in the sense that they are responses to one of the most prevalent sources of core-concern.

Traditionally many religious responses have functioned to help prevent the individual from being depleted of the means of safe passage into the next life at the time of his death (see Van Gennep, 1960). These religions 'prepared' the individual for death by convincing him that he would live again and that his next life could be either joy or agony, depending on how well he was prepared in the present life for the next. The naturalistic shift on preparing people to go on living meaningfully even after the loss of loved ones has replaced much of the concern for preparing to live in the life to come. Needless to say, those who believe that life will continue beyond the grave are concerned that so many people seem not to be preoccupied with the question of safe passage.

Indeed, many religions which do teach life after death do not dwell on it as much as they used to. Some religions have become much more lenient in what they regard as requirements for entering into a happy (or tranquil) next life. Their metaphysical outlook is something as follows: the movement from this present earthly life to the next is more or less 'natural' unless one has been a vile and evil person. This is in sharp contrast to those who regard the way to everlasting life to be narrow and for the elect few only.

E. THE RELIGION OF THE INSIDERS

In many movements that function in part as religious responses to core-concern, the doctrine of hell has been replaced by a kind of subtle doctrine of 'being left out'. For example, some Marxists have portrayed 'the Movement' as something of a unifying cosmic goal, and the appeal is to share in this goal in order not to be left outside that which is historically meaningful. Many decades ago Carl Becker described well this Marxian religion:

> The Russian is most like the French Revolution in this, that its leaders, having received the tablets of eternal law, regard the 'revolution' not merely as an instrument of political and social reform but much more as the realization of a philosophy of life which being universally valid because it is in harmony with science and history must prevail. For this reason the Russian Revolution

like the French Revolution has its dogmas, its ceremonies, its saints. Its dogmas are the theories of Marx interpreted by Lenin. The days which it celebrates are the great days of the Revolution. Its saints are the heroes and martyrs of the communist faith. In the homes of the faithful the portrait of Lenin replaces the sacred icons of the old religion, and every day the humble builders of a new order make pilgrimages to holy places (1932: 164f.).

In the early 1930s it was not uncommon to find in the homes of Americans pictures of both Jesus and Franklin Roosevelt, each of whom was considered to be something of a deliverer in a time of great crisis. In recent years some students of religion have begun to write more of 'the Religion of the (American) Republic'. People stand, and men take their hats off, when a prayer is being offered or when the national anthem is sung or the American flag is marched by. The Jehovah's Witnesses are not altogether misled when they look upon the governments of the world as rival religions. The pomp and splendor of governmental ceremonies have often served as powerful religious rituals and ceremonies. Some of the Nazi pageants were emotionally thrilling and electrifying. Paul de Lagarde, a major figure in the Volkish movement, kept preaching the 'unity' of Germany and portraying the German nation as a spiritual essence.[1]

During times of transition in government, or when the nation is thought to be seriously threatened, national ceremonies may serve as a unifying ritual pulling people of diverse convictions together to pay regard and service to certain commonly affirmed commitments. There are times of national doxology, when devotion to 'the nation' is set to word or music. Also it has been important for citizens to *hear* this devotion verbalized by fellow citizens. The threat of a nation 'coming apart' evokes in some people intense core-concern, and the national rituals and ceremonies sometimes help alleviate this concern. To what extent national religion is a rival with other religions is a complex and terribly difficult question to handle. I have

---

1. See George L. Mosse, *The Crisis of German Ideology* (1964: 31-33). For a humanistic criticism of nationalism as a form of idolatry, see the editorial 'Foresight with Hindsight', *Religious Humanism*, 8:2 (Spring 1974), 78.

tried to indicate in another work how Billy Graham serves as a symbol and leader of both evengelical Christianity and a kind of religion of 'Americanism' (J. E. Barnhart, 1972; 1973).

F. RELIGION AND SEPARATION

Durkheim and others have emphasized the unifying effect which religious symbols, cues, and reward systems have on a country or community (cf. Nisbet, 1974, Chap. 5). One reason that the Supreme Court of the United States prohibited sponsorship of prayer and Bible-reading in the public schools is that the *form* of the religious worship or 'devotions' would be largely dictated by the majority. While children not of the majority faith could simply dismiss themselves from the class until the religious service was over, the harmful emotional effects that this procedure could have on such children was not disregarded by the Supreme Court members. The attempt of the majority to use their own religious symbols to express a kind of national, social, and cultural unity threatened to produce not a unifying effect but a dividing effect. 'In Philadelphia, in 1844, where practically everyone at the time supported Bible reading in the newly formed public school, a riot broke out over which version of the Scriptures would be read. Twenty people were killed, scores were injured, and blocks of the city were burned.' (Yeates, 1975: 19.) There is little doubt that religious symbols and rituals can sometimes embody, and perhaps even help shape, the sense of unity among fellow countrymen so long as the appropriate symbols and rituals are employed. But if they are not the appropriate or accepted symbols, then some members of the nation may separate themselves from others and unite to attack the others.

Hence, we come to the other side of the coin. Religious symbols and practices can manifest, or be an effect of, a powerful separating factor. Behavioral scientists would do well to focus their research on the separation variables no less than on the unification variables. As Dean M. Kelley's controversial book *Why Conservative Churches are Growing* (1972) shows, many religious groups emphasize their great difference from, and disagreement with, many of their fellow men.

Kelley fails to see that this is not a characteristic of so-called conservative churches only. Unitarians make it quite clear that they are very distinct from those who still adhere to what Unitarians regard as superstitions and incredible dogmas, to say nothing of unenlightened social practices. Many religions regard themselves as in some sense 'separated from the world', even though they may differ greatly on what they designate as 'the world',

So, along with the powerful emotional experience of being united with fellow believers or participants in 'the faith', there is also the emotional experience of being separated from that which is regarded as in some sense inferior to the faith. This separateness is often regarded as liberation or freedom rather than alienation.[2]

Konrad Lorenz has noted that animals tend to develop an amity-enmity complex, in which insiders show affection or protective behavior toward one another and hostility toward outsiders. In this connection, a little gospel hymn provides the following revealing line:

One door and only one, and yet its sides are two – inside and outside. On which side are you? One door and only one, and yet, its sides are two. I'm on the inside. On which side are you?

Some religions are willing to 'adopt' new members from the outside so long as those adopted are themselves willing to adopt the ways and beliefs of the insiders. But this may or may not entail respectful treatment of outsiders who refuse to be adopted. Ambivalence toward outsiders remains at the very heart of the teaching of the Jesus of the Gospels. On the one hand he urges his disciples to love their enemies; on the other hand he represents God as sometimes willing to cast his own enemies into outer darkness. (I will ignore here the heated debate regarding what 'the real Jesus' believed.)

The American experiment in religious pluralism has exemplified this conflict between freedom for one's own faith and freedom for outsiders. Relevant to this conflict, a hypothesis worthy of further development and testing is the one which states that many Americans

2. John Stuart Mill's famous essay *On Liberty* stresses diversity and separateness more than unity. From a utilitarian point of view, both unity and separateness are to be evaluated by their consequences and are not to be judged as either good or bad in themselves as such.

participate in two faiths or religions. They may, on the one hand, be Baptists, Lutherans, Unitarians, Catholics, or even members of an Eastern religion. But, in addition, they may adhere to the Religion of the Republic, which has as one of its most fundamental articles the doctrine of religious liberty. To be sure, just as not all Presbyterians are strongly committed Presbyterians, so not all adherents to the Religion of the Republic are steady and consistent in their devotion to religious liberty. I suggest that in some cases a revival of commitment to religious liberty comes about during something of a core-concern crisis in which citizens vaguely foresee what a nasty, brutish, and short existence they might have if the principle of religious toleration should be disregarded by everyone. For many people, the commitment to respect the right of others to live their own faith lies somewhere between short-term expediency and long-term principle. Some profound conceptual analysis would be required before behavioral scientists could develop useful questions and tests to determine what sort of behaviors are associated lawfully with the commitment to religious liberty.

The Religion of the Republic seems to be moving in the direction of encouraging more restraint in punishing criminals and children. Billy Graham – positioned at the more conservative end of the continuum of the Religion of the Republic – was speaking the old dialect when he recommended castration for rapists. The protests that he encountered immediately showed him that he was conspicuously out of step with most other leaders of the Religion of the Republic, and he retracted his statement with apparently no more deliberative thought than that which went into making the original statement about castration.

The 'authority' of the Religion of the Republic is respected by so significant a voice as Billy Graham. Indeed, he may himself be regarded as one of the leading voices in this religion (cf. Streiker and Strober, 1972); but as is often true, a leader cannot lead in just any direction he pleases, especially when leadership has to be shared by many others.

G. BALANCING THE NEED FOR UNITY AND SEPARATENESS

What I am suggesting (for possible future behavioral research programs in religion) is this: The Religion of the Republic (which may even begin taking on more international traits) is a wide circle that includes numerous smaller circles, which are the various religious denominations and movements. Within each of these circles are participants who seem to understand in varying degrees that the *freedom and distinctiveness* of their own circle stands a better chance of survival if the wider circle exists to protect them all from each other and from unknown and underground enemies.

However, this model or analogy is misleading in some important ways if it suggests that every ingredient of each religious circle is an intrinsic part of the large circle called the Religion of the Republic. And yet every ingredient of each religion is in some sense an ingredient of the Religion of the Republic. I suggest that this apparent paradox can be resolved in the following way, using baptism as an example. Baptists and certain others practice adult baptism by immersion. In accepting this practice into its circle, the Religion of the Republic does not thereby declare it to be the universally valid form of baptism for Christians; nor does it deny that it is the valid form. Rather the Religion of the Republic accepts adult immersion as legally legitimate for Baptists and others of similar convictions both to practice and to recommend for others. (Historians have to remind us now and then that baptism by immersion was once regarded as a perverted act and even a criminal act.)

Now in the minds of many, making something legally legitimate comes close to making it *theologically* legitimate. Indeed, some people, translating it theologically, think that such 'acceptance' entails that the Religion of the Republic is advocating the position that it is *theologically sound* for Baptists to practice immersion, Presbyterians to practice pouring or sprinkling, and Quakers to practice neither. There is also the tendency among some to think that to regard a practice or belief as legally permitted is synonymous with regarding it as *morally* permitted. Indeed, as sociologist Phillip E. Hammond (1974: 129) notes, as the U.S. Supreme Court began to provide *explanations* for its decisions, the pressure was created to force it to justify its legal decisions *morally*. This raises the complex issue of legislating morality and religion.

It raises also the question as to whether the Religion of the Republic has a moral dimension – like any other religion. If it does, then it is important to explore what happens to freedom of religion (in its moral domain) when the Religion of the Republic uses its legal power to override the moral convictions of other religions? We turn now to a new chapter to consider briefly the moral dimension of religion. It is imperative to keep in mind that while we may talk in sequence of the cognitive, emotional, and moral dimensions of religion, nevertheless they do not come neatly sorted out for us to examine. Furthermore, these dimensions affect and express each other in a variety of ways. For example, while the mark of bad thinking or bad moral behavior is not shame, embarrassment, or guilt, nevertheless such an emotional reaction as shame or embarrassment will often affect someone who thinks he is contradicting himself, or guilt will plague someone who believes he has acted immorally. Indeed, it is very difficult to speak of morality as a human phenomenon apart from its emotional settings and consequence. And despite the theory of emotivism, a purely non-cognitive morality does not seem possible.

The emotive and emotional dimension of religion has many more threads in its cloth than this exploratory chapter has indicated. Some of the themes begun in this chapter will be expanded in Chapters 6 and 7.

4

The Moral Dimension of Religion

A. THE IMPACT OF POSITIVISM

Some recent writers tend to define religion solely in terms of morality. Even Phillip Hammond (1974: 119) seems to conceive of religion exclusively in terms of 'moral architecture'. Because of some of the misleading efforts of the positivists, a number of twentieth-century thinkers developed the habit of telling themselves that they had outgrown all metaphysical speculations, whereas in fact they were only moving from one metaphysical scheme to another. In most cases they were even working against the background of two or more such schemes. Indeed, by identifying religion exclusively with certain supernaturalistic metaphysical schemes, some of these writers assumed that they had outgrown both religion and metaphysics. Others, no less under the influence of positivism, sought nevertheless to hold on to religion by identifying it exclusively with morality without so much as a hint of metaphysics.

Emotivism, which accompanied the rise of positivism, tried to reduce both religion and morality to emotion, which was regarded as divorced from cognition. Hence the talk of emotivism as non-cognitive ethics. Emotovists treated 'attitudes' as if they were in stances of pristine phenomenological essence free of all cognitive coloring. I will hold that while morality is not purely cognitive, neither is it purely non-cognitive. It *necessarily* joins cognitive and non-cognitive elements.

There is profound truth in Alasdair MacIntyre's observation that 'men first of all lost any over-all social agreement as to what is the right way to live together, and so ceased to be able to make sense of any [theological] claims to moral authority' (1967: 54). However, this must not be taken to mean that people first modified their morality and only afterwards modified their theology or metaphysics. In another book MacIntyre writes, 'Nor can I look to human nature as a neutral [moral] standard, asking which form of social and moral life will give it the most adequate expression. For each form of life carries with it its own picture of human nature. The choice of a form of life and the choice of a view of human nature go together' (1966: 268). The process of change in morality and theology has been complex, for morality and theology had been entwined for centuries. The likelihood that morality would undergo some change was due considerably to the development of a somewhat new intellectual and technological climate. Indeed, many technological and intellectual developments grew into and out of one another. My point is that cultural moves are more like an awkward octopus than a two-legged pacer who neatly places one foot forward before following with the next.

B. THE PROBLEM OF MORAL CONVENTIONALISM

In his excellent article 'A theological approach to moral rights' (1974), Professor Joseph Allen argues that throughout the Bible the rights and special considerations that individuals enjoy 'are inseparably connected with and discerned in certain social relationships or past transactions, imbedded in a concrete social history'. Furthermore, in contrast to 'secular theorists of natural rights', 'biblical and Christian sources . . . have often rooted the rights belonging to all persons in the divine law, which is portrayed as a historical transaction between God and his children' (p. 126).

Professor Allen then adds that 'the symbols of divine law and covenant can be demythologized in ways that see general rights as having meaning only within a social context' (p. 127). Following this suggestion, one might conclude that the authority which bestows rights is the community, which naturally raises the issue of cultural or social relativism in ethics. Allen wishes to disassociate himself from the view that 'all moral rights are simply conventional', for he fears that if the community should fail to bestow a right on a group of human beings, then the individuals would have no recourse, no higher moral appeal than the community itself.

However, the same problem of conventionalism exists for those who appeal to a theological solution. In *Euthyphro* (XII, 10) Plato portrays Socrates as raising the profound question, 'Do the gods love piety because it is pious, or is it pious because they love it?' In other words, Is the definition of piety simply a matter of the convention of the gods? In the book of Genesis, Abraham is represented as reasoning with God about the latter's behavior: 'Far be it from thee to do such a thing, to slay the righteous with the wicked, so that the righteous fare as the wicked! Far be that from thee! Shall not the Judge of all the earth do right?' (Gen. 18:25 *RSV*).

It would seem that Abraham is here not reasoning as a hypercalvinist, who holds that whatever God does is good simply because he does it. Rather Abraham's reasoning is as follows: because the indiscriminate killing of at least righteous people is morally wrong, we may expect that surely the Lord will not engage in such killing. Here we have the odd situation in which the Judge of the earth seems himself on the verge of not living up to moral expectation. He is on the verge of committing an atrocity. It is as if he were about to step outside all community relationships and moral regulations in order to take revenge on his enemies. It is as if Abraham were trying to socialize or civilize him, to restrain him from simply setting up his own arbitrary standard or convention.

C. THE PROCEDURE OF MORAL APPEAL AND INQUIRY

The question comes up as to where to appeal when God has presumably spoken. When the U.S. Supreme Court speaks, there is no higher legal court in the nation. But this does not entail that there is no *moral* appeal superior to the Supreme Court. Some theists may think it irreverent to ask to see the process by which God arrives at his final moral decisions. It is supposed that God simply knows everything at once, which is to say that he goes through no procedures, or at least none which mere mortals could understand.

Some shamans, political leaders, judges, priests, etc. have always wanted to function behind closed doors, which is the mortal equivalent to 'the secret councils of God'. One way of viewing the process of 'secularization' is to see it as the opposite of the process of 'mystification'. The secularization process tends to look behind the temple veil, the closed doors, and the secret councils. If viewed in this way, secularization need not be regarded as irreligious but as simply in opposition to mystification, whether in government, in certain religious responses, or in management procedures.

Numerous societies have portrayed in story form how their regulatory social principles and moral codes were received from the hand or mouth of the deity or the gods. Outside the society the stories were not readily believed; but inside, the tendency was to feel shame and guilt for raising the question of the validity of the stories. Indeed, even in so-called secular America the public school system on the whole is quite ambivalent about its task of teaching students the procedures and processes by which the Bill of Rights and other regulatory principles developed. The degree of fiction taught in 'civics' and 'government' is high, and the degree of critical inquiry very low. Demythologizing 'the Religion of the Republic' (Sidney E. Mead) is no less disturbing an undertaking than demythologizing the sacred Scripture (cf. Smith, 1970).

D. ON TRANSCENDING CONVENTION

If a judge in a community, tribe, or society does not draw his conclusions from divine dictates, then do his sources reside in the community itself? It is a mistake to think of the community as simply the people of a vicinity who happen to be alive on a given Wednesday afternoon. As Joseph Allen suggests, it is 'imbedded in a concrete social history' (1974: 126). What bothers Allen, however, is the question of how a community ever rises morally above itself. He writes:

> If all rights were merely conventional, then a society would be entirely justified in not adopting the convention, and in its absence no individual would have any basis for claiming that anyone owed him any special consideration on any occasion. But on the

contrary, where a society does not recognize basic human rights we think it justifiable to protest that it should do so. Any such protest that claims to be valid against that society must appeal to more than convention in any ordinary sense (p. 127).

The theory of a heavenly Lawgiver has been used in the attempt to 'transcend' the conventional voice of the community. The voice of a transcendent God is thought to be a stopping point beyond which no further appeal is possible.

However, as the Calvinists themselves have been forced to spell out, *theology cannot really lift morality above convention.* Rather, Calvinists assure us that morality rests squarely on the convention of the sovereign God. Calvinism in its boldest form, following the logic of its premises, asserts that some people simply accept God's preferences and some simply do not. Those who do not will suffer the consequences. This is not simply a morality of 'might makes right' but rather is a morality of '*supreme* might makes right'.

Leaving aside the issue of predestination, one might ask, Why should God's conventions be accepted? The answer often comes in terms of alleged consequences. God rewards those who comply and punishes those who do not.

But the evaluation of consequences themselves presupposes a prior interest, desire, or preference. A number of Christians and other theists do not seem to grasp that they must deal with the 'naturalistic fallacy' when they say that God's will is good. To raise again Plato's question and to revise it in a somewhat different setting. *Does God do and decree the good because it is good, or is it good because he does it and decrees it?* Plato still insists on a transcendent good that would *transcend all conventionality, even God's convention.* Hence the Form Goodness, which usually in Plato's works is distinct from God. But Plato, too, faces the naturalistic fallacy. If one asks, 'Why should I commit myself to this Goodness?', Plato can only say that the wise and virtuous person will do it. But this is to beg the question by failing to deal boldly with the question, 'Why should I be wise and virtuous?' Is, then, the appeal to wisdom an appeal to *prudence*? Plato is so eager to talk about the eternal Good itself that he loses sight of the question of why anyone should be interested in it. Or, to be more exact, Plato thinks that once one has glimpsed the Good, he will desire it above all else. Metaethical analysis, however, has pretty well shown this sort of argument to be tautological: 'The Good is that which is desired above all else.' But if we ask what is that which we desire above all else we are given a stone, or rather a word – 'the Good'.

Plato must face also the question of the relationship between the Good and everyday practical moral behavior. The Philosopher-King was supposed to resolve that problem, but eventually Plato began to doubt that such a being would emerge. The messianism in Plato's earlier thought has been largely ignored by many Platonists, although it seems evident that he was deeply concerned with the question of transcendence. He feared very much that his society would fragment and pass into chaos. In the end, the Philosopher-King proved to be almost as transcendent as the eternal Good itself. (One cannot help but compare this to the notion of the transcendent God of Christianity who had to send his Son as mediator.) Apparently Plato regarded Socrates to be the best candidate for becoming the Philosopher-King, but Socrates died without setting up a kingdom or republic, and Plato could not bring himself to believe that Socrates would return to earth again a second time.

E. MORAL AUTHORITY

Professor Allen (1974), we recall, says that 'where a society does not recognize basic human rights we think it justifiable to protest that it should do so'. But Allen is speaking from an advantageous position, namely, from within a society that already thinks it justifiable to protest until basic rights are respected. Not only that, the very society in which he lives and moves has taught him to designate certain things as 'basic human rights'.

Still the crucial question to be asked of the conventionalists is this: Upon what authority does the community or society designate anything to be a right? Or upon what authority does someone within a society protest against what he regards as society's failure to recognize a certain claim as a 'basic human right'? Conventionalists have sometimes obfuscated and confused this significant question. I should like to make a few comments that will at least point in the direction where a more adequate answer might be found.

First, borrowing some leads from Henri Bergson (1956), I suggest that it is the dynamic and open society which makes it possible for individuals to begin protesting and to begin seeking to justify human claims that were never before justified within the society. In other words, dynamic and open societies tend to enjoy a good measure of self-transcendence, which is often sufficient to make a change in morality more likely. Those who insist that a supernatural, transcendent moral authority is required to make any advance in morality are often willing to concede that moral *deterioration* is possible without a supernatural, transcendent source. However, in order to escape this intellectual inconsistency, they sometimes feel that they must add that Satan (or the like) is the supernatural, transcendent authority of all immorality. But this drastic step takes morality completely out of the natural-cultural realm and turns human moral existence into a kind of play of shadows reflecting moral interaction on the transcendent, supernatural scene.

F. THE INTERCHANGE BETWEEN COMMUNITIES

Second, there is the empirical fact that societies, tribes, and families have for thousands of centuries been crossing paths and encountering one another. Each time a human group meets another having a history and culture somewhat different from its own it has the occasion to transcend itself. It would seem that those theists who insist that morality could never progress in any way without some special intervention from the wholly transcendent God have still much to learn from anthropology, social psychology, and other behavioral or social sciences, to say nothing of family relations. Even a child, once he had learned the most elementary concept of fairness in continuing a game that he and others have hit upon, will extend the concept and use it for himself and his group year after year. Given centuries of human interaction, it is no great mystery that in time, and under diverse conditions, various extensions of 'fairness' would come about. This process has not stopped to this day. Fifteen years ago, for example, the idea of guaranteed annual income was not seriously considered a 'right'. Today, however, an increasing number of people have come to speak of it as a live option. For many people the fundamental objection to it lies in the belief that it is not economically or materially *possible* to have such a program. Beyond this, no 'moral' objections are raised.

The Hippocratic oath is a major breakthrough in the codification of professional ethics. Long before the rise of Christianity, this oath formalized the imperative to provide healing for even one's enemies. This moral mutation, which has survived many centuries, was not the result of special divine revelation but rather the result of a number of contingencies, one of which was simply the physician's concern to practice his art without having to become embroiled in partisan and political controversy. Those physicians who did not find reinforcing the burden of choosing who was and was not worthy of healing were able to institutionalize their preference over the preference of those who mixed medicine with politics and intrigue. My thesis here is that this is something like the procedure that many other moral regulations and codes followed in becoming a part of the social and cultural fabric.

G. THE GIFT OF NATURE

Third, what is missing thus far in the attempt to deal with the above debate over moral conventionalism is the fact that individual human organisms have *desires*. It is in desire that conventionality is partially transcended. One must say 'partially' because even the community helps to mold, shape, and even produce desires in the individual. Taking this significant qualification into account, we still may conclude that the human physical organism does transcend convention and society. That is, it has roots in nature, which is a physical system existing prior to human society. Without a physical organism in which desires and satisfaction arise, there could be no society, no culture, no conventional moral rules. Furthermore, there are certain characteristics of nature which, in their vast scope and complexity, provide any and every human society with both necessary resources and limitations for development.

This is not to argue that 'human nature' is a primordial 'given' that society simply receives ready-made from nature. Rather, each human organism is raw material with genetic potential and limits; and the society, along with the forces and contingencies of nature, conspires to transform a cerebral infant into eventually a human person.

H. THE ANIMAL AND PRIMITIVE ROOTS OF SOCIETY

The more we learn of the behavior of primates and other animals the more we come to see that society as such has deep and ancient roots. Primates monitor and cue each other in such a way as to obtain responsible behavior from individual members of the troop. Even wolves show affection and family devotion. And despite the fact that they have had no Moses to give them a divine injunction against killing, it is rare indeed for one wolf to kill another even though wolves have lethal built-in weapons. In the evolutionary process the wolves that had no biological check against aggression toward members of their own pack simply reduced their own population.

The human species is still an evolutionary test case, so to speak. Some societies have developed ways of reinforcing peaceful and cooperative behavior; others have done so only to a lesser degree. Criticizing the writings of Konrad Lorenz, Robert Ardrey, Desmond Morris, and Raymond Dart in the debate over human aggression, Alexander Alland, Jr. (1972), and Robert Claiborne (1974) have recently argued that the adaptable human species is capable of developing cultural and institutional cues and reinforcers that make for mutual aid and peace as well as war. War is no more 'natural' than 'unnatural' to human beings.

The human species is not tied down by stringent instincts in the way that most animals are. Even aggression has no specific releases that are fixed and determined. Culture, then, with its developed institutions and symbols, is all the more important in the case of humans, for cultural structures make more specific what human biology often leaves as indefinite and indeterminate. With his brain and thumb, his language, and his deep roots in the trials and errors of socio-cultural experiments, the human species has, sometimes unconsciously and sometimes deliberately, developed regulations and controls, to say nothing of positive imperatives and visions both creative and destructive, which affect in countless ways the manner in which man lives in his world. Without the community, the individual simply would not be a human individual. Nature has left the human animal only half formed. 'His culture . . . gives him his selfhood' (Eccles, 1973: 292). He is what he is only because of the trials and errors of thousands of ancestors, both human and prehuman. He is the recipient of both their blessing and their curse. To lose completely one's inherited community is to lose one's identity, for the community not only has assisted nature in transforming an infant mass of potential into a person, but continues to sustain him every day of his life (cf. M. A. Barnhart, 1976: Chaps. 3-4).

I. SOURCES OF SOCIAL AND MORAL TRANSCENDENCE

The open society is still a society, and in many settings it is a more enduring society than the closed, for it has made flexibility itself a moral imperative.[1] Seen from a naturalistic point of view, transcendence for an open society comes from *many* sources. Every new organism, every visit from 'outsiders', every environmental shift, technological development, intellectual mutation, artistic venture, and commercial venture is a new tug at the community's institutions, regulations, cultural symbols, and moral and religious manifestations (cf. White, 1949). Furthermore, the dim and remote past of any society transcends its present existence at least temporally.

---

1. A number of naïve treatises have been written to attack strictness in morality. Without moral strictness, the freedom which depends on it would collapse into chaos. The question as to whether to keep or change the moral regulation already in use is quite different from the question as to whether the regulation – whether old or new – should be treated with seriousness, that is, strictness. The point of a regulation is to obtain strict compliance from those for whose behavior it is designed to control or shape. In many cases, a society will obtain *greater strictness of compliance when there is some flexibility in modifying the regulations by public agreement* whenever appropriate conditions indicate the need for modifying them.

J. RELIGIOUS COMMITMENT TO THE SOCIETY PERCEIVED AS PROTECTOR

Now and then individuals look down the side of the ship of society, so to speak, and see the raging chaos against which the institutions and structures of society are believed to protect them. Now and then they receive a glimpse of the meaningless existence that would settle down upon them were it not for the protective bosom of society. When, in the face of this threat of chaos and disorientation, people begin suffering core-concern with finitude, then their renewed commitment to society (or one of its modes) begins to take the appearance of a religious response. When it is perceived as protector and deliverer from chaos, meaninglessness, moral corruption, or emotional deterioration, the society begins to be treated as a God or Savior. Today in especially the United States sociologists of religion and scholars in religious studies are looking deeply into the question of a 'civil religion' or 'the Religion of the Republic', in which the Republic is symbolized, adored, sung to, praised, and in general treated with reverence and awe.

God is said to have created mankind. Society, too, taking nature's infant organism, literally *creates* from it a human man or woman. Besides protecting for fourscore years and ten the hairless ape against the forces of nature, which eventually take him back, society in a more positive sense feeds the organism a diet of stimuli and patterned cues and reinforcers, and in so doing breathes into the organism the breath of personhood, which was not there at the time of his natural birth.

K. BORN AGAIN

Society takes the naturally born human organism and in various ways 'converts' it, makes it into a 'new man', 'transforms' it (cf. Mowrer, 1967: 49–51; Berger and Luckmann, 1966: 50f., 132). Every child that is eventually socialized is 'born again'. He is adopted into a kingdom that is not of the 'natural' world only. He is taken into the fellowship of society and culture and is taught the language of Zion. Although the 'old Adam' survives, the enculturation process is so effective that he can no more return to his 'natural' state than he can by taking thought shrink to a fetus.

L. THEOLOGICAL ETHICS

In a recent article in *The Journal of Religious Ethics* (1974) Glenn C. Graber argues that 'a logical and/or linguistic relation between religion and ethics is much stronger than is generally recognized in the philosophical discussions of these issues' (p. 54). Moving steadily against the winds of contemporary philosophy, Graber contends that God's 'commands form the foundation of all ethical reasons' (p. 60). If we ask why we should so regard the divine commands, Graber replies simply that we *will* if we have already an 'attraction' to God.

What this argument is designed to do is to escape the dilemma that would require us either (1) to make a moral judgment about God before accepting his commands as the foundation of morality, or (2) to accept his commands simply because he is the supreme power. Graber appears to be saying that we may accept, are attracted to, God because of some non-ethical (but not anti-ethical) or pre-moral quality about him. And having once been attracted to him, we then come to love him and consequently to find ourselves willing to take his commands as the foundation of all ethical reasoning (pp. 60, 66, 67).

I wish to develop a few arguments in response to Graber's very fruitful article. First, I think he has prepared the way for a more profound appreciation of the intricate ties between ethics and religion (in the sense of responses to core-concern). These ties have been terribly neglected, in my opinion, by both philosophy and theology. Graber fails to follow through with his significant argument because he becomes preoccupied with establishing a supernaturalistic foundation for morality. By 'detheologizing' his argument, however, I will press his insights beyond his own personal intentions.

But, before doing that, I would like to say in passing that in some sense his argument for a supernatural foundation for ethical discussion is not an argument at all but a matter of defining words. When he says that we may be attracted to God because of a pre-moral quality of God, we naturally want to know what such a quality might be. Graber is ready with an answer – 'benevolence and loving-kindness' (p. 66). I should think that such qualities *are* instances of moral behavior. Indeed, Graber comes close to admitting this point inadvertently when he insists that 'pre-moral' certainly does not mean 'anti-moral' (p. 67).

Inasmuch as Graber offers no argument at all to show that benevolence and loving-kindness are not moral qualities, I can only hope that his case for a supernaturalistic grounding of ethics will be set forth in another article. I will not myself argue a case for regarding benevolence and loving-kindness as moral qualities because I think this particular debate is trivial.

M. FROM INVOLVEMENT TO MORAL COMMITMENT

What is not trivial, but profound, in Graber's article (1974) is his argument that the believer is first *attracted* to God and then, on that basis, is led to accept God's commands as the foundation of moral discourse. In 'detheologizing' this insight, I suggest that this is very much what happens in social interactions. The new human initiate into society is attracted to it, or to certain aspects or members within it. He is first involved, and if the *involvement and interaction* is reinforcing (attracting), he does not withdraw but is pulled deeper into human social relationships.

This, it seems to me, is a broad naturalistic account of how a moral authority (or foundation) gets established in the life of the individual. Instead of becoming personally involved with a supernatural Being, the initiate into society (family, neighborhood, etc.) becomes involved with what George Herbert Mead calls 'the significant other(s)'. If children find their parents (or someone else) to be benevolent, loving and kind, then the children will more likely become more meaningfully involved with the parents, even to the point of sometimes thinking that their parents are omniscient and omnipotent, and are the final arbitrators of what is right, wrong, and fair.

As the child develops, he may come to feel that the society or the nation in which he grew up has fed, loved, and protected him. He becomes *further involved* in the society and finds himself rewarded when he shows respect, and even awe and reverence, for national and societal symbols. He will be told stories and myths that in numerous ways tell him how indebted he is to his fatherland and all the heroes who made it possible for him to live in such a good (or at least promising) society or nation. Indeed, a sense of obligation and duty in the sense of societal bonds may develop. Even guilt will quickly come about in certain societies when the societal bonds are questioned.

There may also be smaller societies – e.g., cliques, hunting parties, Girl Scouts, church bodies, etc. – which reinforce him, get him involved, and impress him with their history, myths, and heroes. He and the next door neighbor may become friends; and, as parents and psychologists have observed, the friendship relationship among children (as well as adults) leads into the phenomenon and issues of moral authority, for the younger child may come to 'worship' his friend and take him as a moral authority on a variety of subjects.

Perhaps one of the most dramatic and powerful forms of involvement and attraction leading into a possible shift in moral authority is to be found in 'romantic involvement'. I have long been struck by the numerous similarities between romantic passion and dramatic religious conversion. In either of these conditions the individual is prone not to doubt or question the object of his love and commitment. The other's moral opinions become not mere opinions but rather begin to carry special significance and weight. After all, one is involved with a new 'significant other'.

There is no need to develop further this point about religious conversion and romantic passion. (Kierkegaard took 'the leap' twice – with infinite passion in one case, and with abandon in the other.) I simply wanted to appropriate Professor Graber's case and argue that the psycho-social starting point (or Graber's 'foundation') of moral discourse is *involvement* (Graber's 'attraction'). But instead of speaking of a personal involvement between a human and the supernatural Being, I have argued from a more naturalistic stance that the personal involvement lies more conspicuously between the individual and the various human and mythical significant others, as well as the cultural symbols and reinforcement structures, which in a thousand ways bind (obligate) the individual initiate to his society. My argument has not ruled out theism, for there may be a God who is the enduring context sustaining all societies. What I have done is to charge Graber and certain theologians of resorting to supernatural explanations of moral authority when they could more directly account for it in naturalistic (including psycho-social) terms. There may be a God, but I have argued against taking theological shortcuts in trying to do ethics. Graber's short cut never leads him to his destination, but in his wanderings he has hit upon some extremely important insights that naturalists would do well to heed.

One of those insights is that both psychologically and socially, morality develops through involved relationships. Without involvements, moral questions would not arise.[2] Indeed, it is probably in the conflict between multiple involvements, as well as the conflict between (1) one's own desires, and (2) the binding implications of one's involvements with others, that moral questions are born. (This is somewhat similar to the way that epistemological questions are born. If my committed actions based on certain of my perceptions had not clashed with committed actions based on certain of my other perceptions, then I would never have bothered to ask which set of perceptions is the 'right' one.)

N. THE QUEST FOR A ROCK-BOTTOM ETHICAL FOUNDATION

The quest for a rock-bottom ethical foundation beyond human and social involvements may be compared to the search for a perpetual motion machine. Stated more positively, if such involvements are not themselves reinforcing and rewarding, then an 'ethical argument' qua argument will have no motivating power. And if the argument cannot *move* anyone, there is no point in inventing it. Even most versions of moral conventionalism fail to take seriously the details of actual

2. It is important at this point not to overlook the serious involvements that people – whether children or adults – have with mythical entities, romanticized heroes, fictionalized villains, invisible playmates, gods, demons, and even symbolized consequences in the form of visions and 'goals'.

empirical involvements. Trying to tell someone that he *ought* to be morally involved may be compared to a neophyte therapist giving a manic depressive the general advice that he ought not to be depressed or ought not to worry.

The so-called 'Is/Ought' controversy that has long plagued the field of ethics has too often engaged disputants in a question of *why* without permitting any answers in terms of *how* and *what*. I see no possibility of answering the haunting question of 'Why be moral?' so long as it is forced to remain a question neither of pure logic nor of empirical inquiry. And even if it were made into a question of pure logic, it still would have no necessary bearing on empirical motivation. Indeed, there is always the question, 'Why be logical?'

There seems to be no escape from hypothetical imperatives always in the background of moral discourse. Hence, the question of 'Why be moral?' cannot be answered unless it is transformed into inquiries regarding *how* in fact people do get motivated to carry out this or that moral duty. And this is another way of raising the question of *what*, in the lives and conditions of people, reinforces them to accept certain responsibilities (obligations, etc.). In discussing morality, many theologians have too often ignored the argument of prudence because of their tit for tat notion of prudence and their lack of appreciation of involved social prudence. At the extreme is Kierkegaard's almost complete insensitivity to social philosophy. His theology lacks any doctrine of the church.

In times past, because utilitarians have expressed such a thin notion of society, they have shown little appreciation of the factor of 'extended identification' in the phenomenon of moral commitment. Social responsibility and morality moves from involvement to involvement, and it is in this way that extended identification develops as a condition of social responsibility. Some of the utilitarians – e.g., Herbert Spencer – held to such an atomistic view of the human self that they could not see that even in an ethic of self-interest, the self itself will be transformed (for good or ill) through interaction and involvement with other selves. The narrow self-interest ethic of Ayn Rand is not misleading because it is a philosophy of self-interest, but because it projects a self that ceases to be interesting for many people. Borrowing from Professor Graber again, I can only say that Rand's recommended life-style is not so much self-contradictory (although there are some serious contradictions within it) as simply unattractive, unappealing, and uninteresting. There is the emotional and emotive condition of morality, which Kant dismissed (except in his fascination with Rousseau) and which emotivism overemphasized, on the one hand, but failed to explore in depth, on the other hand.

One does not so much refute a life-style of selfishness as point to another life-style that is more enriching, involving, interesting, and attractive despite its risks. What Rand, with her 'virtue of selfishness', seems never to have grasped is that for many people the price of selfishness is a loss of 'interest' in living. And this is to make a surprisingly simple point which behaviorism has come to emphasize, namely, that if society or any segment of society desires responsible behavior from an individual, then he is more likely to manifest such responsibility if he finds it interesting and rewarding in the more complex and deeper sense of the term.

My point here is that society reinforces (rewards) moral behavior in countless ways – from gentle strokes on an infant's back and kind expressions from a neighbor to a decent job and a chance to be thought well of in the eyes of one's friends. In other words, morality is an empirical matter which behavioral scientists have too often neglected because of confusion about objectivity and values in science. Philosophers who worry about the question '*Why* be moral?' have rightly presupposed that many people are *already socially involved enough to raise the question*. If someone is not so involved, however, a formal argument void of any reference to empirical contingencies, consequences, and interests will be for him a meaningless exercise.

As a young man, Bertrand Russell wrote: 'It is difficult not to become reckless and commit suicide, which I believe I should do but for my people' (1969–70, I: 63). The 'people' he is referring to are his relatives, and what he is saying is that already as a young man he is so involved and vicariously identified with his people that he cannot bring himself to commit suicide. If my arguments thus far are reasonably sound, then no one can produce a purely formal case *against* suicide – nor, on the other hand, *for* suicide.

O. THE RISK OF INVOLVEMENT

Whether a person commits suicide, becomes sensitive about the plight of the aged or the mistreatment of prisoners, or develops the character (disposition) to steal or not to steal – these are largely determined by the kind and quality of his involvements. However, the mere fact that he is involved with other people or with something else strongly reinforcing does not entail that he will be moral or that he will not kill himself. Bertrand Russell as a man in his early forties contemplated suicide once again. This time it was partly because of his short but traumatic friendship with D. H. Lawrence. It gradually dawned upon Russell that he and his friend Lawrence were very much different in their outlook. He came to think that Lawrence was more interested in denouncing the evils of humanity than in trying to make things better. Lawrence, on the other hand, denouncing Russell's pacifism as hypocrisy, charged that Russell was as much interested in war and blood as anyone else. For twenty-four hours Russell was devastated. That his close friend should say this about him was almost more than he could bear. It was during these hours that suicide once again became a live option for Russell. In the agony of those hours he came to feel that perhaps Lawrence had profound insight which he himself lacked with regard to his own motives. But this morbid mood passed and Russell never again seemed to think of suicide as an attractive option (1969–70, II: 12–15).

During the early months of World War I, Russell used to despair of the propaganda, massacre, and agony of the war; but he found some relief in becoming involved not only in his philosophical studies, but in his visits to destitute Germans in England for the purpose of providing them some relief. Working with a charitable committee, Russell was personally *inspired* by 'remarkable instances of kindness in the middle of the fury of war. Not infrequently in the poor neighbourhoods landladies, themselves poor, had allowed Germans to stay without paying any rent, because they knew it was impossible for Germans to find work' (1969-70, II: 8f.).

Moral behavior, sensitivity to the needs of others, responsibility – these qualities are far more complex than theological and philosophical articles sometimes indicate. I will not enter here into a critique of egoism, for I have done that elsewhere (J. E. Barnhart, 1975: Chap. 10; 1976). It can be safely said that no general argument has been advanced that allows us to make the universal generalization that one *ought* to be either an egoist or an altruist. If we want to make inquiry into morality or ethics, it is much more fruitful to explore (1) the interests, desires, and involvements of people, and (2) the empirical conditions and anticipated consequences of certain actions and kinds of actions.

Religion develops a moral dimension when, in response to core-concern with finitude, people show concern about their ties and bonds (and obligations) to others. Feeling an emotional need for one another, they quite naturally, when faced with the terrible threats of finitude, become concerned with keeping the bonds of affection, expectation, and general interaction from unraveling. How they respond to this challenge – that is admittedly a matter of bewildering diversity but also a fruitful field of research for years to come.

Religious Education

A. THE MYTH OF THE NEUTRAL POINT OF VIEW

Strange as it may seem at first glance, the issue of religion's being taught in the public schools forces in the open some very tough epistemological questions pertaining to the morality and metaphysics of religion. Even now one may still hear a university colleague state that the teaching of 'sectarian religion' is strictly out of place in the state university and, a fortiori, in the lower grades of public education. He will concede that religion may be taught at the college and university level so long as it is strictly 'nonsectarian'. He may add that religion must be taught only 'objectively'.

Having argued earlier that all religions have some cognitive dimension or depth even when this dimension is not emphasized by some cultures or individuals, I will follow through by arguing further that to teach *about* religion is to teach religion from a point of view. I would even add that many, perhaps most, history courses deal with some religious themes and problems. However, they are not dealt with in a so-called neutral way but from a particular perspective. It is impossible to teach history from a neutral point of view, for no such point of view exists or could exist. (The word 'bias' often is used pejoratively to describe *your* point of view if it conflicts with mine, which is why I prefer not to use the word in this chapter.)

If a history course purports to 'describe' military persons as both heroes and agents of the thrust of civilization, then it will be propagating a view that runs directly counter to the religious views of most Quakers and Mennonites, as well as many others. A course that teaches the history of the significant movements and ideas of a given period may, by *excluding* certain religious movements and ideas, reflect a definite judgment or prejudgment that what is excluded is less significant than what is included.

B. REQUIRED COURSES – A CHURCH-STATE PROBLEM?

As stated earlier, the teaching of history from a neutral point of view is an impossibility. *Requiring* a person to take a course in history is to force him to listen to a view that may stand in opposition to his religion. *In the public schools there is no more justification for requiring all students to take courses in history than there is for requiring them to take courses in the history of religions, philosophy of religion, sociology of religion, or the psychology of religion.* Furthermore, just as history courses that touch on some religious themes will express particular points of view, so courses in religion will invariably be taught from particular points of view.

There is no more justification for requiring all students to take a biology course which teaches evolution than there is for requiring them to take courses in religion in which the Genesis account of creation is taught as a set of truth-statements about the origin of the universe and the beginning of the human species. To actually compel by law all children and young people under a certain age to go to school and, on top of that, to compel them to study views that they, or at least their parents, regard as strongly in opposition to their religion and its moral codes is to use the state to support something of an establishment of one religion over others.

This needs to be clarified. Consider the following: John is a Unitarian. Some of his metaphysical and moral views are very different from those of his teacher, Mr. Smith, a Missouri Synod Lutheran. The teacher talks of God and Christ now and then, but John does not believe there is a God and does not regard Jesus as Savior and Lord. Mr. Smith regards abortion to be a sin, whereas John thinks that there are times when it is immoral not to have an abortion. He regards certain things as immoral which Mr. Smith holds to be perfectly moral. But because Mr. Smith is the teacher, John must listen to Mr. Smith's views and be graded by him.

In studying the establishing of the American colonies, the flight of Roger Williams, and the movement of Mormons into Utah, does the teacher simply 'bracket' the question of divine providence? Does the focusing on social, psychological, economic, military, and political facts suggest to students that the religious factor is unimportant? Or if the religious factor is considered, will it be treated simply as a human phenomenon – Joseph Smith only *thought* that God told him to do thus and so, or Brigham Young only *believed* that he was moved by the spirit of God to lead Mormons to the desert. Consider the seagulls that came in to eat the insects that were destroying the Mormons' crops. Were they sent by God or is there some other explanation? Will courses in the history of Israel be simply *excluded* from public schools because such courses are regarded as less significant than courses in English history or Roman history? Certainly many Christians and Jews regard the history of Israel to be profoundly significant to the whole human race.

One university instructor in religion charges that the public school system is in effect teaching a religion of Humanism and secularism under the guise of religious neutrality: 'In secular education, the emphasis has shifted from learning about divine truths to examining human questions of meaning and value. . . . Studying the Bible in English classes or from a humanities point of view means to look for significant "revelations" about man rather than Revelations of God' (Huntsberry, 1974: 736). He indicates further that while Protestants and Catholics, and their various branches, are disputing with one another, the real battle is being won by 'what Robert Bellah [1970, 226] sees as "a sort of latter-day embodiment of Comte's 'religion of humanity'".' (p. 738.) Many liberal Humanists and Unitarians, on the other hand, believe that in the public schools the traditional religions, combined with a kind of uncritical nationalism, are the dominant influence.

C. PRESENTING A VARIETY OF VIEWPOINTS

There is no ideal solution to this 'Church-State' problem. The public schools are very definitely teaching certain views about and of religion and morality, even when no separate courses called Religion or Ethics are offered. We must ask, What will satisfy parents who complain that their children are being not only forced to go to school but forced to study under teachers whose views they are very much in opposition to? Having more money to send their children to a private school more in keeping with their own outlook would be one way to satisfy these parents. But this is not likely to happen for a great many of them.

Another, and perhaps more feasible, plan is to require teachers to open their classes to a greater variety of points of view, perhaps even inviting in representative speakers of the several points of view. In the debate over 'prayer and Bible-reading in the public schools', one alternative suggested in the United States was that the students who did not agree with the school-sponsored prayers and Bible-reading could simply dismiss themselves from the class. But this was regarded as probably an emotionally harmful experience to some students in the minority. Curiously, the students today who believe that they are being indoctrinated by a teacher do not in most public schools have even the option to dismiss themselves from the classroom. Hence, a workable compromise would seem to be that of making the classroom experience tolerant of a greater variety of viewpoints.

This plan grows directly out of the epistemological position that the notion of pure objectivity in inquiry is highly complicated at best and thoroughly confused at worst. Presumably, objectivity includes at least some sensitivity to all the relevant facts or data pertaining to the particular issue under consideration. Because it is humanly impossible to consider all the data pertaining to a problem, we must speak of *relevant* data. But what is or is not relevant is partly determined by the theoretical background or viewpoint from which we approach the problem. Hence, it becomes necessary, in the interest of the ideal of objectivity or fairness, to permit a number of theories or points of view to be represented.

In effect, this tentative comprimise recommends a kind of *laissez-*

faire attitude toward the various viewpoints in what has been called 'the free market place of ideas'. However, no one can say that an Invisible Hand will guarantee progess in academic pursuit and social harmony. What can be said is that there is more likelihood that this compromise plan will be acceptable to a greater number of special interest groups than alternatives allowing gross discrimination and religious turmoil. Also, it leaves open the possibility for new hypotheses or viewpoints to emerge in the process of the interplay and interchange of viewpoints.

The term 'compromise' is used advisedly here because there is an infinity of points of view, although only a small number will in a finite amount of time be explored in a class room. The whole idea of required courses is slowly but steadily being challenged simply because we are becoming aware of the great variety of perspectives that it is possible to take on any given subject. If the state forces a student to learn of sex in a way that the teacher characterizes as 'healthy', this may, from some students' point of view, be as indoctrination in something that they regard as immoral. Indeed, a number of people think that the word 'healthy' is often nothing more than a disguised way of referring to certain ethical and moral judgments, judgments which they themselves might very well reject.

D. THE RELIGION OF THE REPUBLIC AND ITS 'SUNDAY SCHOOL'

One writer contends that the public school system of the United States functions as today's 'Sunday school' for indoctrinating children and young people into the Religion of the Republic, or the 'civil religion', which is regarded as a complex of national mythology, rituals, national 'gods', special doctrines, etc. I do not wish to become deeply involved in explicating at length what the Religion of the Republic is (cf. S. E. Mead, 1954; 1967; E. Smith, 1970; R. M. Bellah, 1967). My point here is that by teaching this civil religion in the public schools, Americans most definitely do have a serious church-state problem.

This is not to say, however, that if we had some other plan, we would have no church-state problem. There are many people who wish simply to have only their own view taught and nothing else mentioned, or if mentioned at all, done so in a way as to show them to be inferior views. Indeed, some parents and students are definitely opposed to a class of open discussion and critical debate because it runs the risk of both creating some doubts and turning the mind in other directions. The 'elective courses' system would ideally contain some courses that are pretty much one viewpoint only, with strict limitations on open debate. Those wanting such courses could elect them. But few, if anyone, will get from this compromise plan everything he would like. Nevertheless, the plan that I have suggested would be less threatening and would satisfy more demands. At least this is a prediction worth testing in light of the current situation in the American public schools.

E. A SERIOUS THREAT TO THE PLAN

It cannot be denied that the above plan could be seriously threatened by one special interest group (Humanist, Baptist, Catholic, or whatever) warning its own children that they will be punished in some way if they refuse to take the course recommended by the special interest group.

The threat to the plan could even intensify if the special interest group should pressure severely its own children not to take courses that the interest group strongly proscribes. One of the most effective ways of dealing with conflicting special interest groups is to have another special interest group that will appeal to something common to all the interest groups. The Religion of the Republic is thought by some sociologists, church historians, and others to be an expression of many common commitments and values that transcend 'denominational' conflict.

F. CHRISTIANITY AND THE RELIGION OF THE REPUBLIC

In times past, Christianity was sometimes regarded as a part of the common law of the United States. Despite the Mormon belief in the divine command to practice polygyny, the U.S. Supreme Court in

1890 'explained' that polygyny 'is contrary to the spirit of Christianity and of the civilization which Christianity has produced in the Western world' (cited in Gaustad, 1973: 99). Most Mormons complied with this ruling and eventually many came to believe that there was even divine guidance in the Supreme Court's decision. Hence, the Religion of the Republic received another supporter.

Today, the U.S. Supreme Court is no longer likely to invoke the 'spirit of Christianity' as the authoritative moral norm. Since the time when Mormons made their dissenting challenge, other moral-religious dissenters have made their challenge also, and many were more successful than the Mormons. The inability of the legal establishment to restrict the definition of religion to Jewish and Christian theism made it possible for the U.S. Conscription Law to be shattered beyond repair. Recently a Buddhist clergyman was named official chaplain of the California Senate. Instead of a Methodist minister, a Buddhist minister will offer prayers at the beginning of each session (see *Church and State*, 28(1:22)). It is doubtful that today a Buddhist would because of his Buddhism be denied membership in the U.S. Supreme Court. Pluralism in the United States is constantly pressuring the Religion of the Republic to make qualifications and concessions. For some people, this seems to be a victory for religious freedom; for others it seems to be a serious threat to religion and its moral expression. This curious double response leads one historian of religion in the United States to make the following prediction: 'The heartiest sinners against society will be once more its truest believers (Gaustad, 1973: 141). As Alasdair MacIntyre points out, the very moral concepts that we employ are historically conditioned – 'moral concepts themselves have a history' (1966: 269), which suggests that the Religion of the Republic, for good and ill, could itself die the death of a thousand qualifications and yet find perhaps its very vitality in remaining sensitive to certain qualifications which could not have been tolerated in previous generations.

G. THE INFLUENCE OF THE RELIGION OF THE REPUBLIC

The Statue of Liberty stands as one of the most significant visual symbols of the Religion of the Republic.[1] The very word 'liberty' has in the United States an emotional and moral impact that is rivaled only by the impact of the words 'united' and 'justice'. Everywhere in the land citizens of the *United* States proclaim themselves to be *one* nation with *liberty* and *justice* for all. The vision of justice is perhaps the most tragic and persistent one of the last few decades. Abraham Lincoln stands as the remythologized expression of a leader who is heralded as not only the defender of justice and the liberator of the oppressed, but even the preserver of the unity of the nation when it was on the verge of destruction.

Banks endeavor to capitalize on the names of such national heroes as Washington, Lincoln, Hamilton, Jefferson, and even Ben Franklin. Eventually this pantheon will contain other gods, one of whom – Martin Luther King – was not formally within the politico-legal system, although he had a profound influence on it.

It is not surprising that in the United States many new groups suffering finitude-crisis will eventually try to become a major voice within the Religion of the Republic. There is no mystery here. If a new group thrives in the republic, it will tend to own property and share somewhat in the commerce and activities of the nation. Indeed, in numerous cases the new group or movement may eventually claim to be the truest representative of 'America'. It seeks to take for itself the power and influence of the symbols of 'America'. (In some ways this may be compared to pagans and gentiles who, upon becoming Christians, proclaimed themselves to be the true heirs of Abraham and Isaac.)

As each new group tries to represent itself as the true remnant of all that is genuinely 'American', the Religion of the Republic tends to be pulled into diverse directions and to be divided into various official

---

1. I do not mean to imply that the United States is the only nation with a 'civil religion' (in Rousseau's sense of the phrase). We need only look at the developments in France in the controversy regarding the legalization of abortion.

and unofficial 'denominations'. Each group endeavors to appropriate certain national symbols, heroes, rituals, doctrines, etc., for its own purposes.[2]

In some ways this pulling at the Religion of the Republic serves to test it. But the pulling need not be looked at purely in terms of Functionalism, for it runs risks that are genuine, as any genuine test does. Not *everything* can be tolerated by the Religion of the Republic. Yet every time a new style of freedom is accommodated and protected, the Republic takes on a new supporter who is trapped into helping to defend religious and moral toleration in general (which is different from religious and moral approval). Thus far, religious toleration has become a major principle of the Religion of the Republic, and there are indications that *moral* pluralism is developing, although still within some strict limits. The slogan 'Do your own thing' sounded very much like the Baptists a few centuries ago when they (and others) proclaimed 'Freedom of Conscience'.

Indeed, the rules, procedures, principles, etc., which facilitate the resolution of conflict between competing religions and their moral expressions and associations will tend to be incorporated as 'Commandments' within the Religion of the Republic, and the breaking of these Commandments will be regarded by the divergent groups as a very serious offense.

H. THE SECULAR OUTLOOK AND THE RELIGION OF THE REPUBLIC

It would be a serious error to regard the Religion of the Republic and a secularized way of thinking as one and the same or as even necessarily compatible. Earlier I gave a tentative definition of secular thinking as that kind of thinking which, rejecting mystification, endeavors to look behind the veil, the closed door, the secret chambers. The National Socialism of Hitler's Germany was clearly not a secular movement but the very opposite, with its myths and

---

2. In his own day Thomas Jefferson was denounced as an 'infidel'. Decades later, when Jefferson became a part of the sacred pantheon, Christian ministers began to include him in the camp of 'godly Founding Fathers who established this nation on God'.

idols and sacred taboos. 'The Nazis', says Alasdair MacIntyre, 'desecularized society with a vengeance'. He points out further that 'Christianity, especially Protestant Christianity, was itself a powerful secularization agent, destroying in the name of God any attempt to deify nature, and so helping to rid the world of magic and making nature available for scientific inquiry' (1964: 131f.).

When the people of a nation regard their nation as threatened, or a society regards itself as in a crisis, then core-concern may ordinarily be said to exist in some form or another. The responses to the concern will be religious. What concrete form the religious response (or responses) take may vary anywhere from ruthless nationalism to a withdrawal into a small elect community. The Religion of the Republic could develop into a desecularized set of uncriticized dogmas and pronouncements protected by law from being exposed to the light of empirical testing and rational probings. 'A common religion which only sacralized* the nation without bringing it under the judgment of a transnational referent would not accord with the best in the heritage' (Michaelsen, 1970: 44).

The danger of nationalism is not that it may be secular or atheistic, but that it may tend to become closed and thus not capable of transcending its most destructive limitations. It loses the capacity to learn to respond creatively. Atheism in the sense of the rejection of classical theism may or may not be a secular view; for atheism, strictly speaking, is not yet a view of its own. One may reject classical theism and yet embrace a mystified dogma that is the very opposite of secularity. In an article entitled 'Should Christianity be secularized?' Martin E. Marty (1967) makes the following insightful comment:

Unreflective religion can be subtly transformed into unreflective secularism. People may retain symbols which have lost all cognitive import. They may see these symbols reduced to routine in the service of new ideologies or practices.

---

* Not secularized.

I. CONCLUSION

In this chapter I have tried to show that because human beings are finite they will probably continue to have crises of core-concern. I have endeavored to show that the study of religion in the sense of the study of the responses to core-concern is almost impossible to eliminate from the public schools. I have suggested that even in the study about religion we are, whether we see it at the time, actually favoring one kind of response over others. The plan of increasing elective courses and reducing required courses was offered as a compromise in the perpetual church-state controversy. Indeed, the first four chapters of this book should throw some light on why the church-state controversy is a continuing phenomenon.

Of course, there are many who, like Professor Benjamin Ladner, insist that the academic study of religion simply misses the boat and that God is found in 'prereflective' knowledge. The 'body with its essential relationship' to God and the world is declared to be the root of knowledge: the brain simply comes in late on the scene (1974: 742).

Well, this is, of course, a point of view itself, which doubtless deserves serious attention. It makes bold epistemological claims. Thus, we must move into the next chapter, for the question of whether there is a God has yet to be explored in this book. In opposition to positivism, I will argue that theistic statements may be cognitively meaningful. Professor Ladner, with his insistence on 'prereflective' knowledge, calls for nothing less than epistemological inquiry in order to make 'religious studies' more than simply the cataloging of religious beliefs. The challenge seems justifiable, and I wish now to try to meet it as best I can.

6

The Mystic and God

A. MYSTICISM AND ONENESS

Students of mysticism often agree that the 'sense of oneness' is a defining characteristic of mysticism. Mystics speak of being 'caught up' into something more than themselves, of being 'a part of' this One (or whatever it may be called). They sometimes describe themselves as 'being absorbed' or as 'losing themselves' in the One. Yet they often insist that while losing themselves in such a state, they nevertheless find themselves to be more truly real than they had ever experienced themselves as being.

Students of mysticism underplay the fact that most descriptions of the so-called mystical state are used in other situations also. For example, it is not uncommon to hear of someone who is wholly *absorbed* in such activities as doing research, driving a racing car, or playing Chopin on the piano. I have observed individuals, wholly absorbed in 'watching' a football game, forget who they are or where they are. Yet by losing themselves in the game they nevertheless may in some sense be said to find themselves. Let me give an example. Consider Vincent, depressed and withdrawn in the mental hospital, and unresponsive to treatment. Then one day something happens. He 'comes alive'. There he sits, arms waving, shouting, and thoroughly 'lost' in a football game on television. The attendants will not describe his 'absorption' in the game as somehow a loss of his identity. Yet is he not absorbed or lost? And has he not come alive?

Mystics may regard this comparison between the mystical state and the football experience to be mundane and entirely insensitive.

After all, one cannot live by football alone, or even by absorbing research activity alone. But in reply I suggest that neither can mystics live by their apex experience alone.

I recall catching myself using the word 'trance' to designate one of my own kinds of experiences. I know of no better way to describe it. I did not begin to notice it until I was just beginning to think and study wholly on my own personal projects, without regard to Ph.D. qualifying examinations or preparation for classes as either student or instructor. It was *freedom* in the sense that I could be wholly 'caught up' in the problem itself, transported and carried by the dictates of the problem without regard to any interfering practical cares. My wife and I learned quickly not to try to communicate with one another during these hours of trance.

During such periods of trance, one has a feeling of *certainty* about one's conclusions. It is also a period of inspiration. Descartes thought that a conclusion which he reached or received during what was probably a period of trance was actually a divinely inspired conclusion. Furthermore, not only feelings of certainty and even divine inspiration, but convictions of being transported beyond temporality come to people who undergo the trance. They explain that at the time they were oblivious to time, which is very close to sounding like one of the 'paradoxes' of mysticism. Being 'caught up' to the extent of losing all sense of the passage of time is not an experience limited solely to those persons classified as mystics.

Plato's 'rational mysticism' involves a kind of metaphysics, which he thought was necessary to account for the trance that most serious scholars and students enter if they are to do any rigorous thinking at all. Plato presupposed that this trance (cf. Socrates' long trance!) must have one common object, namely, the realm of Forms. Psychologically the trance is pretty much the same for the artist as for the mathematician. But does it follow of necessity that the object of the artist's trance-concentration is the same as the mathematicians? Does the oneness of the *psychological* state carry over to the oneness of the alleged *objective referent* of the psychological state?

Those who are classified as mystics receive this horrific title not because their psychological state is different from others 'caught up' in their problem, but because the mystics claim that what they are caught up in is 'the All', 'God', 'the One', or whatever. Of course, there are cases of some liberalizing of the requirements for classifying something as mystical. For example, the Pythagoreans were mathematicians of a sort who regarded their numerical schemes to be manifestations of the universal harmony of the whole of reality. The Pythagoreans regarded their schemes to be both religious and scientific mysticism.

B. MYSTICISM AND INEFFABILITY

After completing his book on logic (entitled *Logisch-Philosophische Abhandlung*), Ludwig Wittgenstein wrote in a letter (on March 13, 1919) to Bertrand Russell that '*nobody* will understand it: although I believe it's all as clear as crystal [sic]' (Russell, 1969-70, II: 157). In another letter (on August 19, 1919) to Russell, Wittgenstein, complaining that not even the great mathematician Frege could understand the book, wrote that 'it is *very* hard not to be understood by a single sole [sic]!' (Ibid, II: 160). Students of mysticism sometimes give the impression that there is something extraordinary about not being able to verbalize certain experiences, or at least not being able to find other people who can understand one's verbal accounts of them. But it seems that the inability to communicate to other people some of one's own experiences – whether they be noetic, emotional, or whatever – is not extraordinary at all but is rather common.

It will prove fruitful to look briefly at the ineffability of mystical experiences in light of B. F. Skinner's position on introspective reports. Contrary to popular legend, Skinner neither denies the existence of feelings nor treats them as unobservable (1953: 35). Rather, 'that which is felt' is, he says, capable of being 'introspectively observed'. In other words, some of the world of events inside the body may be observed introspectively by the individual himself (1974: 16-17). But because of the *private* nature of this sort of observation, introspective reports are difficult to formulate into *public* language.

If mystics complain that public language is not very reliable for communicating the mystical experience, Skinner complains that the language used to express introspective reports is not very reliable (1953: 260). So-called mystical experiences are not the only experiences that are difficult to symbolize into words of ordinary discourse.

Nevertheless, mystics do often try to verbalize their experiences, just as we all try, with only partial success, to verbalize our private feelings. In fact, each person's feelings and responses are private or personal in the sense that his responses are distinguishable from those of other people, even when they and he are all in the presence of similar stimuli and circumstances existing outside the observing human organisms.

Describing a pain or one's felt sickness to the physician is not always easy. A pain in the chest, for example, may not be exactly sharp, nor is it a dull pain. It is very difficult to describe what the felt pain is like because, for one thing, we are not trying to describe something that exists publicly, that is, outside the organism. Rather, we are attempting to offer a verbal report of something taking place inside the organism.

C. OBSERVING THE 'INNER' WORLD

Skinner seems to be saying that *observation can take place through media other than the eyes and ears.* Using our hands to touch something – a tree, for example – is a way of observing. We may be told that a large tree exists just around the bend. But we may wish to observe – or, in this case, *see* – it for ourselves. The blind individual, however, will have to *observe by feeling the tree with his hands.* Similarly, whether blind or not, each of us can feel certain events inside his own body. We readily admit that we feel with our hands because, in part, the hands may themselves be observed with our eyes and the eyes of others. But we are uncertain as to whether we should speak of feeling with any particular organ behind our skin. True, the phrase 'gut feeling' is a kind of vague way of designating in a general area of our bodies certain organs which feel certain parts of its environment. (The body's various members and parts may be regarded as environment to other members.) Seeing a tree is a response or reaction. Similarly, we sometimes have a 'gut reaction' *to our seeing* certain things. Admittedly, this is a very imprecise and rough way of talking, and in polite Victorian circles it was thought to be socially improper to speak of responses taking place inside one's own body. Such talk, regarded as too 'personal', was not appropriate at public gatherings.

'Personal feelings' of things inside the body are not always possible to check out. People feel with their hands, and other people can check out the reports of what outside the body they, too, feel. I can feel the same tree that you feel, and we can compare what we feel. Each of us reports his feelings but the emphasis is upon *what* one feels rather than upon the feelings themselves. In fact, because the emphasis is so focused on the *what* – in this case, the tree – that is being felt (or responded to) outside the body, we are likely to ignore altogether the individual's feeling *qua* feeling. (This is, of course, to bring up the old issue of primary and secondary qualities, and the more important epistemological problems spinning off from it. I will not try to review here arguments stemming from this issue.)

The feelings *inside* the body, however, are a different matter. The linguistic community has thus far not developed a very adequate public language for reporting *what* one feels inside one's own body. The emphasis, rather, seems to be primarily on the feeling itself. A person may say that he feels nauseous, but this does not designate the particular member of the body that is malfunctioning, although a person may locate the general area when he says, 'I feel sick *at my stomach*'.

There are what we call emotional reactions or responses that are sometimes called feelings. John feels upset. The physician may ask *where* the patient feels upset. That is, he wants to locate the reaction inside the patient's body in order to deal with it there. But if the 'upset' is a reaction or response to something outside the organism, then the question becomes not '*Where* are you upset?' but '*What* has upset you?' The physician is usually concerned with what comes into the body by way of eating and breathing. Did the green apples that the patient ate cause the upset? Does the patient have an allergy? Which is to ask, 'What sort of things that the patient breathes into his own body create an irritation or infection inside his organism?'

The psychotherapist, however, seems more concerned with the things which the client takes in through his eyes and ears. What did the client see and/or hear that upset him. What was said to him to cause him to react or respond in such a way? Cultures often differ as to how they classify responses and reactions. In some cultures the reaction that takes the form of visions or that is characterized as 'a sense of oneness with the cosmos', or 'being absorbed into the universe', is treated as improper talk. It is a bit like burping in public. In other cultures, however, verbalizations, overt body language, and ritual may be taken as perfectly respectable and acceptable reports of a 'sense of cosmic oneness', just as in some cultures burping in public is an acceptable way of reporting satisfaction with a good meal.

Religious officials of certain cultures serve to encourage reports of the 'sense of oneness'. Other cultures, by contrast, use therapists and others to discourage such talk. In some groups, reports of seeing angels, spirits, and the like are highly reinforced, whereas in other groups such reports may be ignored and perhaps even punished. The case of Joan of Arc is only one of many such examples of a group's punishing verbal claims that deviated considerably from the official line.

In some groups people are taught to 'express their feelings' publicly through crying, laughing, gesturing, speaking, dancing, fighting, etc. Many rituals serve as demonstrations – a way of being demonstrative. The Bali culture, however, is one of those which rewards those who do not express their own personal verbal reactions to conflict situations (Geertz, 1973: 402). Of course, the Balinese did not teach this life-form to their children without also developing institutional conditions making it possible. Until in recent years, at least, the Balinese seemed to have all sorts of social machinery for preventing the individual from demonstrating overtly his responses to conflict situations. Indeed, the very notion of time in Bali was quite different from what it is in other cultures. 'Balinese social life lacks climax because it takes place in a motionless present, a vectorless now' (Ibid, 404). This is to say that the social patterns of stimuli and reinforcers were such as not to punish people for failing to meet certain kinds of time schedules. Instead, other patterns of responses were cued and rewarded. Another way of saying this is that the Balinese developed social guidelines for preventing individuals from being put into situations of conflicting cues.

D. THE SOCIAL CONSTRUCTION OF REALITY

But what has all this to do with the so-called mystical experience? It has a great deal to do with it. One of the most forthright spokesmen of the experience of being at one with the cosmos and of developing what he calls 'higher consciousness', Andrew Weil, concludes that the physical and social setting is more important than drugs in bringing about the higher consciousness (1972: 29). In other words, in developing the higher consciousness, what the individual takes in through his ears and eyes is more important than what he takes in orally. Ludwig Feuerbach said that man is what he eats, but we now know that he consumes daily a diet of words, syntax, ritual, and a vast complex of cues and stimuli which 'play' upon his eyes, ears, skin, and other 'organs' of his body and central nervous system.

We are, thus, forced to face the issue of the 'social construction of reality' (Berger and Luckmann, 1967). Indeed, even the phrase 'higher consciousness' reveals an evaluation or judgment which one social group places upon certain experiences in contrast to other experiences. But some groups evaluate quite differently and may use a phrase like 'reality oriented' to distinguish certain experiences and responses from others. Businessmen have the habit of seeing their system of interchange as 'the real world', whereas many other groups speak of a different system of interchange as the 'spiritual realm', which by implication is judged as the 'permanent and enduring realm'. Religion is often said to be able to put us in touch with those realities that are not dependent on the transient, fleeting things whose reality is here today and gone tomorrow. The hard-nosed realist, by contrast, tends to regard the realm of spiritual phenomena to be the imaginative play of people who cannot function in 'the real world'. And so on.

Similarly, groups will vary markedly as to what experiences and behaviors they classify as 'real freedom' or 'true freedom'. What will be classified as 'illusionary freedom' by one group will be called 'genuine freedom' by another. Those who designate a certain experience as a 'sense of oneness with God' (or whatever) are prone to designate it also as an experience of 'true freedom'. In addition it may be designated as 'the truly real'. Most people feel that they always have some doubts, and that they are never one hundred percent free. But the so-called mystical experience leaves some people saying that somehow the fragments of knowledge and freedom have all been made whole. In other words, the 'sense of finitude' has been overcome.

Is the mystical sense of oneness a religious experience at all? The primary reason for arguing that it is *not* is that it appears to be in conflict with the version of theism which denies that a finite creature can be absorbed into the Infinite. However, in keeping with my earlier distinction between the *preliminary* definition of RELIGION and the *response* definition, I would argue that the experience that is characterized (rightly or wrongly) as a 'sense of oneness' may very well be in *response* to the concern with one's finitude, which is the preliminary definition of RELIGION. Whether the mystical response is anything other than an extraordinary and highly charged experience which is mistaken for metaphysical and cosmic knowledge is, of course, another question. The mystical experience may or may not have a place in the *ideal* definition of RELIGION, but there can be little doubt that in many cases it is certainly colored by the concern with one's finitude.

In our attempts to move toward some ideal definition of RELIGION, we discover that those who insist that they have experienced a sense of oneness with God (or whatever) quite naturally make far-reaching noetic claims for their experience. Unfortunately, when we call attention to particular areas of knowledge in which we desire more knowledge, the mystic seems to be no more enlightening than others in closing the gap between our ignorance and the ideal of superior knowledge. The mystic may indeed speak on a given topic, but he will usually be very vague when he attempts to show how the sense of oneness throws light on the problem. It is very possible that the term 'ineffable' is a polite synonym for this vagueness. It is difficult to know what, if anything, is meant by the mystic's claim that he just knows that all reality is one. Presumably this does not mean that people in Los Angeles can now relax all smog control standards because the oxygen-smog combination there is completely *the same* in every respect as it is in Alpine, Texas.

Perhaps more revealing than the mystic's phrase 'truly real' is the phrase 'truly free' or 'true freedom'. The 'sense of oneness' may be a report of the individual's feeling 'at one with himself', which is to say that his sense of oneness is the enjoyment of feeling no conflicts and frustrations. In this state the individual may be filtering out the stimuli and cues that have in the past led him to respond in conflicting and ambivalent ways. If we keep in mind that the physical and social 'diet' of each human being is outrageously complex and subtle, with countless stimuli bombarding him at every hour, then it is not surprising that he will value a technique for filtering these cues and will highly value the end result, which he may designate as 'true freedom', 'harmony with everything', or 'higher consciousness'.

Unfortunately, as the so-called mystics agree, this sense of oneness does not last. St. Theresa, for example, seemed all her life to be 'coming down' from her 'true freedom' and living in a life of dualism or fragmentation, which presumably is a life confronted with countless cues and reinforcements that elicit conflicting and ambivalent experiences. Usually those who wish to cultivate the 'sense of oneness with God' (or whatever) insist that they must retreat to a physical place that is without disturbance. In other words, the peace that comes in being free from the conflicting cues and stimuli can best be had if the organism is simply removed from the disrupting and conflicting stimuli. There is nothing particularly mysterious about this technique.

E. MORE THAN ELIMINATING EXTERNAL STIMULI

No one can attend to his 'inside' world if he is being bombarded by conflicting cues. I suggest that at least some of those people called mystics do more than simply filter out certain external 'noises' and conflicting cues. In addition to this, each mystic comes into fuller touch with his own body. In other words, through various techniques and disciplines the individual learns to feel his own 'insides', as if various parts of his inner parts had become something like a finger that feels the inner events and enjoys the 'inner sensation'.

St. Augustine is one among many who have claimed to meet God in the depths of their own being. A naturalist might attempt to explain that some people are taught by their religious community to classify certain feelings inside the body as experiences of God. The naturalist does not find it surprising that the apostle St. Paul would speak of Christ 'inside' him. 'I live', says St. Paul, 'yet not I but Christ liveth in me' (Gal. 2:20 *KJV*). In keeping with his ἐν Χριστῷ doctrine, St. Paul speaks of his body as the temple wherein the Holy Spirit dwells (1 Cor. 3:16).

According to the naturalistic perspective, Christians and others are more correct than they realize when they say that they meet God within themselves. But it is not really God that they meet, says the naturalist, but the stimulus-response-interchange taking place inside their own bodies. The following revealing quotation is from an article in *Psychology Today*:

> *P.T.*'s questionnaire moved 40,000 readers to answer. God is alive, but the address has changed. Their religious search is turning hard, away from a Supreme Being out in space toward the inward and personal mysteries. The grab for Eastern insight, E.S.P. and the occult are but part of a deeper, broader move to find the spiritual in the temple of the living self.
>
> God is not dead; he has simply changed clothes and come down from the clouds into the body (Wuthnow and Glock, 1974: 131).

In his article 'The experience of the body and transcendence', Bernard Aaronson, referring to what he calls 'the true path of the mystic', states that 'it doesn't involve putting down the body, it involves getting *into the body*, enhancing bodily sensations, enhancing feelings, seeing what is there and responding to it' (1974: 49. Italics added.)

Some theists, charging that naturalists try to make themselves into God, point to the example of Feuerbach, who wrote that 'there is no other essence which man can think, dream of, imagine, feel, believe in, wish for, love and adore as the *Absolute* than the essence of human nature itself' (1957: 270).[1] Then in a footnote to this grandiose statement, Feuerbach explains that 'external nature' belongs to the essence of human nature. Feuerbach makes it clear that he is asserting a monistic philosophy. Naturalists, therefore, could reply that, far from being a spokesman of their position, Feuerbach is still too much the Hegelian.

Unlike Feuerbach, naturalists do not identify the human species with the Absolute, for naturalists reject the whole notion of an all-inclusive Absolute. In saying that the God which mystics and others meet inside themselves *is* none other than the mystics themselves, naturalists are saying that there is no God at all. Believers do not 'encounter' or 'confront' God in the 'inner depths of their being'. Rather they encounter the inner world of the body. In *Honest to God* John A. T. Robinson contends that God is not 'out there'. So where is he? Well, claiming to follow Tillich, Robinson comes close to thinking that somehow God is found in the inner walls and muscles of the body. Some traditions have taught that God dwells in a temple, which is said to be the house of God. In our own day, with its new emphasis upon the human body, God is thought of as dwelling in the bodies of the human species (at least).

Thanks to hundreds of years of astronomy's searching and scanning the heavens, we have pretty well been forced to give up the naïve medieval notion of God's existing somewhere in outer space. But the naturalists contend that the recent retreat to the 'inner space' of the body will offer no better sanctuary for God than did

1. The translator does not capitalize the *a* in *Absolute*, but I have done so because Feuerbach has in mind the Hegelian Absolute. Of course, in German the first letter of every noun is capitalized. Feuerbach's italics.

outer space. Physiologists, neurologists, internists, and the like are busy exploring the inner world of the body in a way that astronomers explored outer space.

So long as we were without the telescope and other instruments for scanning the heavens, naïve theists could still have at least a vague notion of the Father in heaven. So long as they lacked the microscope and other instruments for exploring the world enclosed inside the skin, naïve theists could speak of God as existing in 'the heart' or 'mind' or in some vague inner sanctum of the body-temple. Indeed, the soul as a kind of inner being was thought by some to be residing in the body, where it communed with God. But because the soul is no longer believed to reside inside, it follows that God cannot meet it there.

In ancient and medieval times God's permanent address was thought by many to be in a third or seventh heaven. Other homes – such as earthly temples – were only temporary abodes for God. The inner space of the self was similarly divided into various levels or spheres. In the book of Romans (7:22), for example, St. Paul spoke of his 'inmost self', which is somewhat like the third or seventh heaven. That is, the inner self is insulated from the inferior members of the body. St. Paul's own body was composed of 'members' which he himself regarded as under the dominance of sin, just as parts of the lower heavens were thought to be dominated by evil powers and principalities. This lower *vs.* higher distinction is found in both the inner space of the self and the outer space of St. Paul's cosmology. It is as if the human body is a kind of microcosm of the whole of reality, with its gradation. The higher realm of outer space and the higher self (which sometimes turns out to be 'Christ within') are thought of by St. Paul as coming together in some 'mystical' way.

One recourse for theists is that of saying simply that all this talk of the body and cosmology, of the higher and the lower, is only metaphorical and figurative talk. God does not 'really' live in some place in outer space; nor does he reside somewhere inside the human body. Indeed, he does not exist in any location at all. According to this view, because God is Spirit, he transcends spatial dimensions. Nels Ferré's book *The Living God of Nowhere and Nothing* (1966) pretty much expresses this point of view. As expected, Ferré claims that the best way to think of God is not in terms of a person but in terms of Spirit.

What Ferré seems to want to do is to let God manifest himself here and there, in time and space, without 'God himself' being located in space or time. In this way the deity can literally come in from nowhere. It is a way of having a God who is thoroughly involved with the world of change and yet never running any genuine existential risks. All the divine risks are peripheral. In this sense God himself is above religion, that is, he does not really suffer core-concern, but rather, for Ferré, provides the *solution* to humanity's core-concern with finitude.

Theologians claim that in speaking about religion, the individual always speaks from some perspective, commitment, or theoretical framework. I accept this, although I would add that one and the same person may learn to speak from more than one perspective. For example, I am not myself an evangelical Christian, but I have little doubt that under a pseudonym I could write a book explicating certain evangelical beliefs in such a way that evangelicals would think it to have been written by one of their fellow believers. Indeed, it is quite possible that a non-evangelical could make a *creative* contribution to evangelical literature. Still, all writings are produced from a particular perspective, which is not to say that having once begun within a particular perspective a writer may not discover that he had written himself progressively into another perspective. Now, the purpose of this paragraph is to say that in the next chapter I will be writing from a non-supernaturalistic (or naturalistic) perspective. It is useful to look at religious responses from many perspectives.

F. THE MYSTIC'S 'KNOWLEDGE' OF GOD

Not all mystics claim that it is God who is known through mystical experience. The monist interprets the theist's 'experience of God' to be a valuable but still misleading way to speak of oneself being absorbed into the Absolute, which is said to be beyond the subject-object distinction or beyond all pluralistic categories, including those of theism.

Both in his disagreement with other mystics and in his own claim to superior knowledge, the mystic forces us to rethink what we mean when we say we 'know' something. If one has an epistemology rooted in the scheme of Darwinian evolution, he will see continuity between human and animal knowing. Biologically the primate has a curiosity drive or a disposition to explore. Or, stated somewhat differently, the primate is deprived or restless and cannot 'cure' this state until he explores, searches, or exhibits certain kinds of behavior which we designate under the heading of 'curiosity'. It is a bit misleading to say that a primate – including a human – is motivated by curiosity. Rather the deprived or restless state and its accompanying searchings *are* the curiosity.

There is a biological base to epistemology. The mystic comes to cease to be restless. His searching ends – at least for a while. Completely absorbed in this fulfilling mystical experience, he is no longer 'driven' to seek fulfillment in any other direction. 'This is it!' The restless heart has found peace for at least a while. However, this is only a biological and psychological report. The fact that someone's felt deprivation has come to a point of fulfillment (temporarily at least) does not tell us too much about *what* provided the fulfillment. A good meal may fill full (fulfill) the stomach and thus temporarily stop hunger deprivation. But that in no way gives the satisfied individual the authority to speak about the vitamin content of the food he has eaten or anything else about it except that it satisfied him.

'Adam knew Eve'. But it is doubtful that sexual intercourse constitutes a special epistemological state even though, like the mystic's experience, the sexual experience seems to invite repeated experiences throughout one's life. Does a Don Juan have more understanding than a psychoanalyst does of the problems and lives of women? To be sure, Don Juan may be in a position to make certain observations that the analyst cannot make, but sexual intercourse seems not to provide profound knowledge of a person of the opposite sex. It is doubtless an opportunity to learn something under very special conditions, just as traveling on a ship with someone doubtless provides special conditions for learning something special about him.

The point is that when the mystic says he knows God in his mystical experience, it is not clear what he means, and he may himself be very misled or mistaken. Oedipus 'knew' his mother but still did not 'know that' the woman he had had intercourse with was his mother. According to the thirty-eighth chapter of Genesis, Judah knew Timar his daughter-in-law, that is, had sexual intercourse with her, but did not know that it was Timar until many months later. 'She conceived by him', but he did not so much as conceive of the possibility that it was Timar he had lain with.

The task of sorting out the subjective belief from objective knowledge-statements is difficult but necessary if we are not to bind ourselves to accept as objective knowledge every claim to knowledge that is made. The important thing about human belief is that it can be formulated into knowledge-claims. When put into language forms, our beliefs become objects (objective claims) that can be scrutinized. The mystic is very reluctant to objectify his claims. He seems to want to make his claims in public formulations but not to want to have his claims scrutinized.

The mystic practices a linguistic trick, which perhaps is played on himself as well as others. It is the trick of using the word 'know' in an equivocal way. It is conceivable that in the dark two people could 'know' each other by having intercourse with one another, but not know who the other is or at least not know very much about him. It is likewise conceivable that the mystic knows very little about the 'objective referent' of his special experience. He might be even more mistaken than Judah was in his particular experience with Timar. St. Theresa never doubted her mystical experience, but it often worried her that she could not know whether she was making contact with God or Satan. A person can 'know healing' (i.e., can experience being healed) but be wholly mistaken as to what brought about the healing.

Core-deprivation and the Promise of Fulfillment

A. THEOLOGY: PROBLEM OR SOLUTION?

What Professor Nels Ferré (1966) seems to have done is to postulate that there must be an eternal answer or resolution to the human core-concern with finitude. But because he knows the history of theology so thoroughly, he is quite sensitive to the many problems plaguing theology, which is one reason why he rejects a great deal of traditional Christian theology, even though he regards himself as a Christian. As often happens, when a solution is brought in to deal with certain questions and problems, the solution itself generates questions and problems of its own. If Jesus as the savior resolves the human sin problem, he also creates the problem of his relationship to God the Father, to say nothing of the problem of somehow uniting the deity of Jesus with his humanity. And that, of course, brings forth the embarrassing questions as to whether the *humanity* of Jesus was itself deified and whether all human beings who are 'in Christ' have their humanity also deified. This solution, in turn, creates a thicket of new problems for those insisting on drawing an absolute line between God and man. In short, the Incarnation was said to solve some profound problems rising out of the core-concern with finitude, but it also became a fertile seedbed of new and complicated problems.

As noted in the first chapter, religion may have many dimensions – emotional, moral, and cognitive. If the belief in Christ as the savior does heal emotional wounds, it also, for many people, cuts new wounds of at least a cognitive nature. It is not uncommon for a religious response to a problem of one dimension to become a great burden or even outrage in another dimension. There is some evidence to conclude that religious responses have created as many problems and resulted in as much grief and sorrow as they have created successful solutions. There is in religion a high divorce rate, as it were, as well as a high rate of second and third marriages. That is, individuals are divorcing themselves from one religious pattern of responses and moving into another that seems more promising.

Another example of how theology purports to solve one problem but in the process produces another, perhaps even a worse one, is found in the doctrine of heaven and hell. It is often said by orthodox Christians with Arminian tendencies that God respects human choice so much that he gives everyone the option of going to hell for eternity. Ferré speaks for many Christians and other theists who do not find this to be consistent with their view of God's perfection. So, they conclude, if God is really going to be regarded as solving the sin problem, then he cannot be seen as having completed only half the job.

B. PERFECT BEING AS PERFECT SOLUTION

Norman Malcolm, in defending the ontological argument, suggests that the longing for Perfect Being stems psychologically and religiously from the need to have someone who is equal to all our sins. Malcolm explains:

> There is the phenomenon of feeling guilt for something that one has done or thought or felt or for a disposition that one has. One wants to be free of this guilt. But sometimes the guilt is felt to be so great that one is sure that nothing one could do oneself, nor any forgiveness by another human being, would remove it. One feels a guilt that is beyond all measure, a guilt 'a greater than that which cannot be conceived'. Paradoxically, it would seem, one nevertheless has an intense desire to have this incomparable guilt removed. One requires a forgiveness that is beyond all measure, a forgiveness 'a greater than which cannot be conceived'. Out of such a storm in the soul, I am suggesting, there

arises the conception of a forgiving mercy that is limitless beyond all measure (1963: 160f.).

Malcolm then goes on to quote Kierkegaard (*The Journals*, 1938, Sec. 926):

'There is only one proof of the truth of Christianity and that, quite rightly, is *from the emotions*, when the dread of sin and a heavy conscience torture a man into crossing the narrow line between despair bordering upon madness – and Christendom.' (Italics added.)

It is well known that Kierkegaard felt such intense guilt that he bordered on madness. To save himself from this fate he required a conviction that he had been forgiven. His need to feel saved was prior to everything. Malcolm, however, has a need to come to terms with the *cognitive* dimension of his religious concern. Hence, he writes what he regards as an intellectually defensible version of the ontological argument.

Kierkegaard and Ferré are saying that if we have an infinite depth of sin, there must be an Infinite Forgiver. Ferré is like a number of Christians who, while not terribly concerned with the ontological argument, nevertheless are committed to the belief that there is One who is perfect in the sense of being sufficient to the task of saving us from sin and death. Here we raise the question of the *kind* of Perfect Being to be adored, worshipped, or called upon. It is as if the idea of Perfect Being, having been sketched out by St. Anselm, now needs to be 'colored in'. Various schools of theism color the Perfect Being according to their own deep needs and desires. For Ferré, this Perfect Being is conceived to be the Perfect and Eternal Spirit of Love. For the Muslim and many Calvinists, perfection is thought of in terms of a superlative *will*; that is, the power to carry through what God has begun, to accomplish what he declared to be his purpose. This is not to deny that Ferré rejects the notion of God's *will*; for, after all, his God eventually gets his way, although by means of persuasion and time. Calvin and Muhammad do not deny God's love and grace, but they 'color' love with a shade different from Ferré's shade. The difference in emphasis between them, nevertheless, is significant and far-reaching.

C. CORE-CONCERN AND UNIVERSAL RECONCILIATION

The appeal of universalism, on the one hand, and a kind of neo-Calvinism, on the other hand, are both embraced by Karl Barth. Unlike theologians H. H. Farmer and John Baillie, Barth has not clearly drawn the conclusion of universal salvation, but Brunner thinks that Barth may, nevertheless, have accepted the premises which demand such a conclusion. Desiring to emphasize both divine grace and divine freedom, Barth is reluctant to say that all human beings will in fact be reconciled by divine grace; for that would turn this grace into an *obligation* to mankind. Barth detests the notion of divine grace being conceived of as automatic. Yet, at the same time, he believes that this grace cannot be thwarted, not even by human sin. In this position Barth's theology of salvation remains suspended (1960, IV/1: 135, 834-835).

Other theologians, however, believe that God's obligation to reconcile all creation and every human creature to himself is an obligation essentially to *himself*. It is God's remaining true to his fundamental character. This is more or less the position of Farmer, Ferré, and Baillie. F. W. Farrar also seems to be thinking in this direction when he complains that the doctrine of eternal damnation belittles the sacrifice of Christ. Hence, Farrar writes, 'How frightful a result, in spite of how infinite a sacrifice' (cited in Berkouwer 1956: 212).

D. RECONCILIATION OF DESIRES

Theologian G. C. Berkouwer (1956), rejecting the conclusion of universal reconciliation, asserts that 'the doctrine of apokatastasis[1] can find its roots in the *desire* to elevate God's triumph above every resistance. . . .' (p. 212. Italics added.) The naturalist, agreeing with Berkouwer at this point, conjectures further that religion and theology themselves are born in human desire – the desire to find some way to overcome finitude, to relieve human beings of their deepest frustrations and defeat, to overcome whatever resists

1. Distributive and collective total reconciliation.

humans absolutely and completely. (This is, of course, expressed differently from one context to another.)

In keeping with the naturalistic thesis is the view that the complexities of theology mirror the conflicts and complexities of human desires. Berkouwer is correct to say that 'a speaking about the triumph of grace and of the love of God is always a *complex* speaking' (p. 212). But the naturalist takes this in a different light: Because human desires are complex, their theology will invariably become complex. For the humanist, there is no special theological mystery here; there is, rather, enormous complexity. Because human beings desire numerous and diverse things of their deity, not all of their desires could conceivably be met even by omnipotence.

Hence, in postulating a superior, perfect being, theists have always had to resort to a kind of procedure of conflict and compromise even in what they postulate as perfection. That is, if the perfect God is to be adequate to deal with one problem, he will necessarily be *in*-adequate to deal with a problem that is in genuine conflict with the former one. This is not because God is conceived of as being low in resources, but because not even an infinite supply of resources could deal with problems whose solutions mutually exclude one another. Theology, therefore, will continue to proceed in the manner of 'conflict and compromise' so long as the desires of human beings are in conflict.

E. 'ORIGINAL' CONFLICT AND 'ULTIMATE' SOLUTION

B. F. Skinner once stated that original sin might better be seen as 'original conflict' (1962: 104). Barth himself seems to postulate a kind of original conflict in or with God – *das Nichtige* or chaos.[2]

---

2. See Karl Barth, *Church Dogmatics*, III 1: 108–109, 117, 123; III/4: 366. Of this term *das Nichtige*, Harry R. Boer explains: 'It does not mean "nothingness" but connotes active, destructive power of a wholly negative character, as is suggested by the corresponding German and Dutch verbs "vernichten", "vernietigen", which mean: to annihilate, utterly to destroy. The concept "das Nichtige" is a powerful one in Barth's theology and particularly so in his doctrine of creation. It is intended to designate the non-created chaos reality which God in creation "passed by in disdain". It is the everthreatening foe of man and constitutes the enemy over which grace triumphs' (1956: 62, n.*).

Barth's *das Nichtige* is an ambivalent concession to something which Plato (in the *Timaeus*), John Stuart Mill, and E. S. Brightman see as a kind of primordial 'given' with which God must in some way contend because it is not something which God simply created. Brightman, going so far as to say that in his own being God endures conflicts of his own, uses the phrase 'nonrational given' to designate this conflict dimension of the divine life. In other words, for Brightman, not even God has all his aims and interests in perfect harmony. There is struggle in God, despite Aristotle and various Christians who seemed to say that God is always in perfect peace and tranquility, without any frustration whatsoever (1958: 57, 349–350).

God, like the mystics, is portrayed by most theists – orthodox or otherwise – as not always enjoying complete tranquility. In fact, he is portrayed as sometimes becoming quite agitated and upset, as if things were getting somewhat out of hand. What the naturalist wants to say at this point is that it is very difficult, if not impossible, even to *imagine* a perfectly tranquil and peaceful being who also is *involved* in a life or world of conflicting desires. Nirvana-womb may be perfectly tranquil, but the price for such a state may be that of extinguishing the flame of desire altogether, and some Buddhists appear willing to pay this price.

What the naturalistic conclusion seems to be is that *there simply is no perfect resolution to human finitude.* Breaking out with conspicuous propaganda, however, Billy Graham makes a fantastic campaign promise, ostensibly on God's behalf, when he says the following of heaven, the perfect place:

> It will be as wonderful and beautiful as only the Creator can make it. Everything for your personal happiness and enjoyment is being prepared. *Every longing and every desire* will have *perfect fulfillment.* . . . Heaven will be the perfection we have always longed for. All things that made earth unlovely and tragic will be absent in heaven (1966: 220).

Unfortunately, like most campaign promises, not all wants and desires can be satisfied, and in his less sensational moments Mr. Graham has to say that in the first place few people are going to enter the narrow gate leading to heaven, and in the second place those who do make it will have been divested of a great number of their desires – for example, the desire for sexual intimacy.

F. ALL PERFECTIONS ARE FINITE STATES

Throughout the centuries people have *spoken* of a perfect Camelot or Heaven, but they cannot speak in *detail* about it before running into the conclusion that a perfect state is not even *imaginable* unless some desires are eliminated from the picture. The Ancient Greeks seemed to realize that 'the limitless' is chaos, without form or structure and, therefore, is void of discrimination and meaning. All those religious responses which purport to solve human finitude by guaranteeing everlasting life do so in only a compromise form. Even in their free imagination they can do no more than promise that *some aspects* of the individual will live forever, while other aspects will simply have to be sacrificed – annihilated.

Immortality or resurrection can never be even a *promise* of more than partial life. Mysticism tries to promote the finite to the status of the infinite, but sometimes the 'transformation' and 'transportation' resembles *elimination*. If the finite one loses himself in the Infinite, what does he in turn find himself to *be*, if anything? In short, finitude follows us even into heaven, if we are to have any identity at all. The promise-makers finally resort to the very drastic device of, on the one hand, promising that all our desires will be *satisfied*, but adding, on the other hand, the qualification that many wants and desires will simply be *extinguished before* we enter heaven. And that is all that could conceivably be expected.

When the preacher would give *vent to the id* by promising to fulfill all the heart's desires, he must later tell his new converts that he was speaking hyperbolically and evangelistically and that they must not expect more than even God can provide.

G. PRIDE AND GUILT

I wish to return to Norman Malcolm's forthright comment about the psychological and religious roots of the ontological argument.

He says that the individual may come to the point where he cannot find a way to be rid of his heavy guilt. No other person can forgive him. He requires an infinite forgiveness to rid him of 'a guilt that is beyond all measure'. Malcolm, of course, believes that, fortunately, the desperate longing for an infinite reservoir of forgiveness does in fact exist in the Perfect Being than whom none greater can be conceived.

A naturalist, on the other hand, is not convinced that the ontological argument, or any other case defending theism, can hold water. Instead of seeing himself as drenched in *hybris* because he does not believe in the Perfect Being, the naturalist tends to argue that *hybris* is more likely to characterize the individual who sees his guilt in cosmic terms. Without denying the social and personal instrumental value of guilt, the naturalist thinks that those who speak of their own guilt in cosmic, infinite, and eternal terms are endeavoring to make themselves into something they are not. An individual's guilt, says the naturalists, is, when realistic, a reflection of some evil done against other finite creatures who feel and hurt. The evil done may be very far-reaching indeed, but it is not infinite.

This is not to deny that the effects of our evil deeds are subtle and usually impossible to track down in perfect detail. If we are taught, and come to believe, that we have no right either to a place in the scheme of things or to happiness until the infinite effects of our evil deeds are all somehow collected and compensated for, then we will quite naturally and eagerly embrace the promise which assures us that our evil deeds have all been located by an omnipotent observer who is self-empowered to forgive us of everything.

The naturalist tends to look upon the sort of person who is desperately 'under conviction' as being somewhat like the obsessional neurotic who cannot enjoy living in his house until he has convinced himself that it is spotlessly clean. The neurotic may worry to the point of physical illness because he knows that he can never really eliminate all dirt and dust from his house. The psychotic, however, may 'solve' his problem by coming to believe that it is in fact perfectly clean. This, then, gives him permission to live in it.

The naturalist thinks that some theists are like the psychotic. Through various devices and programs they become convinced that the requirement of absolute purity has in reality been met. 'Jesus paid it all'; the slate has been wiped clean; the sins have been washed away; etc. Most Christians who become involved in this elaborate ritual and program leave it at the metaphysical level, for they can see that in their daily lives they continue to do evil. Some of them naïvely believe that God comes along behind them, as it were, to pick up the pieces and to make their evil deeds less harmful than they would ordinarily be. It is this sort of irresponsibility that naturalists and some theists protest against.

Holiness Christians attempt to translate their transcendental views of forgiveness into daily life – to the point of declaring themselves to be empirically, rather than simply transcendentally, sinless. To maintain such a self-image, one must learn to concentrate more on sins of commission than sins of omission. It would be interesting to see whether, as the holiness Christians increase their financial and educational status, they come to regard their sinlessness in more transcendental than empirical terms.

H. RISING EXPECTATION IN RELIGION

In religious treatises, such words as 'ultimate', 'basic', 'fundamental', and 'deepest' appear in comparatively high ratio. Tillich even speaks of religion as 'ultimate concern'. As I attempted to show in an earlier chapter, the concern with finitude is concern with what is perceived as one's basic or central self, although I emphasized that the central focus of the self is defined and perceived variously from culture to culture, and group to group. To a great extent, one's self-identity is considerably tied up with one's interests and desires, which, of course, may differ widely from person to person (cf. Lee, 1959: 70–77).

Interests and desires are central in that, when deprived of satisfaction, the organism expends an enormous amount of energy in overcoming the deprivation. To speak somewhat metaphorically, if you want to know what is in a person's heart, then observe what it is he has his heart in. Where his interests are, there his heart is also. Now, one remarkable thing about human beings is their flexibility in acquiring new interests and desires. The newly married young man and woman are not born with a desire to own a home of their own; it is not 'natural' to either of them. But they may acquire this desire to the point that it becomes an obsession. They will talk about it, think about it, work extra-long hours for it, and even pray for it.

In understanding various religious responses it would prove fruitful to ask just how a person comes to feel profoundly deprived if he does not own a home, or at least does not have a way for eventually getting it. Indeed, the desire may become in his outlook a *need* or even a *right*. Behavioral scientists point out how the individual is cued, stimulated, and reinforced in a variety of ways to take on new desires or expectations. Anthropologist Dorothy Lee expresses this point clearly:

> In speaking of these other cultures, I have not used the term *need*. I could have said, for example, that the Ontong-Javanese needs a large house, to include many maternally related families. But I think this would have been merely an exercise in analysis. On the other hand, when I spoke of our own culture, I was forced to do it in terms of needs, since I have been trained to categorize my experience in these terms. But even here there are no basic needs, but rather part of a system expressing our basic values; and were we able to break away from our substantial or formal categorizing, I think we should find these to be aspects or stresses or functions, without independent existence. Culture is not, I think, 'response to the total needs of a society'; but rather [is] a system which stems from and expresses something [already] had, [namely,] the basic values of society (1959: 76).

What I wish to argue here is that just as no particular style of house is universally basic to the species (but rather is socially, culturally, and individually tailored) so 'salvation' has many forms and styles, no one of which is universal or basic.

An expectation of something is often built up by actually having it more or less regularly and then being deprived of it. There are conditions under which an individual normally received fulfillment of a desire. When these conditions come into existence, the individual begins responding in the way that he has normally responded under those conditions or stimuli. This action on his part is called anticipation or expectation behavior. For example, a child comes home from school and regularly finds an orange and sandwich waiting for him. But on a certain day it is not there. After having looked thoroughly in the refrigerator, and perhaps looking again, he may search for one of his parents. In short, the child has been conditioned to expect the snack. To be *deprived* is to have taken away what one has come to expect. If the child's mother or father tells him each day thereafter that he can still expect his snack to be waiting for him, he will more likely believe that he has a *right* to expect it to be there. Behaviorally he will look for the snack and even complain if it is not where he predicted it would be.

A child may have his expectations raised by being told in July that he will receive a bicycle for Christmas. Similarly, many Christians have come to live in expectation of a life after death, a life in which their particular central desires will be fulfilled. They have been taught through a program of 'Christian education' to believe that their present life has meaning only because it will reach into the infinite future and will never die.

While the naturalist sees no grounds for concluding that anyone will be *eternally* important and *infinitely* significant, he nevertheless can live in peace with those who have been taught that at least their own lives are eternally significant. He might even concede that under certain conditions it might be morally permissible for a parent to tell his child that he will receive a bicycle on Christmas day, even if the parent knows that the child will never in fact receive it. To be sure, this would be a cruel thing to do in most cases. But consider the following case: Having talked with the team of physicians and specialists, the parent now realizes that his child will not live beyond the middle of October. Knowing also that his child will very soon be too weak to ride a bicycle, the parent promises the child that he will receive a bicycle on Christmas day and will be able to ride it to his heart's desire. In looking forward to that day, *the child is made happy.*

Whether this bit of deception by the parent is justifiable I will not go into here. It is certainly understandable. If a naturalist could understand why a parent would give his or her child the promise of a bicycle on Christmas day, then the naturalist could understand why one person might promise another that he will live forever. Indeed, the naturalist himself does not believe that people will actually live for ever, but he might say to himself, 'What harm is there in letting some people believe they will live after death if it comforts them and makes them happy? Why should anyone wish to disillusion them?'

However, many Christians are not willing to leave the matter there. Some are not even willing to acknowledge that those who do not believe in everlasting life after death can have a happy and meaningful life *here and now*. These Christians tell children and adults alike that their lives are wholly without value and meaning if they do not accept the Christian beliefs about life after death and about the procedures for moving into a state of bliss rather than torment in the next life. It is this sort of Christian pressure that naturalists find objectionable.

The naturalist, if he is knowledgable in the social sciences, looks upon the Christian view of sin and salvation as strictly a part of the cultural and social system of Christianity. The 'need for salvation' is no more universal than a learned tribal need to dance before ancestral ghosts. In each case, the cultural and social system creates needs of its own, just as the American society creates a need for gasoline and oil to fuel automobiles. While people do need means of transportation, the means vary greatly. Similarly, many people need a way to feel assured that they belong to that which is designated as supremely significant, but how this assurance is actually brought about varies considerably from culture to culture and from religion to religion. Indeed, what is 'supremely significant' or of 'ultimate concern' is not an ontological category but, rather, is culturally, socially, and individually defined within the limits of 'nature'.

In his book *Prisoner of Mao* (1973) Bao Ruo-wang tells how grown men and women are brought to the point where they *want* to confess their sins against the government of China and how they come to volunteer to speak in glowing terms of the generosity of the Chinese

Communist system. To borrow the language of evangelical Christianity, the individual is brought 'under conviction' by a number of well delivered cues, stimuli, and reinforcers (both positive and negative). The great relief and transformation in the convert's life comes when the systematic pattern of cues, stimuli, and reinforcers surrounding his life are transformed or radically changed. There is no mysterious Spirit at work in the process of changing people into Communists. And the naturalist does not find any mysterious Spirit at work in Christian conversion. There is, rather, a complex of variables and contingencies at play. Some people convert to Communism and some do not – depending on what the natural and cultural contingencies are, including the factors in each individual's unique personal background, with its special contingencies and variables.

The point here is that no religion seems to be warranted in the claim that it meets the 'basic needs' of the individual because 'needs' are contextual, and what is 'basic' cannot be defined in ontological categories. When St. Augustine wrote that human hearts are restless until they find rest in God, he was insensitive not only to the great diversity of the styles of restlessness, but to the numerous ways in which people find what they regard as peace and tranquility. If modern Christians would like to specify some independent criteria of tranquility and then assert as an empirical claim that only Christianity can satisfy these criteria, then there would be the possibility of *testing* the hypothesis. As is often the case, however, the very meaning of 'peace and tranquility' is defined in the categories of the religion making the claim, which makes the claim, then, something of a tautology.

I. TEACHING PEOPLE TO FALL INTO DESPAIR

Promises have a way of sometimes breeding discontent as well as hope. Some branches of Christianity appear to feed themselves by breeding discontent in others. Although the naturalist cannot consistently oppose all rising expectations in religion, he can in consistency raise the question of whether there are foreseeable means of meeting certain specific expectations. Unfortunately, if an individual is conditioned into expecting to be profoundly discontent with this present world, then he will tend to move toward despair unless he can believe the promise of heaven or the equivalent for which he feels he is destined or elected. The naturalist points out that many people cannot believe the promise of life after death or believe in certain other Christian doctrines. Nevertheless, these people need to be equipped intellectually, morally, and emotionally to defend themselves against the Christian who sets out to sew the seeds of despair so that he may, when the time is ripe, take advantage of the persons suffering the despair.

Kierkegaard thought that his only options were either Christianity or 'despair bordering on madness'. Finding in his own life that Kierkegaard's dilemma is a false one, the naturalist gives his own 'witness' that there are other ways which are intellectually, morally, and emotionally worthy of commitment outside the circles of Islam, Christianity, and theistic Judaism.

J. THE RIGHT TO LIFE AFTER DEATH

If an individual learns to expect life after death, he will more than likely come to believe that he has a *right* to it. True, Christians are concerned to say that life after death is not a right but a gift of grace received by faith. However, once the requirement of *faith* has been met, some Christians believe that they then have a *right* to resurrection or immortality.

Indeed, a large number of Christians maintain that God would not have brought people into the world only to let them die in due time without giving them at least a very good chance at everlasting life. Implicit in this view is that God owes them a genuine option for life beyond the grave. With this as background, it is not surprising that some people believe that there is in fact such an option. They think it is somehow *required*; in effect they *demand* it. They have been led to believe that the universe *ought* to be a 'moral universe' that pays them respect and regard for eternity.

According to the position of naturalists, there is no basis for anyone's feeling that he has a right to life after death. Certainly no one can demand it without suffering illusions. In short, the naturalist says that nature does not owe anyone anything. True, if there were a creator who is somewhat sensitive to the longings of finite creatures, then he might come under the moral obligation to give resurrection to his creatures if he had the power to do it. But naturalism does not think the case for belief in such a conscious creator is a strong case.

The task, then, is to learn how to enjoy life and to share in the joy of others even if no finite life is forever. Naturalism believes this task would be easier if some Christians could restrain themselves from trying to make especially children feel unhappy and miserable if they do not embrace the Christian beliefs. Naturalists look upon some Christians as members of a strange tribe who want to tell ghost stories to children outside their own tribe. Sometimes the only alternative which naturalists believe they have is to fight back by exposing what they regard as the illusions of Christians. Unfortunately, this affects believing Christians, disillusioning some of them and making them unhappy. This seems to be a tragic aspect of the interchange between naturalists (most of whom do not believe in life after death) and Christians (most of whom do believe in everlasting life).

The ideal would be to raise children to consider the various sides of the issue (and other such issues) and also to give them moral and emotional support for looking carefully at the various sides. Unfortunately, most parents find it difficult to do this. The bitter conflict in parts of West Virginia regarding textbooks to be used for children reflects the inability of many parents to allow their children to look into views with which the parents themselves do not agree. This is true of many parents, regardless of whether they are naturalists or theists.

K. NATURALISM AND CHRISTIAN *HYBRIS*

The informed naturalist believes that he can appreciate the Christian and Islam appeal. People come to expect to wake up tomorrow, to be alive, to be living. It is disturbing to have to say that this pattern of waking up will someday be completely broken. The chicken every morning zestfully greets the farmer, who has been feeding him morning after morning. The chicken has a kind of behavioral faith or trust in the farmer. But on a certain day the poor bird, coming to be fed as always, is caught by the farmer and killed immediately.

The naturalist is saying that someday human lives, too, will just as surely be ended once for all. True, people, having been rewarded with life everyday, do very reasonably come to expect to live day after day. But, says the naturalist, this life is for only a season and there seems to be no spring after the final winter. It is not that some Cosmic Farmer creates human beings only to snuff out their lives for his own pleasure. Rather, says the naturalist, there is no divine cosmic consciousness at all to either love or hate anyone. There is a cosmic scenery but no cosmic drama in which God and human creatures together carry out a plot.

This chilling thought simply cannot be faced by some people who have been taught to think that their lives are empty and void unless they somehow live forever and are remembered by a cosmic consciousness for eternity. If they raise Karl Popper's question, 'Does history have any meaning?', they think that history must have meaning if their own lives are to have any value, meaning, or significance. The naturalist believes that Christianity, Islam, certain branches of Judaism, and various other religions have made it almost impossible for some people to face forthrightly the possibility of their own permanent death. The naturalist charges also that some versions of theism have yielded to the temptation to tell people simply what they want to hear: namely, that they are in some ways infinite and eternal.

In two ways, concerned naturalists attempt to respond to what they regard as theism's grandiose claims about the human species: (1) First, naturalists seek to cure theism of *hybris* by placing the human species and individual in a less grandiose perspective. (2) Second, naturalists endeavor to establish their own 'religious education' program in order to provide children and adults a different frame work for looking at sin and immortality. They endeavor to teach them not to expect that each of their evil deeds will be individually tracked down, paid for, and forgiven. In other words, naturalism contends that people can both be socially constructive and face the fact that the universe is not a neat and tidy weighing station. There are loose threads and injustices in the mix-up of things, and the task is to increase the *degree* of justice for the purpose of advancing enjoyment and interesting living. Regarding this second point, naturalists argue that the hope of somehow making everything come out even 'in the end', as if life were a Charles Dickens novel, is an illusion, especially when it is projected onto the cosmic screen. The theistic vision of God's 'finally' coming in to restore everything in perfect order is the child's fairy tale, wherein the good fairy waves the wand to restore everything to its proper place and doles out reward and punishment with perfect and absolute justice.[3] Naturalists see no basis for believing in such an 'ultimate denouement'.

L. FREEING IMAGINATION FROM CONVICTION

As noted earlier, those theists who believe that their vision of perfection either is or will be instituted in reality are, nevertheless, compelled to admit, in one way or another, that the perfect state is only an *approximation* of perfection. Theodicy will always have problems to wrestle with as long as there are beings in whom new desires come into existence, that is, so long as people are alive.

Earlier I quoted Evangelist Billy Graham's orthodox Christian promise of euphoria and of complete satisfaction of all Christian desires. But there are many liberal Christians who are equally willing to out-do their rivals in making promises of euphoria. Nels Ferré, for example, writes:

> Imagine actually believing that nothing God has ever made will ever be wasted, that God will not only put all things right, but will make out of the whole heap of human and natural tragedy a result so magnificent that in the experience of it whatever went into the making of it will seem sheer praise (1966: 71).

A former true-believer communist of the Soviet-style, Arthur Koestler, knew personally what a 'strong faith' could do to someone.

3. Evangelical Christian E. J. Carnell in *The Kingdom of Love and the Pride of Life* (1960a) contends that the child's fairy tale expresses the Christian's 'conviction of the heart' (pp. 18-19, 71-72).

He writes: 'Faith is a wondrous thing; it is not only capable of moving mountains, but also of making you believe that a herring is a race horse' (1952: 39). The Communist Party to which Koestler belonged for seven years could not tolerate his doubts as to whether a fish is really a race horse. For seven years he had been married to Leah, but the Party kept telling him that she was really Rachel. Finally, he gave up indulging himself in his illusions about the Party, which had assured him that the atrocities of Stalin and the slave camps in Soviet Russia would 'ultimately' lead to the glorious triumph. The Soviet myth – like the theistic myth of Graham, Ferré, and John Hick – had its doctrine of 'eschatological verification'. It, too, had its 'theodicy' by which it justified revenge and destruction. Such mental acrobatism – whether it is called 'the dialectic' or simply 'the Christian's deep and abiding faith' – adds up to the same thing: self-indulgence. Naturalism, at this point at least, would teach theism a measure of discipline and self-control.

Naturalism cannot compete with the Soviet myth or Christian eschatology in terms of promise-making. Nevertheless, naturalism has vision, hope, faith, and imagination. It argues that creative imagination in art, music, literature, dance, ritual, etc., gives human life much of its joy, sustained reinforcement, and meaningfulness. What it asks is that the rich life of imagination be given a place of its own without its being transformed into transcendental *convictions* – at least not until much more rigorous testing than either the Party or the Faith has undergone thus far. By rigorous testing, the naturalist means something different than simply the test of survival. (If survival were the test of value, the cold virus should be enshrined. And compared to the cockroach, Christianity is hardly an infant in the test of survival.)

M. THE SIN OF DESIRING TO BE *INFINITELY* SINFUL

Finally, the naturalist would criticize those Christians who demand that human sins be given cosmic scope and dimension. This criticism, very bluntly, is that these Christians have once again tried to find a way to make themselves feel infinite or to make an infinite impact.

They believe not only that the universe has a Lord who sees human sin, but that the Lord takes it as a profound personal threat to himself. The naturalist can only laugh at such clever arrogance on the part of these finite mortals. By making their *sins* a matter of eternal significance to the eternal God, these Christians have hit upon a way to make *themselves* eternally important and infinitely significant. Indeed, the 'Christian drama' is a play in which the 'terrible infant' causes a great stir in the counsels of eternity and finally generates enough heavenly excitement to effect a temporary split in the Trinity. It is a grand production – this Christian drama. But the naturalist sees it as another example of human pretentiousness and arrogant presumption. It is Prometheus sporting angel wings.

Is God Verifiable?

A. THE VERIFICATION CRITERION

In the previous chapter I wrote from the viewpoint of naturalism. My purpose was to show how it is possible to use the naturalistic perspective from which to talk at least intelligibly about theology without adopting the supernaturalistic perspective. Needless to say, the preceding chapter offered only a bare indication of what the naturalistic position is able to do. Whether it is a more credible position than supernaturalistic theism is something that I will not go into with any philosophical depth.

In his book *The Scientific Study of Religion*, J. Milton Yinger writes, 'Science inevitably takes a naturalistic view of religion' (1970: 531). This raises the question as to what naturalism is and what it stands in contrast to. I mean by naturalism the commitment to speak of the growth of knowledge in terms of better formulated and testable hypotheses that are successful in predicting observables. This entails being at least skeptical of claims which, while purporting to reveal truths, resist all cross examination and experimental testing. However, because this statement of naturalism says very little in some respects, and too much in other respects, it needs to be explicated at length.

In recent years the Principle of Verification has been subjected to a kind of erosion and neglect. The Christian theist Basil Mitchell recently charged Kai Nielsen (an atheist and naturalist) with inconsistently applying the verification criterion. Mitchell also thinks that Nielsen has failed to come to terms with John Hick's theistic defense called 'eschatological verification'. I think Mitchell has inadvertently exposed a serious problem in the verification criterion – so serious that not even eschatological verification can be usefully employed by theists (1931: 11–18).

Furthermore, I will in a later chapter try to show that Nielsen has sometimes confused the verification criterion with the falsification criterion. At the same time I am very much with Nielsen in rejecting the 'conceptual relativism' implicit in some of the neo-Wittgensteinians who think that Wittgenstein opened up a profound way to save 'God-talk' from extinction among thinking people of the twentieth century. Nielsen uses the phrases 'conceptual relativism' and 'Wittgensteinian fideism' to label the position of D. Z. Phillips and others who contend that the criterion of meaning and truth in religion is provided by religion itself. Those who think along the line of Phillips insist that 'religious meaning and truth is not the same as other kinds of meanings and truths. . . .' (Campbell, 1973: 163; cf. Phillips, 1965; Hudson, 1968; Nielsen, 1971: Chap. 5.)

However, if contemporary theism and theology are going to defend themselves with such weapons as John Hick's view of eschatological verification and conceptual relativism or Wittgensteinian fideism, then their victory would seem to be hollow or quixotic at best. To say that religion has its 'logic', science its 'logic', and aesthetics its 'logic', etc., is no improvement over Kant's epistemology although it is accompanied by a better appreciation of anthropology than Kant was able to enjoy.

Neo-Wittgensteinians, armed with cultural relativism, seem to regard themselves as defenders of theology in some respect. But, as I will try to show, they are Durkheimian in their approach to religion and theology. Durkheim was very much a naturalist, hardly a theist, and certainly not a supernaturalist. Some have even regarded him as a positivist (cf. Lukes, 1973; Wallwork, 1972). After reading D. Z. Phillips' neo-Wittgensteinian book *Death and Immortality* (1970), one wonders whether Phillips' case for 'religious language' does not turn out to be a subtle denial of what religious language is supposed to be about. Like Durkheim, Phillips is aware of various 'uses' of religious expressions – both verbal ritual and body ritual – within a society; and he even suggests that if religious language and ritual are eliminated from society, then nothing better can be substituted for it (p. 77). But I fail to see that a believer would welcome Phillips' defense.

This raises the question of whether the religious 'life-form' is preserved only if the inquiries of philosophy and science are suppressed. Is the language of religion to be seen as something like what Plato called a 'convenient lie'? Plato thought the social lie which he had in mind was a kind of necessary glue to help prevent the society from fragmenting. The neo-Wittgensteinian conceptual relativists, therefore, may be actually equivocating about the meaning of 'justification' when they say that religious language can be justified. Shifting from talking in terms of epistemology to talking in terms of sociology and anthropology, they seem to forget that social justification does not entail epistemological justification. However, I even question whether their sociological and anthropological case for religious language is defensible, inasmuch as their presumption of functionalism and the homeostasis model has serious flaws in it. But more of this later.

The point here is that the neo-Wittgensteinians seem to have given up the attempt to defend theism except in terms of social function ('meaning'). The issue of the epistemological justification of belief in God is not treated by them with any seriousness. They prefer a kind of sociological and anthropological version of William James's psychological defense of the right and will to believe. James tried to show that it was psychologically and morally constructive to believe in God. Neo-Wittgensteinians think that such belief is sociologically 'justifiable' in that it provides 'solidarity' (Durkheim) and 'meaning' (Weber) in the community. (Later I will try to show that the term 'meaning' is often a weasel term, difficult to hold, but highly charged emotionally. Perhaps it should be called an 'eel word' in that it is slippery, charged, and 'fishy'.)

I do not wish to imply that the sociological and anthropological inquiry into religious problems and behavior is unwarranted. In fact, religion cannot be profoundly understood apart from this sort of inquiry. My point is that when a radical shift in the way of looking at religion has been made, the shift itself needs to be looked at and *seen for what it is. That is, it ought to be seen as a shift and not* simply as the same thing stated in new terms. The sociologist and anthropologist may think that theology is a self-contained socio-cultural form, but the theologian usually thinks that God-talk has reference beyond the human community. For him, theology is not reducible to sociology or anthropology. In other words, the theologian holds that the phrase 'faith in God' is not simply a code phrase that means 'trust in the social structures and institutions of the community'.

B. CONFUSION REGARDING GOD-TALK

A subtle confusion develops among some of the defenders of religious language and God-talk. It comes about somewhat in the following manner: First, relying on the presumption of Functionalism, they claim that religious discourse and ritual are essential ingredients of the community. (Sometimes this is an empirical claim, which is falsifiable or testable; at other times it is only a circular statement.) Second, with a profound appreciation of what Robert N. Bellah (1974) thinks of as 'symbolic realism', they look upon all language as having some intercourse with dimensions of reality other than language symbols. Because the human animal uses language and symbols to relate to other dimensions, all symbols are in some sense in touch with the reality beyond the finite sociocultural system itself.

It is now, at the third step, that confusion is likely to develop. To say that symbols have intercourse with a reality deeper than the symbols is a necessary but only a preliminary position to take. Unless the defenders of religious language acknowledge that it is only preliminary, they are likely to fall into the trap of complete cultural relativism. (In the previous chapter I explored briefly a naturalistic interpretation of 'salvation' and 'perfection'; naturalism is different from absolute cultural relativism. The former seeks to account for the enormous variety and diversity among people without falling into total relativism in epistemology. In ethics, even emotivism has learned to speak of attitudes in connection with facts and belief systems.)

All symbols are in touch with reality, but not necessarily in the way that their utilizers think they are. If a person enjoys success in utilizing God-talk, or other kinds of religious language, within a ritual and churchly setting, it does not follow that he will be able to carry on God-talk in an illuminating way in other settings. (One of the problems with the defense of religious language which Phillips and other 'conceptual relativists' make is that they give us no way for determining when a setting is or is not cognitive.)

A 'believer' may know what to do in a churchly setting when his minister or priest says, 'Let us now bring our tithes and offerings to Christ' or 'Let us come to Christ through Holy Communion'. Furthermore, the believer may know what is meant – i.e., what to do – when he is challenged by fellow believers to 'serve God at the office'. In this latter case, the behaviors and attitudes to be called upon will vary from one Christian group to another. To one group, 'serve God' means, 'pass out gospel tracts, witness verbally, teach Sunday school, etc.'. 'Believe in Christ' could mean 'confess your sinfulness, say that you accept Christ as personal savior, etc.'. To another group it could mean other things. This great variety of meanings naturally raises the question as to whether one is justified in speaking of Christ at all.

That is, granted that one may become a skillful participant in a Christian community and use God-talk and Christ-talk appropriately, there is still the question as to whether one is rationally justified in engaging sincerely in this talk.

Let me state the issue in this way: If D. Z. Phillips himself engages in prayers at church or speaks of Christ's forgiveness of his sin, does he sincerely believe that there is a Christ who is Phillips' Savior and Lord? This is not a question about Phillips' skill at a ritual or a language game but about the reality of something more than human language or ritual. In other words, is Phillips really in relationship with a cosmic Christ, or are all his relationships contained within the human community, so that the symbol 'Christ' simply stands for a very special cluster or network of human relationships?

Some writers hold that one is justified in using Christ-language and God-talk if people in the 'believing community' know what the person means, that is, they know how to respond appropriately to his discourse. But I am asking about justification in another sense. To explicate what this other sense is requires considerable elaboration. At this stage, perhaps the general direction of my concern can be expressed as follows: Suppose Mark asks, 'Does it make sense to speak of God and Christ?' John replies, 'Well, it makes sense to those in the religious community who talk in that manner'. Mark might then ask, 'But does it make sense to participate in that community in the first place? Or if one does participate, does it make sense to participate in that aspect of the community in which Christ-talk and God-talk are essential ingredients?' In a tribe or community in which witch-talk flows freely, there have been some individuals who did not sincerely participate in this particular aspect of the tribe, although they participated in other aspects. So, might not a person, although living in a community in which God-talk is frequently observed, nevertheless choose not to share in that particular aspect of the community because he thinks that there is no God or Christ to call upon, pray to, or speak about in a believing way? The Wittgensteinian fideists, while admitting that theoretically anyone may step out of any community, or any aspect of that community, nevertheless do not like to explore the *reasons* for not playing the game of God-talk or not participating in the religious community.

C. SOCIAL TOLERANCE DOES NOT ENTAIL LOSS OF EPISTEMOLOGICAL RIGOR

Some of the neo-Wittgensteinians seem to confuse political and social tolerance with a kind of philosophical passivity. Open-mindedness is not flabby-mindedness. To 'accept' another culture politically, socially, etc., does not imply that its claims about God, gods, atoms, witches, etc. should not be challenged with regard to their truth-value. Later I will have to return to the conceptual relativism of the neo-Wittgensteinians. Kai Nielsen does well not to give in to relativism, but in this chapter and the next two I will endeavor to show where I differ with Professor Nielsen as well as the neo-

Wittgensteinians. It is now appropriate to examine the notion of eschatological verification.

D. ESCHATOLOGICAL VERIFICATION

As an up and coming New Testament scholar, C. H. Dodd was concerned to show that the Christian faith is not simply a promise about the wholly remote future. He coined the phrase 'realized eschatology' to describe his view that the finger of God could always be detected in the everyday world. The Kingdom of God was not simply on the 'other side' but existed in our very midst. God was thought of as lovingly governing the world while salvation was in our very surroundings.

But when this position was challenged later by such writers as Alasdair MacIntyre (a former Christian) and Antony Flew (whose father, R. N. Flew, was a New Testament scholar as well as a Methodist leader) – when Dodd and others were challenged, then the Christians' emphasis shifted so that we were told that the divine eschatology is not so 'realized' after all. Challengers like Flew, MacIntyre, and others were in effect saying, 'Show us the sign(s) of his presence'. Theologians and biblical scholars were hard pressed to do without also having to acknowledge Flew's list of counter-evidence suggesting at the very least that God was not governing the world lovingly.

The dilemma for theism developed into something like the following: *Either acknowledge the strong evidence telling against the view that God is lovingly governing the world or admit that statements about God's existence are not even verifiable.* Rather than accept the position that theistic statements are unverifiable, John Hick and others developed the argument of 'eschatological verification'. In substance, this view asserts that while the hypothesis of God's loving and guiding presence in the world cannot *now* be verified because of the lack of sufficient evidence, we will *in the next life* be able to verify it. Flew and others had argued that we can now *observe* things in the world that seem clearly to count as evidence *against* the hypothesis of God's loving providence. Hick and his followers replied in effect that in the next life we will be able to *observe* things which will lead us to conclude that all the things which seemed to count against God's providence were actually a part of God's providence. (Hick is not impressed with the appeal to the Beatific Vision or any 'literal vision of the deity' [1973:90-93].)

In essence, Hick's argument gives a new twist to Flew's charge that Christian theism simply will not allow *anything* to count as evidence *against* the belief of loving divine providence pervading the world. The only concession made to Flew is that many things in the world *seem* to count against the Christian's belief. There is nothing original about Hick's argument that 'ultimately' everything will turn out perfectly. What is novel is his assertion that in the next life we will be able to *verify* that God's loving providence was at work all the while. In short, for Hick, God's loving providence can be eventually verified but never falsified.

Unfortunately, Hick's argument can be turned against him. For in the next life one could use Hick's argument to say, 'Well, things *seem* to support the view of God's loving providence, but the final word is not yet in. By and by we will see that what *seems* to us to be divine providence is really a mistaken impression rooted in our failure to grasp the entire picture, for in the eschaton that is still to come after heaven, we will actually verify that things are not at all like what they now seem to be here in this temporary heaven.'

The presumed fact that in heaven no one would dare to assert such an argument is irrelevant to the logic of the argument. In fact, if such an eschaton should come after an interim of heavenly bliss, the subsequent suffering would be enormous, inasmuch as everyone in heaven would fall into disillusionment and bitterness at having been fools for so long a time.

The charge might be made that speaking in this way about the successor to heaven seems to be too fanciful for us to take seriously. But if this charge is justified, then the counter-charge must be leveled also against Hick's talk of heaven. One view of the next life is as fanciful as the other.

Hick does not so much come to terms with Flew's criticism as postpone having to face it. After all, his argument against Flew

leaves wide open the possibility that the next life could be for everyone even *worse* than what it is here and now. Professor H. H. Price writes that it seems
> likely that if we do live after death, we shall find the doctrine of Purgatory, at any rate, is substantially true, although I would suppose that Purgatory is to be conceived as a kind of nightmare-like dream rather than a place (1972: 85).

Price and others, drawing on paranormal psychology, speculate that in the next life people may have all sorts of drives and desires that are in conflict with one another, drives that cannot be satisfied. This suggests that those people who find the most peace and happiness will be, not Christians, but those like Buddha who sought to extinguish or reduce all desires or expectations. Christians lead their own fellow believers to expect to be indescribably fulfilled and happy in the next life and to look forward to it with eager anticipation. Indeed, this anticipation of heaven is often appealed to in order to make the present life more bearable for Christians. But if the next life is meager in terms of satisfactions, then Christians may turn out to be of all people the most miserable. They will suffer a form of hell because their gap of relative deprivation will be so enormous.

But this is only speculation, which is true also of Hick's statements about the next life. The fact that Hick carries out his speculations 'within the circle of faith' does not make them any less speculative. True, knowledge advances through bold and daring speculation plus testability. But it is this latter step which Hick postpones indefinitely.

E. INDEFINITE POSTPONEMENT OF VERIFICATION

If there is no specified *time* in the next life when God must prove that he is actually governing the world lovingly, then why should any rational person believe that he in fact can justify all the misery, suffering, etc. that has gone on? If God keeps postponing a time of verification, then we have no basis for thinking that a verification will ever come about. We may come to entertain the hypothesis that if there is a deity at all, he cannot be a loving agent in charge of the universe.

Also there is the question of just how much misery God will allow to pile up before he makes it all justifiable. The issue here has to do with the logic of the argument, not the determination of believers to persist in their belief. At Las Vegas and at other gambling centers we can find people who still persist in believing that they will win back all they have invested. Their faith in 'the big win' is strong. But we call it a pathological state at worst, and rationalization at best, if the gambler continues despite great losses. (We must keep in mind that Hick is not trying to justify the *lesser* claim that for most of us this present life is worth living on the whole, but rather the *greater* claim that the whole of creation is governed perfectly and lovingly by an omnipotent God. Naturalism can make the lesser claim without the hypotheses of God and life after death.)

Of course, Pascal and other betting individuals in theistic circles could argue that 'the big win' is just around the corner. But my point is that eschatological verification is empty if the verifying payoff is forever being postponed. Hick's argument allows it to be postponed *almost* forever because he specifies no time when he will be able to say that he will *know* that there is a Heavenly Father running the world lovingly. In this connection it is very important to recall that Hick speaks of the possibility of 'a continuation of the purgatorial suffering often experienced in this life, and leading eventually to the high good of heaven . . . ' (1973: 102). In other words, Hick's view of life after death entails temporal process and change, and I am arguing from Hick's own premises that somewhere in the process either we *must* be provided with evidence to verify the hypothesis of the loving providence of God or we must declare the hypothesis unverified. Hick cannot reply that because God is a loving Heavenly Father he will not postpone verification indefinitely, for this is to presuppose the very hypothesis in question.

It is interesting that even in the next life Hick still will have to *appeal to the future*. I call attention to the word 'eventually' in the quotation from Hick in the above paragraph. The word functions like the loose words 'ultimately' or 'finally', only now Hick says in effect that the ultimate state has to be broken down still more so that there is a *more ultimate* time in the future. What this clearly implies is that *even in the next life we will be forced to appeal to the argument of eschatological verification.*

F. INFINITE REGRESS AND EMPTY CONCLUSION

In his 'eschatological verification' argument, Hick overlooks the fact that he throws theology into an infinite process of postponement. That is, with his argument, there is never a time when we have a right to expect sufficient evidence to verify that there is a loving God governing his creation. Hick has already conceded that in this present life we lack such evidence; for if we possessed it, there would be no need to resort to the eschatological verification argument. Indeed, Hick's argument makes it possible for God to always say, 'Well, there's plenty of time to verify. We have all eternity. True, things *seem* to be pretty bad now but "ultimately" you will see how it all comes together into a perfect picture'.

If in the next life the big payoff of evidence seems to be indefinitely postponed – and on Hick's view we cannot say that such will not be the case – then we may find ourselves believing that if there is a God at all, he is unable to verify that he has sufficient control of things to earn the title of powerful, loving Heavenly Father. Hick's version of eschatological verification leaves open the possibility that there is a cosmic agent of some sort who will postpone always just a while longer. Technically the phrase 'just a little while' does not mean 'forever', yet conceivably the 'little while' need never come to an end. An everlasting cosmic agent has an eternity for saying still once more, 'Wait just a little while'. Indeed, in eternity what would be an operational distinction between a 'little while longer' and 'indefinite postponement'?

G. HELL – THE ACHILLES' HEEL OF HICK'S ARGUMENT

Unlike evangelical or orthodox Christians as well as some Catholics – Roman and Greek – Hick insists that there is at least one evil which, if it exists, will *falsify* the statement that God lovingly governs the world of creation. This inadmissable evil is hell as eternal torment. When Professor Hick advanced his argument of eschatological verification he seemed not to be aware that short of a hell of eternal torment, every conceivable evil and misery could be justified by Hick's argument that 'ultimately' or 'eventually' God will restore all things and demonstrate that his loving providence had all along the way been pervading the universe. In other words, God's 'ends' will 'eventually' justify all his means, with the one exception of eternal hell. (I once asked Nels Ferré if this was his view of theodicy. He responded affirmatively. Ferré and Hick hold to very similar views of eschatological verification, although Ferré holds in addition that a religious experience may be a kind of hole in the fence of eternity through which one may attain at least a glimpse of the whole picture into which all the evils fit in perfect harmony with the statement that God as the Heavenly Father is providentially caring for the world.)

Like Ferré, Hick draws the line where eternal torment is concerned. But he gives no argument as to *why* he must draw it, for he has already set up the principle that God is adequate to explain all other evils. Why not travel still further on the train of faith to conclude that God will 'eventually' show how even hell as eternal torment can be justified? If faith can deliver you to one point, why not to another?

In insisting on drawing the line where hell is concerned, Hick would seem to be forced to say that at some specified *time* in the next life God *must* give an account and verify the belief we have in his loving providence. However, as noted earlier, Hick's argument allows 'purgatorial suffering' to continue *indefinitely* even though it is not technically *forever*. (It would seem that a 'purgatorial suffering' that lasts forever *is* hell.) Hick's thesis does not permit anyone to say that anything has *already* continued forever, for that would contradict the very idea of 'foreverness', which has no terminal point (1973: 92f.). My point is that the logic of Hick's own argument allows us to conclude that *indefinite purgatorial suffering is no different from hell*. This is because Hick establishes no *period* when the cosmic agent *must* present sufficient evidence to verify that he is, after all, a Heavenly Father lovingly governing all of creation. (Hick has already ruled out the notion of a timeless heaven.)

H. THE PROBLEM OF INDUCTION

The problem of induction that philosophers and mathematicians worry themselves about poses a very serious problem for theology. Much of my criticism of Hick's eschatological verification is premised on the view that theology cannot answer Hume's challenge pertaining to evidence for trusting in a promise that covers the entire future forever. To state my point bluntly, Hick's case falls more on his appeal to verification than on his appeal to eschatology. What I wish to challenge is the claim of Hick, Mitchell, Nielsen, and the positivists that verification is possible. With Sir Karl Popper I will argue in the chapter after next that the rejection of the verification criterion does not lead to epistemological anarchy. Nor does it allow us to stipulate, with Bertrand Russell and Kant, an a priori defense of induction. Furthermore, to say that God solves the induction problem is simply to say that we are determined to *believe* that the problem can be solved. The need, however, is to show *how* the appeal to God solves the problem. Merely to say 'God solves the problem' is no more helpful than to say, 'The solution solves the problem'. In the previous chapter I accused theism of too often substituting the word 'God' as a synonym for 'solution' – a kind of verbal magic.

The impact of the problem of induction upon theology is that it leaves theology unable to say that Hick or anyone can ever have sufficient evidence to verify the view that God is a loving Heavenly Father. Even if there is life after death, we will never be in position to *verify* our faith in God. Rather, we shall still have to live by faith, that is, by conjectures and courage. If my argument holds, then not even heaven can overcome our epistemological finitude and the risk that it entails. In the chapter after the next, I will deal with religious faith in light of the problem of induction. In this present chapter I have cut myself off from the criterion of verification (and in the next two chapters will show why this was necessary). But neither can I subscribe to epistemological or conceptual relativism, for this seems to be hardly more than emotivism in epistemology. Hare's 'blick' and Hick's 'circle of faith' are simply skepticism and epistemological relativism with positive passion rather than existential despair. Whether a way can be cut between this relativism on the one side, and verificationism on the other side, remains to be seen. We now must turn to the next chapter where the issue of conceptual or epistemological relativism must be faced.

9

Relativism and Contradiction

A. WHAT EPISTEMOLOGICAL RELATIVISM ENTAILS

Very briefly, epistemological relativism entails that there is no rational way for determining whether one general outlook on the world is more credible than another. The noted anthropologist E. E. Evans-Pritchard (1937: 195-476) points out that a society of witchcraft, oracles, and magic forms a kind of coherent system, coherent in the sense that each strand of this system more or less connects with every other strand. But a secular society which rejects such beliefs as witchcraft and magic has also a certain belief-system of its own.

G. J. Warnock has stated pretty well the relativistic view of some of the neo-Wittgensteinians:

Much admirable philosophical work has been done upon the notion of 'ways of seeing', of angles of vision, of . . . alternative conceptual systems . . . It has thus become almost impossible to believe that some *one* way of seeing, some *one* sort of theory, has any exclusive claim to be the *right* way; the notion of 'reality' itself, it would commonly be held, must be given in a sense in terms of some particular theory or view, so that the claim that any such theory reveals or corresponds to 'reality' can be given a circular justification which is also open, in just the same way, to other views as well (1966: 93).

B. NO UNIVERSAL CRITERION OF TRUTH

In trying to meet the challenge of epistemological relativism, I cannot appeal to the criterion of verification; and the relativists also reject it as a universal criterion. Indeed, I am driven reluctantly to the position that there is no criterion which, if met, will justify our feeling assured that we have the truth on whatever particular hypothesis is in question. But I am not driven to conclude that all statements are equally credible and equally incredible. Such a relativistic position would make it impossible even to assert the theory of relativism as more credible than non-relativistic positions.

Rather than search for a universal criterion of truth to replace the retired criterion of verification, one would do well to take an altogether different approach in dealing with the challenge of relativism. This approach would start within any given point of view. Instead of trying to show that one view is better than another, we would do well to test to see just how coherent any given view is, how it answers its own questions, and how it deals with new problems that emerge for it. This approach finds much in common with the neo-Wittgensteinians without having to subscribe to the relativism that some of them seem to affirm.

C. THE METHOD OF INTERNAL CRITICISM

Let me give an example of the method that, following the philosopher of personalism, E. S. Brightman, I will call 'internal criticism'. In the course of writing this chapter I happened to have a conversation with a professor of Education and a staunch Mormon. In our all-too-brief exchange I asked if it were true that Mormons believe that God once upon a time was a man. The answer given was that God started off in a very finite way and has worked himself to fuller Godhead. I was assured by the Mormon professor that God had a body, inasmuch as we humans were created in his image.

My point here is that the Mormon gave me sufficient information about his theology for me to begin with the approach of 'internal criticism'. I asked if his God had weight and height. I received no answer to the question but was assured that God had two legs and other bodily parts. Having previously read some

Mormon theology, I knew that God was believed to be a male.[1] So, I asked if God had male organs, and the answer was an affirmative one. The Mormon volunteered to say also that God eats, which prompted the question, 'Does he have divine excrement?' My Mormon acquaintance had not been taught how to respond to this question, and he was not willing to venture an answer of his own. These questions that I was asking are examples of what I mean by 'internal criticism'.

It is a good guess that as Mormons continue to move further from Utah, they will be challenged more often by biblical scholars, philosophers, theologians, scientists, and thinking laymen. Hitherto in the intellectual world, Mormon theology has generally been ignored as unworthy of intellectual attention. As Mormon intellectuals themselves confront more and more 'internal criticisms', they will very likely be embarrassed by the number of inconsistencies uncovered *within* their theological system. This will effect some revision and refinement in their theology. Also theological changes will probably come as Mormon intellectuals are made to face a number of embarrassing *implications* which the Mormon community had mostly ignored or had never even discussed at length.

In defense, the Mormons will, like other religious groups, fight back with 'internal criticisms' of the views of their opponents. The forthcoming debates should be enlightening. Despite the conclusions of epistemological relativists, communication and debate across widely divergent views can be, and are, carried on either because the views themselves overlap at places or because an individual person can actually embrace many views, some of which are in contradiction with one another at points. A crisis sometimes comes in the individual's life when the contradiction is actually seen by him. In order to square his conflicting beliefs, he may deny one or both, or even revise one or both.

Let me illustrate a possible route which theologically sophisticated Mormons might take. Believing that God eats, they must some-

1. For a very readable and authoritative book on Mormon theology, see Sterling M. McMurrin, *The Theological Foundations of the Mormon Religion* (1965). McMurrin is himself a Mormon.

day ask if God *needs* the food. The Mormon answer would seem to be that he does need it (McMurrin, 1965: 29). This prompts the question as to whether God makes *use* of the food. If he does, then what does he *do* with the waste? If he urinates, *where* does he urinate? Is there a special indoor toilet in the New Jerusalem, or is there an out-house?

To most Christians these questions would seem to be downright crude. Why? Because over a period of centuries the more standard theology of Catholics and Protestants has gradually been forced to 'spiritualize' God. Mormons, however, have the Book of Mormon to draw upon, and it has not yet had enough time to be subjected to internal criticism. Indeed, outside the Mormon Church very few people have even read the Book of Mormon.

While Mormons say that God has a body, they qualify by adding that he has a 'glorified body'. This is one step in the 'spiritualization' process. If asked whether God has blood flowing through his body, an informed Mormon will answer that some other more glorified substance is traveling through the divine arteries and veins.

God's teeth and eyes are regarded as perfect – no cavities, no astigmatism. God can read the finest print or the largest sign. According to Mormon teaching, God does have two eyes. But eyes, if they are really eyes, have to have some *color*, even if they are chalky in color. Mormons tell us that God has excellent eyesight, but they cannot tell us the color of the divine eyes, or whether God ever closes them. We may surmise from Mormon literature that the divine skin is white. But whether or not the deity turns red when angry is not made clear by Mormon theology. Also Mormons do not tell us whether God's body perspires, needs a bath, or has a scent.

Mormons will quite understandably try to ignore these questions, but they arise from what Mormon theology has already asserted to be true of God. There are *thousands* of such questions, and it is very unlikely that Mormon theology can answer most of them from *within* the current Mormon belief-systems. In order not to appear hopelessly ridiculous, the Mormon system of theology will gradually have to undergo modification. But this is not to predict the fall of Mormonism, which is not fueled by its theology anyhow. Rather, we may predict that Mormons, like other theists and polytheists, will very gradually qualify their views. The 'death of a thousand qualifications' in Mormon theology is not likely within this generation, and the necessary qualifications will come slowly, thus giving believers time to adjust to the changes.

D. GOD-TALK WITHOUT THEISM

Turning away from Mormon beliefs about God, we may look at a writer who grew up within a Christian tradition that not only is considerably older than Mormonism, but has allowed theological and philosophical debates to flourish within its ranks. I have in mind Professor Paul van Buren (who received a doctorate in theology *summa cum laude* under the teaching of one of Christendom's most significant theologians, Karl Barth) and his work *The Edges of Languages: An Essay in the Logic of a Religion* (1972).

Van Buren believes that Christianity is religiously much more important than theism. He represents those who have qualified their view of God to the point where the word 'God' is used to call to our attention such qualities as mercy, grace, forgiveness, faithfulness, etc. (pp. 136–148). Having once written that the word 'God' is meaningless and that 'God is dead', van Buren now holds that 'God' is not meaningless, but is a word that can point us to the growing edges of our language (and thus of our experiences). Van Buren explains his position:

> If saying 'God' is an acknowledgment that one has come to the end of language, if it is a religious way of indicating that one longs to say all that could possibly be said on some matter of great concern, then there is a role which lies just barely but legitimately within our language (pp. 144f.).

E. CONTRADICTION AS A TEST OF FALSITY

Where along the continuum of qualification and revision a theologian stops or revises his God-talk is not the concern of this chapter.

Rather, the concern is to show that, while verification is not a universal test of truth, people nevertheless do tend to acknowledge a *criterion of falsity*. Stated plainly, intellectually we are embarrassed most when our views are exposed as having contradictions. There is no need to repeat what was said in an earlier chapter about this widespread criterion of falsity. What is important to see is that the detection of contradiction is an essential condition of the growth of knowledge, or at least of the reduction of bad theories and hypotheses (cf. Popper, 1968: Chap. 4). A careful following of the debates among defenders of various theological views – or any other views, for that matter – reveals that often each side attempts to draw the other out. That is, each attempts to elicit definite statements from the other in order to compare the statement with other statements that the opponent is thought to embrace. The next step is to check to see whether there are statements within the opponent's belief-system that contradict other statements within the same system. This is internal criticism at work.

F. AN EXAMPLE OF EMBARRASSMENT OVER CONTRADICTION

It would be misleading to say that embarrassment is a criterion of falsity. Rather, when scholars are caught making contradictory statements, they tend to act in an embarrassed manner because the academic and scientific community has already conditioned them to respond in this way. I am not sure that conditioned embarrassment is the best way to deal with contradictory statements, but it does seem to be a fact of academic life. What is important here is to understand just how necessary it is for people of science and scholarship to be sensitive to the charge of contradiction. Without this sensitivity, scholarly endeavors would break down.

Indeed, if my argument from an earlier chapter holds, effective communication in every area of human life depends upon maintaining some level of consistency of meaning or of avoiding inconsistency of meaning. Contradiction is inconsistency between statements. When we become rigorous in detecting contradictions within a belief-system, we are engaging in internal criticism.

The disciplined sensitivity to contradiction may be illustrated by a recent case in which a professor wrote a paper directly critical of some of the theodicy of Professor Alvin Plantinga and orthodox Christianity. Plantinga is one of the most outstanding philosophers among evengelical Christians. The critical paper was read by a few orthodox Christians, one of whom responded by saying that in the paper Plantinga 'is made to sound like a buffoon – which he clearly isn't'. Now, the central issue of the paper was not whether Plantinga is a buffoon, but rather whether some of Plantinga's statements in his book *God and Other Minds* are in contradiction with one another.

The respondent to Plantinga's critic seemed to think that the critic had put the words in the mouth of Plantinga and had misrepresented what Plantinga was saying. The critic, on the other hand, believed that he was drawing out what was implicit in Plantinga's arguments. I am not interested in trying here to decide what Plantinga 'really' meant – such debates are often fruitless. Rather, I wish to show how the scholarly enterprise progresses because of the increased sensitivity to the charge of contradiction. Let us suppose, for the moment, that the critic faithfully explicated Plantinga's meaning. This then forces those who agree with Plantinga to either accept the explicated statements (some of which are indeed difficult to swallow) or to reject them. But in order to reject (or at least revise them), Plantinga's *prior* statements may have to be revised. In short, the threat of being pushed into making *explicitly contradictory* statements forces the academically sensitive mind to qualify and revise in order to beat down the threat.

But let us now suppose, for the moment, that it turns out that the critic had indeed misrepresented Plantinga and that he had made Plantinga say things to which Plantinga would not subscribe. This, nevertheless, could be very useful, if the misrepresentation is not too far afield; for it affords someone like Plantinga the opportunity to clarify his position and to show more exactly where he has avoided contradiction.

In this case, one of the respondents commented that the critic making the attack on Plantinga and 'orthodox Christianity' should have considered also the theodicy of John Hick, whom the respondent classified as an 'orthodox Christian', along with Plantinga.

Now, while the critic and the respondent may have their feelings mixed in with the arguments, what is important to understand is that cognitive progress can be made in this sort of interchange. For example, if Plantinga is indeed in the same camp with Hick, then the critic's particular attack on Plantinga's theodicy will not hold up, for the critic had supposed that Plantinga is one of those Christians who believes in an eternal hell. Hick, as we saw earlier, professes to be something of a universalist.[2] If the critic eventually 'smokes out' Plantinga's beliefs about hell, etc., then he will have served the cause of cognitive progress.

In order to meet the criticisms raised, Plantinga or his associates must *either* give up some of their beliefs and replace them with new ones (or with drastic qualifications) *or* deny that the statements which the critic attributed to Plantinga are accurate representations of Plantinga (and *show* where they are not accurate). Of course, Plantinga may choose to obscure the debate by writing so that the readers are still left wondering what he is saying. But in making such a choice Plantinga would earn the reputation of not making a scholarly and intellectual contribution. If the embarrassment of contradiction is too intense for him to face, he may continue to obfuscate rather than deal with the apparent contradictory statements in a scholarly manner. Academic debate is sometimes heated as well as enlightening, and sometimes writers have to wait until the heat dies down before they can gain the poise to address the fatal issue of contradictory statements.

G. THE ROLE OF DOGMATISM

We tend to use the word 'dogmatism' to refer to the tendency to hold on to statements that are in contradiction with one another. It is often forgotten that there are degrees of dogmatism. One

---

2. In at least one book John Hick has clearly come out in defense of universalism, cf. his *Evil and the God of Love,* 1968: 380f.

becomes increasingly dogmatic as he confronts more and more significant statements contradicting his belief. There is no easy rule telling us when exactly to modify our beliefs and when to cling to them. Dramatic conversion often comes when a person has clung for a long time to a belief-system that has suffered much from the rise of new contradictory statements to challenge it. 'Dogmatic theology' is composed of statements that are believed to be based on divine revelation. This implies that statements that appear to contradict 'dogmatic theology' (i.e. dogma theology) are to be revised and qualified rather than force dogmatic theology to qualify itself. The statements of dogmatic theology are regarded as established and canonical. In especially the latter part of the nineteenth century the conflict between canonical statements in theology and canonical statements in biology, astronomy, and geology became intensified. Among those Christians who became sensitive to these contradictory statements, a tendency developed to 'harmonize science and scriptures'. Over a decade ago the Wheaton College faculty of Wheaton, Illinois, decided that the flood of Noah's time was not, after all, global in scope but simply a local flood. The pressure of the newly established statements in geology forced evangelical biblical scholars to 'see' that the correct interpretation of the scriptures dictated the conclusion that the flood was limited to only a small area on the globe. Robert Rimmer, in *The Harmony of Science and Scripture* (1936), endeavored to show that the Bible is actually a very advanced scientific book if only scientists would learn from it. Writing a few decades later than Rimmer, Bernard Ramm, realizing that Rimmer and other such writers had made a number of outlandish and indefensible statements, sought to find a more respectable way of protecting 'biblical theology' without exposing it to ridicule. In his book, *The Christian View of Science and Scripture* (1954), Ramm sought to provide a hermeneutical principle for evangelical Christian biblical scholars that would help them to clash less often with the hypotheses and laws of science. Ramm's principle, very simply, is that the Bible uses phenomal language rather than scientific language.

What this means is that the Bible is written in popular, not technical, language. 'The language of the Bible is phenomenal.' 'By phenomenal', said Ramm, 'we mean "pertaining to appearances". The Bible uses a language that is not only popular but restricted to the apparent.' (p. 67.) Rather than watch his evangelical Christian faith engage in all-out battles with the physical sciences, Ramm hoped to limit the battles to what he regarded as substantial issues rather than phenomenal appearances.

More than he realized, Ramm has given orthodox Christians one way of qualifying their statements without losing face, that is, without being embarrassed by contradictory statements. His principle allows Christians to declare as 'phenomenal' whatever has to be modified and qualified. This naturally raises the question of just where to draw the line between what is phenomenal and what is technical and substantial in the Bible. For example, when Paul speaks of the atonement of Christ, is he utilizing the popular religious forms of his own time in order to express a substantial Christian revelation? If so, where does the popular religious form end and the Christian substance begin?

Ramm does not help in answering this sort of question. There are numerous 'forms' of expression which St. Paul took from his culture. Are the forms to be taken in a phenomenal sense only? Clearly, this raises the whole issue of Form Criticism. In fact, it may be that the Savior-God form which was prevalent in St. Paul's time was borrowed by him rather than revealed to him.[3]

H. THE PRESSURE OF CONTRADICTION

The notion of various 'forms' of expression in the Bible might never have arisen had biblical scholars not come upon what appeared to them to be contradictory statements within the Pentateuch, within the Gospels, or within other parts of the Bible. Detected contradictions demand either creative harmonizing or else some new conceptual scheme to account for the contradictions.

---

3. Ramm tries to deal with the issue of 'forms' in his later book, *Special Revelation and the Word of God* (1961).

Sometimes those evangelical Christians who regard science as something of a 'general revelation' feel it necessary to overcome contradictions between science and scripture. Ramm's distinction between phenomenal and noumenal language is one of various attempts to deal with apparent contradictory statements between science and theology. Another evangelical Christian, N. H. Ridderbos (1957), feeling the pressure that science brings to bear on biblical exegesis, writes the following:

It is true that natural science may not at any point decree how Scripture should be interpreted. Still, we may not in our exegesis ignore the results of natural science. The fact that there arise objections of a scientific nature to every more literal conception may and should occasion the question, Is it possible to offer some other acceptable exegesis? (p. 46)

In the final paragraph in which he discusses whether Genesis I and natural science are making statements that contradict each other, Ridderbos says in a disarmingly frank way that

often natural science has posited that the human race has existed several hundreds of thousands of years. It is obvious that this cannot be easily squared with the content of Genesis (p. 71).

My thesis in this chapter is that the presence of contradiction, while not a criterion of truth, is a criterion of falsity. This is why the sensitive recognition of contradiction usually accompanies a recognition that something is required to be done about the contradiction. Indeed, since the time when Ridderbos wrote the above lines, the human species has been estimated to be over a million years old, which squares even less with the evangelical view of Genesis.

It is not accurate to say that God-talk and theology are meaningless, as I will try to show in the next chapter. But it is accurate to say that the presence of contradictory statements within theology is sometimes conspicuous. This is particularly true when theology extends itself beyond the so-called 'spiritual' and 'ritual' realm. Many believers insist that because religion is of the heart and not the head, theological statements pose nothing more than worthless stumbling blocks. Such believers try not to concern themselves with correcting contradictions. Or, to be more accurate, they have their own special way of coping with contradictions, which is by desensitizing themselves cognitively. That is, they condition themselves, through a rather elaborate program, to avoid 'arguing' religion. They will 'give their witness', which is to say they will present their views and answer questions about their beliefs so long as the prospect being 'witnessed to' does not point out contradictions in the believers' presentation.

I. EXPANSION OF THE BELIEF-SYSTEM

A religion as a complex of patterned responses to the core-concern does not thrive completely in isolation. New contingencies emerge even in the most stable tribal community. New moral and emotional-ritual responses develop. Verbal statements and communications pertaining to these new responses increase the cognitive scope of the religion. As these verbal responses become more or less standard and even institutionalized, they come to be recognized as a part of the religion's cognitive belief-system. In many cases the expansion of the belief-system to incorporate the new statements increases the probability that contradictions will develop within the system.

An illustration from Southern Baptists in Tennessee will throw light on this point. The Tennessee Baptist Convention publishes a journal, *The Baptist and Reflector*, which in 1974 began to call attention to the fact that both inside and outside the Baptist churches people were getting divorces. Statements by Baptist leaders are now being made to the effect that divorce does happen to decent Christians. Not very long ago, divorce was something that could be expected to happen to people 'of the world' but not to dedicated Christians. Today Southern Baptists are even being forced by social events to make statements that will make it acceptable for divorced people to hold positions of leadership within the local church. There are even divorced people working in the Southern Baptist Convention headquarters in Nashville.

The point here is that recent statements having to do with Baptists' coming to terms with the fact of divorce among their own people are in contradiction with some of the statements made by Baptist leaders a decade or so ago. For example, Billy Graham (an ordained Southern Baptist minister who has spoken many times at the Southern Baptist Convention) stated a number of years ago that 'divorces in America are mostly among non-religious people. . . .' Graham also complained, 'There was a time when a divorced man would have no chance in American politics, but with our shifting ideals of today, whether or not a person is divorced seems to make little difference' (cf. Flint *et al.*, 1966: 62f.). Telling of a well-known family counselor who obtained a divorce, Graham proclaimed that the divorce demonstrated the failure of the counselor's 'humanistic philosophy' (Ibid, p. 147). But when some of Graham's fellow Southern Baptist ministers and deacons became divorced, he declined to conclude that this demonstrated the failure of the Christian faith.

In order to avoid being caught in contradictions, Southern Baptists are having to modify and qualify their statements about divorce. The daughter of Billy Graham's own pastor married a Baptist evangelist and shortly thereafter divorced him. It is very unlikely that Southern Baptists today will hear the kind of sermons on divorce that they heard a decade ago. In the November 13, 1974, issue of the Texas *Baptist Standard*, the book *Divorce – The New Freedom* by Esther Oshmer Fisher (1974) was treated very favorably and the reviewer recommended 'the wisdom of this author' to the Southern Baptist ministers of Texas. It is doubtful that ten years ago such a book could have been reviewed in this influential Baptist paper.

The point here is that epistemological relativism fails to observe carefully the process of *how people do in fact modify or change their views* on a variety of topics which are of profound concern to them. So long as people attempt to relate their religious faith to various old and new areas of human living, they will run the risk of having to make statements that contradict religious statements made a few years earlier by leading spokesmen of their own faith.

Southern Baptists will continue to accommodate divorce and will probably not worry themselves greatly about contradicting previous stands taken on divorce. They will on the whole try to prevent the contradictions from being spoken. But if, for some reason, Southern Baptists are forced to face this contradiction in open and prolonged debate, they will undergo a very serious crisis. Indeed, the epistemological consequences could become a denominational disaster, for it would compel even some of the most conservative ministers to acknowledge that they either have disobeyed the teachings of the Bible or have qualified their view of the inspiration and authority of the Bible.

If the second horn of this dilemma were to be dealt with in the open debate with regard to the question of divorce (and adultery), then many conventional ministers would more than likely find themselves shifting in their view of the authority of the Bible. It is safe to predict, however, that the Southern Baptist Convention will not tolerate a prolonged debate on divorce because the Convention cannot risk the enormous epistemological impact that the debate would likely have on the churches of this large Christian denomination. Facing contradictions usually forces some kind of epistemological modification. But the contradictions which the issue of divorce would expose to the light would create a radical change at the very heart of the main stream of Southern Baptist theology.

J. SUMMARY

In this chapter, I have replied to epistemological relativists by suggesting that people do not simply exchange one worldview for another as if they were replacing one garment for another. Rather the *process* of cognitive change is much more piecemeal and gradual (despite Thomas Kuhn's thesis) – and very real. We observe people with one foot in one view and the other foot in another. Discovered contradictions force some sort of change, adjustment, or conversion.

To be sure, looking back over an individual's life one may see that he has indeed moved from one worldview to another. But I have argued that this movement is not done by blind 'blick'. Rather, people are trying to solve problems, and in the cognitive realm the basic problem is the presence of contradictions. When they are made sensitive to these contradictions, people often move cognitively to resolve the problem.

In this chapter, I have not dealt at length with how people move away *from* felt contradictions *to* beliefs that they can live with (at least until new contradictions break out). This must be discussed in the next chapter, after the issue of induction is discussed with regard to religious motivations and implications arising in connection with the issue.

Finally, I have tried to show that cognitive problems in religion are not simply language games with no relevance beyond the game. To the contrary, cognitive problems emerge because they involve *statements* purporting to refer not only to hypothetical entities (i.e., entities that may be real although not *directly* observable), but to directly observable events in the empirical world (e.g., the increase of divorces among Southern Baptists).

David Hume's Threat to Faith

A. KARL POPPER – OPPONENT OF VERIFICATIONISM

The verificationists and positivists seemed unable to either answer or accept David Hume's threat to all knowledge claims (including so-called inductive generalizations). Sir Karl Popper is one philosopher who perhaps more than any other has faced Hume on his own grounds and dealt with the threat to all inductive statements, whether in science or in theology. Unfortunately, because Rudolf Carnap and other positivists tried to claim Popper as one of their own, the epistemology of Popper has often, but erroneously, been classified with verificationists. In this chapter, I will set Popper in a different light because I believe he has advanced some profoundly significant arguments that theology, philosophy of religion, and religious studies need to come to terms with. Popper can perhaps be best understood against the background of David Hume's brilliant critical treatment of induction.[1]

B. HUME'S POSITION

Very briefly, Hume's argument leads to the position that we have no basis for saying that the sun will rise somewhere tomorrow. We have

---

1. D. Stove challenges the thesis of Popper (and most philosophers since Hume) that Hume was dealing with the problem of 'inductive probabilism' ('Hume, probability, and induction', 1970: 212–232). Stove acknowledges that his thesis is historical in nature. I do not find his thesis very convincing. But even if it were, it would have no substantial bearing on the *problem* of induction. Stove throws little light on the problem itself even though he says he believes that 'inductive probabilism is true' (p. 213).

no basis for making the so-called inductive generalization that tomorrow will come somewhere. We have no basis for stating that the whole of reality will not simply vanish. Extending this further, theology is forced to admit that it has no cognitive basis for believing that God (assuming that he exists) will not simply vanish.

The theist Basil Mitchell asserts that the theist, but not the atheist, raises sincerely the question 'Why is there anything at all?' (1973: 69). But Hume in his critique of induction clearly raises the issue of necessary and contingent being, and in doing so he is not conspicuously a theist. Popper deals with the issue even though he, too, does not accept the theistic position. Theists themselves disagree as to whether God's being is such that it could not *not be*. Apparently it is Mitchell who fails to see the impact of the question – 'Why is there anything at all?' – as it pertains to God. Why is there God at all? Might God cease to exist?

The ontological argument for God's existence quite obviously is an attempt to overcome the position that everything that exists (including God) might *not* exist. I am very much impressed with Charles Hartshorne's process panentheism, but his ontological argument does not even begin to answer Hume. One might pull an argument for God out of a logical hat if one has such a hat, but Hume's argument calls that hat itself into question. If the universe depends on God for its existence, then in that sense God is a Necessary Being – that is, necessary to the existence of the universe.

But on Hume's argument, both God and the universe might vanish. I taught one year in a school where the students said of a certain professor that they could pass his tests if somewhere in the essay answers they would mention God a few times. There are some religious writers who seem to think that they have advanced an argument when, upon finding their cognitive backs against the wall, they pronounce the name 'God'.

As noted in an earlier chapter, theology too often becomes this sort of verbal magic. Merely to say 'God solves problems x, y, or z' is of no cognitive worth, although it may have considerable emotional and ritual worth – comparable to pulling beads, crossing oneself, facing the East, or even saying ritual words. To say that God solves the problem of induction is to do no more than announce that the problem of induction can be solved. The crucial question, however, is, '*How* is it solved?' Whether the solution comes through God's being or Hans Reichenbach's 'posit' is a secondary matter. Even the 'Ground of Being' is the ground of all things *only* so long as the Ground of Being itself does not cease to be. (Tillich does not like to say that Being 'exists'.) But unable to answer Hume, Tillich, like Spinoza, falls back on a definition as though it were an argument.

C. THE RADICAL IMPLICATIONS OF HUME'S ARGUMENT

Hume is saying more than that we simply do not yet have sufficient evidence to venture the hypothesis that God or the universe will continue to exist a hundred years from now. Hick's eschatological verification argument is based on a premise which Hume cannot accept. Let us assume that Mary Ann has been playing the piano regularly for many years. Taking into consideration that she is still in excellent health and that no drastic changes in her life-style have developed, we predict that she will continue to play for the coming month.

Now, this prediction presupposes that the future will, in at least Mary Anne's case, be somewhat like her past, that there will be sufficient continuity between past and future for us to predict Mary Ann's playing the piano. Unfortunately, we are only assuming something that Hume insists we have no basis for assuming. We are making an inductive generalization that, inasmuch as in the past some continuity has continued in the course of things, then this continuity must be repeated in the future. But Hume correctly contends that we have made this statement with no justifiable grounds for doing so.

There are, of course, conjectures as to *why we go ahead* and live as if we could make justifiable inductions, but this is not to say that induction is *justified*. It is one thing to conjecture how people carry on their affairs on a large ocean liner. But it is another to explain how the liner itself keeps afloat. When people make statements about the future, they are simply engaging in activity on the boat, so to speak. Hume, however, is wondering how the whole ship of inductive generalization keeps afloat. And his radical conclusion is that it does not keep afloat. In short, inductive generalizations are impossible. The ship of induction never even gets built. We are in error to think that anyone makes inductions. Hume has never been successfully answered. I do not deny, however, that *if* human life continues somewhat as it has, many humans will probably continue to imagine that they make inductive generalizations.

Karl Popper states Hume's argument in the form of the following question:

Are we justified in reasoning from [repeated] instances of which we have experience to instances [conclusions] of which we have no experience? (1972: 4. The words in brackets are Popper's.)

In attempting to answer this question we need to distinguish (1) the question of whether *inductions* are justifiable from (2) the question of whether *we* are justified in acting on the basis of some of our conjectures and hypotheses. Popper answers the first question negatively, the second affirmatively. Later this second question can be dealt with, but now we must deal further with the first question. According to Popper, 'there is no induction because universal theories are not deducible from singular statements. But they may be refuted by singular statements, since they may clash with [i.e., be contradicted by] descriptions of observable facts' (1974a, II: 68. The words in brackets are my own additions).

The emphasis in the previous chapter on the role of 'contradiction detection' as a tool of rational inquiry and cognitive movement can now be better understood in light of Popper's and Hume's case against induction. Against Carnap, I deny that the justification of a belief is possible. But this denial does not entail epistemological relativism, for we can conclude that some hypotheses or beliefs have been falsified. We have other beliefs or statements which, if they are not mere circular statements, *may* be approximations of truth. So long as these beliefs stand without being falsified by contradiction, *we are justified* in holding to them.

This is not to deny that we frequently act upon conjectures that we know are not fully self-consistent. But such is born of a practical necessity to act. If we had a non-circular conjecture pertaining to a certain issue, we might be more likely to act upon it if it were without self-contradiction. This is to speak ideally, at the unmixed cognitive level. In actuality, our other desires and needs may influence us to *pretend* that the contradiction is not there or to trust that the self-contradiction will be overcome 'eventually'.

D. NEW CONJECTURES AND INSPIRATION

In the previous chapter, I indicated how in religious discourse revisions of theological statements often come about. It is the same with scientific statements. Embarrassed by contradictions, individuals may qualify their statements in the hope of overcoming the contradiction. (Whether the qualification is called a 'basic change' or even an 'exchange' of one view for another is in some ways less an epistemological than a conventional matter. What is regarded by one group as a slight change might be regarded by another as a radical departure from the position.)

(1) Dissatisfaction with contradiction, combined with (2) imagination, and (3) familiarity with the cognitive problem under consideration – these seem to be some of the distinctive ingredients of the creative process by which new testable hypotheses and conjectures come into existence. Those who stress the role of imagination, intuition, and inspiration in the growth of knowledge understand that mere criticism without imagination is the death of all cognitive life. Without bold and daring conjectures, our knowledge would be composed of bland and trivial tautologies at best. Karl Pearson's book *The Grammar of Science* (1892) misleadingly portrays scientific work as a sort of butterfly collecting – a kind of putting together of a hypothesis from bits and pieces until the final piece is fit together with the others into a new hypothesis.

But scientific development is considerably different from this ant-like activity. The world is riddled through and through with 'data' and 'evidence', so much so that finite scientists could not possibly 'collect' all the data, not even all the data relevant to a particular issue. Here is where imagination enters the picture as a necessary short-cut. One brilliant imaginative conjecture or hypothesis can direct the scientist's attention in one direction rather than another.

Sir Peter Medawar of the Clinical Research Centre of Harrow, England, is correct to say that 'the bold use of imagination was the rule in the science of discovery, not the exception' (1974: 281. Paraphrasing William Whewell).

There is no special 'scientific method' different from rational thinking in every area of life. Rather, science is the discipline which *intensifies* (1) imagination, (2) critical discussion, and (3) experimental testing in the quest for truth. Science happens whenever these three activities are intensified. The creation of art, too, depends upon intensified imagination and experimentation. But art as an activity is not the pursuit of truth; rather it is the process by which certain problems peculiar to itself are worked on. (What the problems of art are, in contrast to those of science, I am not qualified to say.)

The point is that, without daring and bold conjectures and hypotheses that grow out of the attempt to solve cognitive problems, we could not improve our knowledge. Claude Bernard, a biologist, states this point crisply:

> A hypothesis is . . . the obligatory starting point of all experimental reasoning. Without it no investigation would be possible, and one would learn nothing: one could only pile up barren observations. To experiment without a preconceived idea is to wander aimlessly (Quoted by Medawar, 1974: 288).

E. DOUBT AND BELIEF

Religion and science do not differ with regard to vision and imagination, for either will perish without vision. Those who think that science is not visionary are confusing science with the proliferation of bureaucritic ritual that sometimes is called science. Belief is also a major part of the scientific process. If science were nothing but skepticism, nothing would ever come of it, that is, no scientific advances would be made. Belief is the tendency to act on the basis of expectations. When scientists put their hypotheses and conjectures on the line, they are then living up to the scientific ideal. There is a certain amount of useful dogmatism in science, and the cognitive venture in general; but beyond a certain point – which is not always easy to specify – the dogmatic attitude ceases to contribute to the growth of knowledge.

Karl Popper notes that it is good to hold dearly to hypotheses and theories that have content and scope. To give them up just because they are contradicted by a few observations is to act too hastily. To believe in the theory is to defend it rather than give it up. Science profits from a dogged defense of its more far-reaching theories, for even if a theory turns out to be in excessive contradiction with relevant observations, nevertheless the dogged defense has forced the contradicting observational statements to be checked out more thoroughly and to specify more precisely where the contradiction lies.

There is another kind of dogmatism. Refusing to defend its view by argumentation and critical debate, it obscures the issue in order to prevent any possibility of 'contradiction detection'. It also resists formulating clearly the view held, and it in general thrives on the intimidation of those who try to put the view to empirical tests. This sort of dogmatism does not contribute to the cognitive venture, but rather scuttles it. It gives the appearance of making profound statements but fights off attempts to probe to see whether the statements are what they at first glance appear to be. Oracles practice making very vague and equivocal *predictions* but making very definite statements about what has *fulfilled* the prediction.

So far, religious commitment and scientific commitment are seen to be psychologically very similar. Both require belief. But this leads to the question of the role of doubt in the form of severe critical discussion and crucial experimentation.

There is a certain equivocation in the term 'doubt'. In some contexts, to doubt is to welcome questions, to throw open the door of criticism. In this sense, to doubt is to raise questions and propose tests which might falsify the hypothesis in question. But in other contexts, to doubt something is not to suspend judgment, but rather to have *already concluded the falsity* of the claim or view under consideration. Popper's concern is to encourage the opening up of questions and crucial tests. If the scientist expects the hypothesis to survive the test, then he may be said to *believe* in it. If he expects it to fail the test, then he *doubts* that it will survive. But Popper thinks that this psychological factor (whether belief or disbelief) is epistemologically irrelevant. The requirement in science is that nothing be allowed to prevent crucial tests and the critical scrutiny of the conjectures, hypotheses, and theories.

F. SCIENCE AND RELIGION – SOME DIFFERENCES AND SIMILARITIES

It might be thought that unlike science, religion lacks *critical* inquiry. But the study of the history of religions indicates that, regardless of the psychological state of believers and unbelievers, religious statements of various traditions have often come under scrutiny and critical inquiry. In this process of critical debate, religious claims have been qualified, revised, rejected, reformulated, or changed in a variety of ways. It is true that many religions (i.e., traditions manifesting their distinctive responses to the core-concern) have resisted probing into their claims. But if one religion refuses to probe into its own views, another will without invitation probe for it.

It is sometimes said that science differs from religion in that the former requires critical debate, whereas religion tends to resist it. But this is an oversimplification. There are plenty of examples of scientists' resisting critical inquiry (cf. Kuhn, 1970). It is quite possible that the development of science is partly the result of the growth of new 'denominations', which is not without bitter controversy. Currently within the discipline of sociology is a group of 'radicals' who are challenging established, canonical, catholic science of human behavior. This group forms the 'Anabaptist' wing of science and has probably been either a cause or an effect of the recent emphasis upon 'participatory observation' in particular (cf. Deutsch and Howard, 1970).

It is perhaps permitted to say that science is concerned with the growth of knowledge, whereas religion is concerned with salvation, that is, with the question of core-finitude. However, anyone who has associated with physical scientists knows that for some of them science is a 'ship of salvation'. Messianic claims have often been made on behalf of science. Doubtless such claims are made more by non-scientists than by scientists themselves. Nevertheless, scientists have sometimes been naïve in not admitting that they in effect contributed to this propaganda by not attacking it publicly and relentlessly. The counter-culture upsurge was probably an excessive reaction to excessive propaganda. The propagandists for science are a bit like the evangelists of religion – they are a source of embarrassment but also serve to bring in money and other material means.[2]

Many people still believe that science saves them from the cognitive dimension of their own finitude. Suffering the illusion that the latest theory in science is the final theory, they are consoled that the vast sea of human ignorance now has a bridge to span it. They do not yet realize that there is no such bridge; there are only cognitive ships and boats resting precariously on the vast sea of human ignorance. We may expect that sooner or later our scientific theories will sink, and the hope that we have is that science and other cognitive endeavors will have constructed sturdier hypotheses and theories for us to step into before the old ones break apart into a thousand pieces. Otherwise, we shall have only folk-knowledge to cling to like survivors clinging to floating planks and scraps.

G. FAITH IN RATIONAL INQUIRY

There is little question but that human beings, whether they be just or unjust, have no choice but to live by faith. But the committed Christian will not say that just any faith will do. Nor will the humanist, Marxist, Muslim, or Hindu say this. Some Hindus claim that they are tolerant of all religious faiths; but except for strictly political and social tolerance, this boast of tolerance has little meaning. A Hindu *cannot* consistently hold to both Hinduism and Christianity, for there are points where they stand in serious opposition to one another. Every religion – including Hinduism – makes exclusive claims for itself. If the Hindu apologist wishes to advocate political and social tolerance, he will be joined by many other faiths. But epistemological tolerance

---

2. For a sociologist's attempt to check some of the outlandish promises made on behalf of sociology, see Gynn Nettler, *Explanations* (1970).

is a category mistake – like a happy briefcase or a thoughtful hammer.

Each religion regards as unwarranted some of the claims of other religions, at least as those claims stand unrevised. Even the attempts of one religion to make room for aspects of other religions extract a price for admission. Sometimes it is not easy to determine when one religion fulfills another and when it abnegates it.

Rational inquiry as itself a faith-commitment stands in contrast to certain other kinds of faith-commitments. At the heart of rational inquiry is the faith that critical debate, imaginative speculation and conjectures, and empirical testings are more likely than any other faith-commitment to move us closer to the ideal of truth. However, it is not possible for rational inquiry – of which science is a branch – to proceed consistently on a philosophy of 'as if'. It is like being consciously unconscious. As noted earlier, if we agree with Hume and Popper, we cannot rationally believe that we are rationally justified in holding induction to be valid. Hume says that we may go on believing in induction nevertheless, even though there is no rational way to justify induction. According to Hume, we believe in induction because we have developed the *habit* of doing so; it is our custom, a very useful one, although wholly without any rational basis. Here Hume gives us a kind of epistemological 'convenient lie' similar to Plato's sociopolitical 'convenient lie'.

But Popper is in effect saying that a lie is still a lie no matter how convenient it is or how habitual it has become with us. So, he concludes, the rational mind must give up faith in induction. It is an epistemological dead end (1972: 97-100). This quite naturally raises the question, If we cannot act and believe 'as if' induction were justified, are we left with no distinction between rational inquiry and irrationality? Are all beliefs nothing but biases and prejudices? In short, does the loss of induction throw us into absolute or total relativism, with no one view being more warranted than another? Popper is not arguing that the theory of inductions is lacking in sufficient evidence. He is saying something more radical, namely, that the very notion of induction is 'a kind of optical illusion' (1974b: 1015).

It may come as a surprise to those unacquainted with Popper to learn that he is not an existentialist. Yet like many existentialists, he confronts contingency, looks into its bottomless throat, just as Ralph in *Lord of the Flies* faces the peering skull of the beast. Standing on the premise that the universe has the possibility of dissolving into nothingness, Popper nevertheless does not fall into fits of despair and anguish. This is perhaps because he was not brought up to expect the universe to underwrite his dreams, hopes, and expectations of eternity.

Popper cannot be classified with the irrationalists who claim to pay no regard to the recommendations of the intellectual inquiry. Yet, at the same time, he insists that 'from a rational point of view, we should not "rely" on any theory, for no theory has been shown to be true, or can be shown to be true (or "reliable")' (1974b: 1025).

H. TWO MEANINGS OF 'RATIONAL'

A careful reading of Popper reveals that he uses the word 'rational' in two distinct ways. In *epistemological* contexts he uses it to describe theories, hypotheses, or conjectures that have *good reasons* for our taking them as true or reliable. As noted above, he denies that in this sense there are any rational views.

But in *pragmatic* contexts, Popper uses the word 'rational' or 'rationality' to refer to the selection of 'the best tested theory as a basis for action' (1974b: 1026). A theory can be the best tested even though it cannot be known to be true. This needs clarification. An imaginative hypothesis or theory can be tested by deducing predictions from it in connection with specified 'initial conditions'. So long as the predictions do not fail, the hypothesis or theory may be regarded as a good one. This does not mean that it is *guaranteed* to be *true*, for we have no way of knowing in advance whether the next predictions will or will not fail. If 'the world as we know it may completely disintegrate in the next second' (Ibid.), then we can say of a hypothesis or theory only that up to now it has either passed the tests or failed them. (A theory which has not been brought up for testing is strictly not yet in the race.)

It would be irrational to act on the basis of hypotheses and theories that have been *refuted*. Given the fact that we have to make choices, the rational choice is the one based on a theory or hypothesis that has thus far been well tested and has not been falsified or refuted. If it has withstood the tests thus far, then it is better than a hypothesis that has failed to meet the tests.

I. FROM FAITH TO FAITH

To choose not to act is itself an act. Popper and Sartre are in agreement that we are 'condemned to be free'; that is, so long as we live, we cannot escape making some choices. Even suicide is a choice. Popper would seem to be in agreement with William James that we have a right to believe and that we cannot avoid believing something. But *what* we have a right to believe rationally is a matter of debate. James himself, reacting against the 'block universe' of Hegel and Absolute Idealists, asserts a pluralistic universe. But it is also a chancy universe in which even God is conceived of as a 'fighter for ends'. James seems to want to believe that our human moral efforts help God to carry on better his own struggle for value. Having rejected the apriorism of Spinoza and other monists, James gives up any basis for guaranteeing that even God will win his fight forever. The pluralistic universe might become so fragmented as to leave God exhausted in the endless endeavor to do battle with the chaos.

Nevertheless, living here and now, we must make practical choices. Popper writes, 'From a pragmatic point of view, . . . most of these possibilities [of the world's disintegration] are not worth bothering about because we cannot *do* anything about them: they are beyond the realm of action' (1974b: 1026. Italics added). A theist might object that we can do something: we can by faith get into right relationship with God and thus be saved from the possibility of disintegration; but this objection fails to consider Popper's position that disintegration is a possibility for God, too. We may *define* God as the One who will not disintegrate, but a definition is only a verbal tool of communication, not a reason for believing something. I think that Kant is correct to hold that the cosmological and teleological arguments tend to turn into the ontological argument, which is an attempt to demonstrate that God *must* endure all threats of contingency.

If Popper's arguments stand, then God, too, would seem to have to face the possibility of his non-being. He, too, must consider his 'thrownness'. God is being-unto-death, not in the sense that his dissolution is certain but that it is a possibility. For most theists, this way of speaking of God is strange for the simple reason that God functions in their scheme of things as the absolute solution to the possibility of nothingness. He is, for them, the Ground of Promise. Without him, all other promises are always conditional. A child sometimes finds it difficult to accept that his father will break a promise. And theists find it threatening that the Heavenly Father may not be able to make good the promises which he has made, or at least which have been made in his name. When God swears by his own name, he can appeal to nothing more secure. His word is his word. But Hume and Popper have found the loose thread that could possibly unravel all theistic promises that reach into an everlasting tomorrow.

Religious responses, it seems to me, cannot with a metaphysical doctrine overcome the analysis of induction that Hume and Popper have set forth. Nirvana, the Absolute, the One, God, Heaven, the Logos, and the infinite wheel – these are one and all infected with the possibility of not being. Yet religion is a very desperately practical matter which has for centuries called upon magnificent theoretical cathedrals for protection. But if Popper and Hume are right, we cannot be secure in believing that the winds of chaos will not crumble our faith-fortresses. Theology cannot recover fully from the analysis of Hume and Popper. But religion with its various dimensions will always be a part of human existence – so long as humans live. The practical necessity of acting in a universe of multiple levels of contingency will dictate needs of various kinds. The ways in which people come to terms with their sense of finitude will demand both sympathetic and critical study. Just as no species in the evolutionary interchange is guaranteed survival, so no religious form is guaranteed survival. We may expect religious faith to continue, and our best prediction is that religion will continue to go in diverse directions.

J. FROM CONJECTURE TO CONJECTURE

If our present physical and biological conjectures are good guesses, then we as 'thinking reeds' must conclude that we live in a universe that is mostly chaotic dust. According to Popper, even if induction were

> the method of science, then modern cosmology is at least roughly correct . . . ; and . . . modern cosmology teaches us that to generalize from observations taken, for the most part, in our incredibly idiosyncratic region of the universe would almost always be quite invalid. Thus if induction is 'inductively valid' it will almost always lead to false conclusions; and therefore is inductively invalid (1974 b: 1027).

It would appear that in our practical lives we have no alternative but to live from conjecture to conjecture. Faith and belief are but the psychological side of conjecture. Like Abraham, the 'father of faith', as he has been called, we journey without knowing for certain where we will arrive. Practical reason, like natural selection, is the tool of eliminating error. However, instead of dying wastefully and too soon, we can sometimes let our conjectures and hypotheses die in our stead. The imperative of imagination develops in the need for it if we are to do more than repeat all the errors of our ancestors. In fact, the conjectures of our ancestors came with a setting; but today, because we do no longer have the old setting, some of the old conjectures are of no practical use. They are Saul's armor on David – more lethal than protective to the wearer. We live as dwellers in a marsh, who drive down into the marsh stakes on top of old stakes. But we never hit bottom. We will have to drive down still more stakes in due time.

Scientific, psychological, and religious conjectures eventually become refuted. But as cerebral animals we cannot live without conjectures, which is why the development of new conjectures is imperative. They are like new mutations, most of which prove to be of little value, but some of which help the species to continue still a while longer.

The positivists were in error to regard religion and morality to be mere private utterances and meaningless nonsense. Understandably the positivists of decades past wanted to find a short cut to positive knowledge. But their expectations for science were too high and their cavalier treatment of religion naïve. Indeed, Otto Neurath never seemed to realize that his own Marxism was cognitively meaningful and, for him, an intense and steady response to Neurath's own core-concern. Popper's controversial and sustained critique of early Marxism did not deny that it was cognitively meaningful. His point was that it failed to appreciate the conjectural status of scientific statements. This was in many ways Bertrand Russell's critique of the Russian version of so-called scientific socialism. But let us now move into the question of meaningful religious language. There are various meanings of 'meaning' and 'meaningfulness' in the vast field of religion and theology, and it will be very fruitful to look at some of them. A meaningful but refuted theory with scope is often more important than the trivial statement that has not yet been refuted. The cognitive appeal of religions lies neither in trivia nor in meaninglessness, but in its daring boldness and imaginative scope.

Meaning in Theology

A. CAREFUL ABOUT PROCEDURES

To say that everything – including God – might disappear into nothingness is not to predict that everything will in fact disappear, God included. There may be a God, or some Being upon whom all else depends in some sense, who will endure forever. Or the universe of the naturalist may endure forever in one form or another. Some of the claims about the existence of God seem to be at least cognitively meaningful, and this issue will be explicated later in this chapter.

Agnosticism is the view that we simply lack sufficient evidence to say that God does or does not exist. But if induction and empirical generalizations from the known to the unknown cannot be made, then we cannot talk in the way that agnostics used to talk. Popper argues convincingly that we can never have sufficient evidence to justify any conjecture or view. Hence, agnosticism cannot be a question pertaining to the evidence or lack of evidence in support of a conjecture about God or anything.

Nevertheless, it is possible to suspend judgment regarding certain conjectures or hypotheses. For example, regarding a certain experiment that has not yet been made but which is projected, we may sincerely assert that we do not know what to expect from it. If we expect the hypothesis *not to fail* the test, then we believe in it to that extent. If we do expect it to fail, then we disbelieve in it to that extent. Indeed, this gives us some behavioral way of talking about belief, disbelief, and agnosticism. For example, if we believe in the existence of the sea 'monster' of Loch Ness, we will under various conditions state that at least sooner or later certain clearly designated signs believed to be of the monster's presence in Loch Ness will be detected through carefully controlled experiments. This, of course, will not prove that the monster exists. But the greater variety of testable consequences that we can deduce from the 'sea-monster-in-Loch-Ness' hypothesis, the better this hypothesis will fare in competition with rival testable hypotheses. That is, the monster hypothesis will fare better if it withstands tests of falsifiability while its rival hypotheses fail.

We cannot talk of the absolutely best hypothesis; our best is only in comparison with competing hypotheses. The door is always open for the possibility of a still better hypothesis – a Jacob hypothesis to supplant our favored Esau.

Here we see that practical belief in something's existence is tied in with the instruments used in the testing. Transposing this way of thinking into religion, we recall that in various religions some individuals are regarded as outstanding instruments for receiving communication from the gods, God, or other extraordinary beings. Sometimes the receiving agents seem to fail the test, which in turn demands that qualifications be made. For example, the special agent of revelation (or whatever) has to be in a certain condition; and if the *procedures* for getting into this special condition are made public, then other people may observe whether or not the special agent meets the conditions by going through the appropriate procedures. If the conditions are met but the experiment fails nevertheless, then either the hypothesis has to be qualified or the statement designating the proper procedures has to be qualified. This is very similar to what we find in scientific experiments, except that science requires a more intensified and rigorous record-keeping, note-taking, calculating, checking, rechecking, and repeating the experiment when possible.

In religion the 'receiving agents' have often insisted that the ritual or other procedures must be carried out properly and strictly – otherwise the visitation or whatever will not come about. This strictness to the detail of procedure is a forerunner of scientific experimentalism. Even the attempt on the part of the 'receiving agent' to account for his failures by blaming a devil, witch, or other hostile being is not out of step with the way scientific experiments are carried out. The question of 'intervening variables' is a thorny one even in the experimental laboratory. As I will show later, pre-scientific thinking is primarily a failure to keep pushing the inquiry with increasing rigor and more precise formulations of procedure and predicted consequences when appropriate. When the oracle told the general that a mighty power will surely fall, the general should have asked *which* mighty power! Also when? Fall to what extent? And so on.

If a shaman, priest, or whatever claims that he cannot get into the proper condition so long as *other people are observing* to see whether or not he goes through the publicly announced procedures, then the question arises as to whether *non-human instruments* may be used to monitor the 'receiving agent'. Almost all religions seem to speak of some conditions and procedures that are supposed to increase the so-called probability of the occurrence of the special revelation, experience, or whatever. The issue becomes one of how rigorously these procedures are kept track of and used in test cases.

B. THE QUESTION OF MEANING

If certain statements are made but we have no means of testing them, then are we justified in declaring the statements meaningless? This is a terribly difficult question, but also a very fruitful one to explore.

The first point that I wish to make in dealing with this question is that the term 'meaning' has various meanings. A dance movement has a meaning in the sense that it belongs to a pattern of responses, reinforcers, and stimuli. A movement by one dancer 'means' something to another when it serves as stimulus or response to the other; or the movement may be in response to a stimulus or reinforcer within the dance pattern. Within the whole painting, certain lines and shadows have 'meaning' in the sense of being necessary, or at least contributory, to the painting. A meaningless line on the canvas is one that contributes nothing. Sometimes, it is said that a person's life is without meaning if it contributes nothing to society or to someone.

The second point is that one way of determining whether something in art or music has any meaning to the painting or score is to remove it and see what is left. (I am not here speaking psychologically in terms of the painter's or musician's self-expression, but rather suggesting that a painting or score develops problems, directions, and solutions of its own – somewhat in the way that a mathematics problem does.)

It seems that theological discourse – like art, music, and mathematics – can develop patterns, structures, directions, and problems of its own. In Christian theology various statements 'mean' something in that they have an intricate place in the theological context and structure. The statement that God neither sleeps nor slumbers means something, but it means little or nothing to say that God yawns but never dozes. There is a kind of open-ended dance to the movement of theological development or discourse. Some statements are profound cues and reinforcers in the theological community. However, this is to begin speaking somewhat psychologically and sociologically. Tightening my argument a bit, I want to say that theological *statements* may have meaning with regard to other theological statements or a network of statements, just as lines in a painting may have meaning with regard to one another. Whether or not someone *psychologically appreciates* the meaning is an altogether different question.

Now, in the movement of theological discourse, certain statements may come to cease to have meaning, although they may still be meaningful in the study of church history or in the ritual. For example, statements about angels occupy very little place in contemporary theological literature, whereas in the day of Thomas Aquinas they were very 'meaningful' or integral to the theological structure of statements. Without structural statements, theology simply ceases to be. The need for new statements is created in either contradiction crises or when something theological has to be said in a new area. For example, in light of discussions on abortion, can a theological statement be made regarding when an organism becomes a person? Or perhaps theology can talk of personhood rather than the status of the fetus.

In this century, many theologians have emphasized the 'faith encounter' and have de-emphasized the 'proposition'. This came about in reaction to the evangelical's and fundamentalist's emphasis upon 'verbal inspiration' and 'propositional revelation'. Unfortunately, reaction against this stress on infallible propositions in the Bible has perhaps made theology somewhat loose and careless with its statements. Ninian Smart, insisting on new theological theories, deplores the failure of theology to attend carefully to its statements. He writes with dry wit the following: 'Propositions [i.e., statements] are indeed heaven-sent, though not in the way we once thought' (1974: 236).

C. DO THEOLOGICAL STATEMENTS HAVE COGNITIVE MEANING?

A line in a painting may not have cognitive meaning, for it lacks verbal statements about the world. (I cannot become involved in the fascinating but complex issue of whether art may be non-verbally cognitive, or whether it offers 'insights' that might later be formulated into statements.) Theology, on the other hand, is composed of verbal statements that, within the structure of theology itself, may be tested for contradictions. Often it is forgotten that theology undergoes *changes*. It is a more or less dynamic structure that drops some statements and picks up new ones. In many ways Karl Barth's famous formulation of the Trinity (as one personal God in three eternal modes) was to Sabellius and the Cappadocian Fathers what Newton's new physics and astronomy were to Galileo and Copernicus. The old conjectures were not simply absorbed by the latter; rather they were found to contain serious contradictions. Fortunately, imaginative persons like Newton and Barth, working with the contradictions, came up with new, bold, and daring conjectures that arose out of the original problem. (It doubtless will sound strange to some to have Barth's genius compared favorably with Newton's, for the impact of Newton seems far greater than Barth's. However, Barth was working on problems that were 'metaphysical research programmes' (Popper) for Christians primarily, and of no direct intellectual importance for those outside the field of theology. Incidentally, despite his views of biblical prophecy, Newton advanced some rather ingenius and daring conjectures of 'higher criticism' of the Bible. Unlike Goethe or Bishop Berkeley, Barth never turned his imaginative genius loose in the field of astronomy or physics.)

Barth's theory of the Trinity is regarded by many as superior to its trinitarian predecessors because it still makes meaningful statements – i.e., it connects in numerous intricate ways with the whole structure of Christian theology – while at the same time it eliminates a number of the most embarrassing contradictions of the predecessors. Note that two ingredients are necessary for progress within the theological boundaries. First, it must keep intricate ties with much of the theological system of statements (of which there are very many) and, second, it must reduce the level of inconsistency at the critical points. Had Barth stated simply 'The Trinity is!' and left it at that, he would not have made *theological* progress because this statement does not specify very many intricate ties with the rest of the theological structure. True, within the theological structure, this statement might have stood without contradiction, but it would also have been without profound meaning or contact with the many basic parts of the structure. In summary, Barth's theory of the Trinity meets the two tests of cognitive meaningfulness in theology in that it is an intricate part of the system of Christian theological statements and it is more or less self-consistent at the critical points.[1]

---

1. Shortly after writing the above paragraphs on Barth, I happened to come across H. Martin Rumsheidt's analysis of the relationship between developments in twentieth-century physics and Barth's theological method. See his *Revelation and Theology: An Analysis of the Barth-Harnack Correspondence of 1923* (1972: 177ff.). I will not go into the considerable difference between Rumscheidt and myself on Barth's theological method.

D. EXTENDING THE BOUNDARIES OF THEOLOGICAL MEANING

Of course, a theological theory or doctrine could lose its self-consistency if it should extend itself into new areas by making theological statements in those areas. It is always a problem for any established body of doctrines to determine whether to venture new statements or to rest content with the old creeds and formulations. In the new 'secular' areas themselves statements are sometimes made which force theology to make either accommodating or opposing statements. Martin Luther, for example, feeling the challenge of Copernicus' new astronomy, ventured to make statements to the effect that a choice had to be made between sacred scripture and Copernicus. John Wesley, in a time when belief in witches was on the wane, made the statement, 'The giving up of witchcraft is in effect the giving up of the Bible' (quoted in White, 1960, I: 363). In recent years the evangelist Billy Graham has taken some comfort in a rising belief in witchcraft, demons, and other such despicable characters of the spiritual underworld; for Graham's own cosmological and psychological conjectures have never been very compatible with those of modern science.

Graham's view of original sin includes a kind of theological chemistry or alchemy in which human blood somehow transmits from generation to generation a disease called sin (1966: 56-57, 60-61). That is why, according to this theological chemistry, God had to spill the blood of Jesus as an atonement, for Jesus' blood is thought by Graham to have been pure and undefiled. (Many fundamentalists hold that Jesus had to be born of a virgin in order not to inherit tainted blood, cf. DeHaan, 1951.) In science, a theory is sometimes used to direct the energies of research toward an area in which new phenomena are expected to be discovered or detected. But the adherents to 'theological chemistry' seem unwilling to suggest what to look for as the 'sin factor' in the chemistry of the blood. Graham seems clearly to be speaking of literal human blood and not a 'spiritual' blood. But he does not care to be more specific than that.

There are numerous areas in which theology has ventured to make statements in opposition to new scientific theories. Rector Hensel's textbook, *The Restored Mosaic System of the World* (1734), was written for Protestant students in Germany in order to show them that the Copernican theory of astronomy led to atheism. Sometimes theological writings oppose new scientific theories on the grounds that they are unscriptural. At other times, when the new scientific theories become established, theological writings may be found boasting that the latest scientific discoveries were already suggested in the Bible. Prediction gives way to ad hoc hindsight. For centuries, such phenomena as comets, storms, and other such events were regarded as 'signs' of divine intervention into the affairs of human beings to bring divine judgment upon evildoers. But Newton and Halley provided as less moralistic framework for understanding especially the movement of comets. In 1770, Semler, professor at Halle, tried to strike a compromise by both accepting the new astronomy and stating also that while comets were not God's judgment of human evil, they were nevertheless signs, warnings, or reminders of the Just Judge of the Universe (White, 1960, I: 205).

The positivists were excessively puritanical in their attempts to render all theological and moral statements as cognitively meaningless. Or, to be more exact, their whole notion of 'evidence' and 'verification' was misconceived. In the above few paragraphs I have tried to argue that theological statements have sometimes been found to be in contradiction with one another, especially when theology has attempted to maintain its old statements while at the same time extending itself by making definite statements about the central formulations of the sciences. Luther, Wesley, and others realized that many of the old statements of theology would be contradicted by the new ones sensitive to the new sciences. They attacked these scientific systems in order to get to the root of the problem. Graham still attacks the conjecture-scheme of evolution because he can see that, once accepted, it will create consistency crises for evangelical theology. Evangelical theology cannot incorporate statements of an evolutionary nature without qualifying, i.e., reformulating, some of its central statements. Some evangelical Christians talk of 'threshold evolution', but they do not come to grips with any significant points of contention.

Thus far in this chapter, I have attempted to make essentially one point: if theological statements were all meaningless, no one could legitimately fear that they would be contradicted, and no one would – or could – expose the alleged contradictions. But various theological statements are both attacked for being inconsistent with one another and defended against this attack. This debate has not been meaningless; not all theological statements are cognitively meaningless. In fact, I would argue, because it has made both cognitively meaningful statements and has been caught making statements that contradict one another, theology has been forced to qualify, revise, reformulate, and sometimes to develop bold new conjectures.

Therefore, the evangelical Christians are correct to take the daring conjectures of such men as Brightman, Whitehead, and Wieman to be, not classical theism simply revised, but rather replacements of classical theism. These daring new theological conjectures would replace the old, just as Newton's conjectures replaced those of Copernicus and Galileo by exposing their contradictions, learning from their mistakes, and boldly projecting a new theory dealing with the old problems in a revolutionary and bold way.

E. THEORY AS A DISTINCT REALITY

I am aware that theological statements can have ritual and other kinds of meaning. Neo-Wittgensteinians have argued well this fundamental point. Nevertheless, emotive and ritual meanings are in *addition* to the cognitive meaning, and are not instead of it. There is no case for reducing religion to exclusively a 'functional' meaning and definition. Even though theological formulations may have been written down by human hand, this does not mean that theology is reducible to psychology. The first automobile was made by human hands, but once it was made it became a reality of its own. Today theological treatises and arguments exist in libraries and elsewhere and are as real as jet planes and works of art. Theological arguments, once constructed, take on a character and direction of their own. They are cultural objects at least.

Before working through the content of this chapter, I did not have the arguments tucked away neatly in my 'mind'. Rather, I had to follow some of the leads that other arguments had already initiated. That is, in some sense 'my' arguments have led me. After writing down and later rereading my arguments, I was sometimes made to see that still earlier statements I had made could not stand in harmony with my more recent statements. Needless to say, had I been able to predict the contradictions, I would not have set them down on paper in the first place. It was in seeing the contradictions that I was led to qualify, modify, or even desert some of my arguments in favor of new conjectures and arguments.

I will not here attempt even to outline the various contingencies and patterns which directed and controlled the content of this chapter, for my point is simply that arguments as set forth on paper or before an audience have their own special reality. Strictly speaking, an automobile that is constructed may run quite well even though its inventor regrets ever having made it. Similarly, a theist may write a brilliant defense of theism and then in later years become an atheist. But the brilliance of the defense still stands regardless of what happened to its original composer.

The question of what a person does with theological expectations (beliefs) is not primarily a theological question but one which social and behavioral science may wish to explore. A theological statement may have profound cognitive meaning within the theological structure even though it may have almost no ritual or moral meaning. That is, it may be intricate and central to the *theological* system of statements of which it is a part while at the same time not function as significant cues, responses, or reinforcers within *ritual* behavior. The present chapter has been concerned almost exclusively with cognitive meaning within the system of theological statements.

Some writers regard theological discourse itself to be always ritual behavior, and I have no strong objection to this so long as 'always' is not translated as 'nothing but'. One serious objection to thinking of theological discourse as ritual behavior might be that ritual is too routine and repetitious, with tightly fixed patterns. If ritual is understood in this way, then theology in its more dynamic and creative surges is definitely not ritual.

F. THEOLOGY AND TRANSCENDENT OBJECTIVE REFERENCE

In reviewing Paul van Buren's book, *The Secular Meaning of the Gospel* (1963), the late Bishop of Durham, Ian Ramsey, raises pointedly the question to be pursued in this section. Drawing from his own thesis of 'cosmic disclosures', he contends that in religious faith (in the *ideal* sense of the word) 'there must be an element of transcendence in both the objective reference of the disclosure and in our own subjective responses and commitment' (1974b: 255). Not content to view religious literature as stories that motivate us morally, Ramsey insists that 'the loving [human] response presupposes some sort of objective challenge about the stories, the art, the music, and so forth' (p. 253). It is not enough simply to become religious in the sense of taking on a 'new way of looking at things'. Rather, argues the bishop, we need to say something about the transcendent, objective challenge that elicits our response. Bishop Ramsey admits that his call for an 'element of objectivity and transcendence' will probably be 'too metaphysical' for van Buren (pp. 253–255).

However, the issue of *whether* one writer is more metaphysical than another is not the issue. It cannot be said that the bishop is heavy on metaphysics whereas van Buren has only a light touch of it. Rather, it is a question of *which* metaphysical view is being asserted or presupposed. Indeed, Ramsey correctly interprets van Buren as more the naturalist than the theist. But naturalism is just as much a metaphysical view as theism. Van Buren seems to be one of those who, having once embraced the theistic metaphysics, later rejected it, although he still sees great value in the ritual, communal, moral, etc. meanings of Christianity. Of him Ramsey writes:

His secular sympathies and his serious Christian concern lead him to see 'natural religion' not as a first stage on the way to Christianity: instead he offers his readers a 'natural religion' derived from Christianity (p. 253).

Ramsey is justified in insisting that we inquire into not only our own responses, but what it is that brings about the responses. Aware of some of 'the complex logical rules that, e.g., Trinitarian and Christological doctrine embody' (1974a: 254), he nevertheless contends '"it is *a sort of fact* that God exists, not unlike the fact that we exist".' (1974d: 239. Ramsey is quoting approvingly Ninian Smart, but the italics are Ramsey's). In my book *Religion and the Challenge of Philosophy* (1975: Chaps. 3–8), I have already dealt with various arguments for the existence of God and will not repeat here what was said there.

Ramsey says further that '"God" is a word which talks of what is objectively disclosed in a disclosure of a cosmic kind' (1974c: 237). Somewhat like Popper and Quine, the bishop recognizes that all claims to factuality and objectivity 'depend on some background conceptual scheme' (p. 238). Unfortunately, he does not indicate whether God is a part of the background or a fact standing out from the background. My guess is that he is saying simply that the theistic conceptual scheme is different from the naturalistic one and that the former allows God-talk to be carried further than does the latter. Most naturalists will use God-talk only in the sense that an anthropologist who does not believe in witches will nevertheless use witchtalk in order to describe, or converse with, the tribe that does believe in witches.

The naturalist and the theist each tries to fit the other into his own conceptual scheme. It is generally agreed that the theist views natural phenomena as the direct or indirect work of God, whereas the naturalist views religious and theological practices and works as arising out of the interplay between human beings (individually and in groups) and the complex energy system which is called nature. Yet this is not quite the case, for the theist views the world both theistically and naturalistically. It is difficult to know what to make of this observation. Perhaps theism is analogous to colored glasses by which the events of the world are seen in their naturalistic relationships but with a theistic color. For example, looking through green sun glasses we see, say, an automobile crash. We observe this happening but we see it as green – or, to use the analogy – we see the act as somehow the providence of God.

Or perhaps being both a theist and a naturalist is somewhat like being both a physicist and a father. When with his fellow physicists, Dr. Pollard converses in the language of physics and mathematics and focuses his attention on the special problems of physics. But when talking with his children, he utilizes everyday language and dwells with various problems and interests that are usually not regarded as problems of physics as such. Similarly, if Dr. Pollard is a theist, he might speak in theistic terms under certain conditions and with certain people. But when talking with his children he uses ordinary or everyday language. To be sure, he might now and then speak to his children about physics and teach them some of its principles or even do some experiments with them. Similarly, if a Christian, Dr. Pollard might talk to his children about God and Jesus, teach them a few elementary theological principles, and pray with them. But ordinarily he would not as a Christian say to his children, 'Would you please pass the butter, which God has so wonderfully provided'. Nor would he say, 'Please pass the swirling molecules in the pink dish'. He would not ordinarily say to his wife, 'God willing, I will be home at 4 p.m.'. Nor would he say, 'If the atomic structure of the universe does not fall apart, I will be home at 4 p.m.'.

As a physicist, he believes that the streets on which he travels home are a part of the atomic structure of things, and as a Christian he believes that the atomic structure is held together by God. But in every day discourse he does not ordinarily mention this because to do so would be inefficient. It is simpler to say, 'I will be home at 4 p.m.' or 'Pass the butter, please'. No reference to God or atomic weight is necessary to communicate what is desired in these cases.

G. THE PROBLEM OF TRANSLATING FROM ONE LANGUAGE GAME TO ANOTHER

No profound problem would emerge for a Christian physicist if, say, his inquisitive son were to refrain from asking for an explanation of prayer. Even Christian ministers endeavor to explain prayer by using both everyday language and theological language. But using the language and concepts of physics to explain prayer is not something about which physicists claim to be able to do. The believer says in theological terms that 'God provides common grace to believer and unbeliever alike'. Then in ordinary language he can talk of a rain that came during the night and can even report the number of inches that fell. The physicists can speak of rain in terms of molecular structures, velocities, capillary attraction, and so forth. And what seems so impressive about the physicist is his ability to *connect* his language and concepts to the language of everyday description, and to do so in terms of prediction and law-like formulae. In all candor, it must be said that the theologian simply cannot make *comparable connections* between theological language and concepts and everyday language.

True, the theologian can jump from God-talk to ordinary discourse about rain or whatever. But this tells us more about the skill and ability of the theologian than the *law-like connections* between theology and everyday descriptions. One may carry on two conversations at once, but this does not entail that the conversations are even remotely related. The fact that a person can be both a theologian and a physicist may indicate his remarkable ability to carry on two 'inner dialogues'. But this in no way demonstrates that there are theological law-like connections between theology and physics. Indeed, if there were, their discoverer would do the world a genuine favor by publishing them in either a journal of physics or a journal of theology.

To be sure, ministers are frequently heard talking about 'spiritual laws', but no systematic and precisely formulated statements have been set forth to indicate what exactly these laws are. At best they are vague suggestions connecting an assortment of procedures with a very wide range of consequences, so wide as to make predictions and law-like connections impossible. Oral Roberts' prediction that 'something good is going to happen to you' is an extreme example of the vagueness of theological prediction. It is doubtful that any 'spiritual law' that is intricately bound to theistic language comes even close to the scientific prediction that at a specified elevation water will boil at a specified temperature.

H. TRANSFORMING ONE LANGUAGE GAME INTO ANOTHER

The theologian could object that the language game (or conceptual system) called physics is not really *connected* with our ordinary language descriptions. Rather, the physicist must do either of two things (and often both). He must either (1) transform ordinary language descriptions into the language of physics, or (2) practice talking in the two languages without connecting them.

This objection by the theologian has some important implications. From the start, it raises the question about our ordinary language descriptions. Take, for example, the phrase, 'The sun went down this evening at 7 p.m.'. Well, this statement simply will not fit into the system of statements and formulae that we call physics. It will have to be transformed to say something else. To be sure, the ordinary language description is a starting point, but the physicist cannot leave it there. He must insist that the expression about the sun's going down is inaccurate when seen from the broader context of physics and astronomy. This is not to say that the experienced red of the sun is not 'really' red, but rather that the phrase 'sunset' belongs to a conceptual scheme which physics and astronomy has *eliminated* and *replaced* by a different scheme.

It seems, therefore, that the theologian is correct in objecting to the assumption that the language of physics and the language of everyday descriptions and explanations are systematically connected. Rather, one system is made to yield to the other. But this raises a question about another implication of the theologian's objection. Is he implying that the conceptual scheme of physics should be replaced by a conceptual scheme of theology?

This develops into an even more fascinating problem. Is theology to become a new superscience that will supercede physics and astronomy? Will theologians someday be able to speak in theological formulae in such a way as to render the statements of physics inferior because their theological replacement has proved itself to be superior? (It is epistemologically irrelevant to say that the theological scheme is superior *because* it promises a more optimistic view or a 'moral universe'.)

Another possibility is that of regarding theology, not as a science at all, but as a kind of metaphysical recommendation. That is, theologians recommend that the laws and concepts of physics, astronomy, chemistry, and perhaps biology be viewed behaviorally – as the overt behavior of God. In short, the language of especially the physical sciences is God-talk. Borrowing from behaviorism, a theologian might conjecture that the various realms of nature are really the overt behavior of God that is publicly observable. If this position were accepted, then theology would not be required to have extra-scientific sources of knowledge. Whereas biblical theology would be required to check its statements with the Bible lest they contradict what is taught in the Bible, 'behavioral theology' would be required to check its statements with the laws, etc., of science in order not to contradict science.

However, many theologians and believers regard this alternative to be much too confusing. The acts of God must not, for them, be bound by the doings of nature (even if our sciences could formulate objective laws of nature). There must be super-nature acts. There must be supernatural revelation. God-talk, according to these protesting theologians, is not simply science-talk plus humanistic culture-talk, but rather 'special revelation' with a special authority of its own.

If this biblical theology is accepted, then the option is left open that God-talk may even instruct science and perhaps even render it an inferior conceptual scheme, much in the way that physics and astronomy leave as inferior and naïve the ordinary language talk of 'sunsets'. I have no objection to theology's setting for itself this magnificent task. I ask only that the theologians start talking and keep talking until they show us how their superior scheme explains in a way that the sciences do not.

I. WILL GOD-TALK TALK ITSELF TO DEATH?

Positivists tried to find a way to prevent God-talk from getting started. By contrast, my thesis in this chapter, based in part on the previous chapter, is that God-talk needs to be both encouraged and scrutinized. Karl Popper admits that the line between critical discussion and empirical testing is not always easy to draw. I do not think it very useful to demand that theology formulate some sort of single, one-shot critical experimental test that will either falsify God's existence or else leave the God-hypothesis standing victorious, at least until some other test can be devised.

The more fruitful approach is to encourage theology to make *more* statements, to talk at length. Mystics were perhaps no less clever than pious when they tried to tell people with inquiring minds not to pay their statements any mind. Although apparently unable to refrain from engaging in God-talk, mystics seemed to realize that the more they talked, the less they could defend their conviction that they had rubbed noses with the transcendent or the transcendental.

To say that theologians and religious spokesmen should be encouraged to engage at length in God-talk is not to encourage just any sort of talk but rather the sort that is relevant and material to the issues. When a physicist is trying to explain a point or resolve a problem, he is deviating from his task when he resorts to exhortations or begins to classify as blind those who are skeptical of his position. Similarly, a theological treatise purporting to explain and to develop a point should be reinforced for doing just that.

The phrase 'linguistic therapy' reveals considerable insight, although Wittgenstein was mistaken to think that philosophy as linguistic therapy is the cure for metaphysics. As F. H. Bradley realized, there is no cure for metaphysics per se (1955: x). Phenomenologists and positivists are deluded if they think they can talk without coloring their conversation with metaphysical expressions. The very language we use is drenched in metaphysics. An 'ideal language' divested of all metaphysics is at best a very vague promise.

Claiming that linguistic therapy can eliminate metaphysics is a bit like claiming that, say, non-directive therapy can eliminate problems. Carl Rogers can help in the elimination of some problems that are particularly destructive. But even Rogers has problems and regards it as quite desirable to have them. In the same way, linguistic analysis has helped in exposing and eliminating certain particular metaphysical claims and assumptions. But they are replaced by new ones. By paying close attention to what theologians have said, the individual practicing language analysis is able to compare and contrast statements, first to see what is being said, and then to determine whether a contradiction has been made. In many ways the linguistic analyst has paid theologians the high honor of attending to their statements and treating such statements as though they were set forth to be taken as serious *cognitive* statements.

Apparently, theologians have learned that if they are going to be read with analytic scrutiny, they had best learn to think like analytic philosophers. When the theologian's words are returned to him and he sees that some of them are void, then he must reply either that he was himself misled or that he was simply moving his readers ritualistically and exhorting them. Indeed, as the habit of linguistic analysis became more widespread, some theologians and some philosophers writing in the field of theology began to turn on one another. Ninian Smart, for example, says very frankly that what he has learned from linguistic philosophy has made it difficult to read Tillich without seeing in his works 'Obscure ineptitude', 'trivialities', and 'loose talk' (1974: 233-234). Malcolm L. Diamond, however, much more impressed with Tillich, tries to restate some of Tillich's views so that they will not appear to be so loose and equivocal.

But Diamond ends up telling his readers that the famous Christian theologian Paul Tillich actually is an existential humanist. Diamond claims that 'Tillich manages to avoid most of the pitfalls of Christian thought', which is to say he does not make as many contradictory statements as Diamond thinks other Christian writers make. But this is not surprising if Tillich is using Christian code-language to express a metaphysics and morality that is essentially non-theistic. In the words of Professor Diamond:

There would seem to be little reason to talk Tillichese, for anything that he says in terms of Christian symbols could equally well be communicated in terms of the symbols of another faith, especially that of existential humanism. It is not, therefore, altogether surprising that one of the movements strongly influenced by Paul Tillich, a Christian thinker, called itself the 'Death of God Theology' (1974: 388-389).

J. TILLICH'S TRANSITIONAL LINGUISTICS

Needless to say, many Christians read Tillich not as a humanist but as a theist. But this is not altogether surprising either – given what Ninian Smart calls Tillich's 'loose talk of "being"' Tillich cannot be said to have developed a bold and daring theory either of God or of humanistic atheism; but rather he has developed a kind of transition language which has helped many Christians to begin thinking as naturalists and existential humanists while at the same time enjoying the ritual and emotional ties with their Christian background.

It should be acknowledged that for many people such words as 'God', 'Christ', and 'new being' are highly charged in terms of positive emotion. The symbol 'Christ', for example, is a kind of magnet around which are drawn such profound values as forgiveness, love, concern for the down and out, meaningful living, humility, and the like. For some people, dropping such words as 'God' and 'Christ' is like dropping also all the values associated with them. Tillich understands the non-cognitive and quasi cognitive function of symbols; he rather smoothly, which is not to say deceitfully, substitutes more neutral words for the traditional words. For example, God and Ground of Being become emotionally associated. Those who protest against Tillich's loose talk of 'being' are cognitively justified. Whether Tillich is justified in other ways for using such vague terms transitionally is a difficult and very complex question. Indeed, it is debatable as to how 'transitional' Tillich regarded his own work.

Tillich's theology, then, is no important or daring theological venture. It is more of a venture in what should better be called 'transitional linguistics'. It is a mushy 'synthesis' having minimal intellectual significance. Nevertheless, words and symbols (especially traditional and highly charged ones) can be used in various ways to move people and to give them 'courage to be'. There is little doubt that Tillich has with great skill used words and contexts to help shape the responses and attitudes of many people. He has helped to save people from 'losing their faith' by, in effect, teaching them to lose only half of it and to retain and cherish the other half. He has helped them to give up the Zeus-like God (the God 'up there') of some versions of Christianity, without at the same time becoming disoriented and bereft of ritual, fellowship, associates, and other social reinforcements that come in 'religious association'.

Many traditional theists, it must be admitted, still think of God as 'up there'. In June 1974 I happened to attend a sermon which Billy Graham preached to the large audience of the annual meeting of the Southern Baptist Convention. Graham spoke in all sincerity of 'King Jesus' coming literally on a white horse through the sky to earth. This is what I mean by the Zeus-like God of traditional Christianity. Paul Tillich, son of a Protestant minister, describes his own position as 'self-transcending or ecstatic naturalism' (1961: 341). The word 'self-transcending', containing a cognate of 'transcendent', pays at least lip-service to transcendent supernaturalism. Yet Tillich is also a naturalist. It is not clear as to who or what is ecstatic – presumably nature is standing outside itself, which suggests the phrase 'out there' rather than 'up there'. Again, this is a mushy 'synthesis', not an intellectually daring venture.

When Bishop John A. T. Robinson wrote his now-famous *Honest to God* (1963), he made it quite clear that 'the truth of the Christian Gospel' is not to be confused with 'traditional orthodox supernaturalism' (p. 8). Such words as 'Gospel' and 'Christian' have deep roots and very subtle overtones for many people; and Bishop Robinson, like the Tillich from whom he borrows so much, was not about to drop these cherished and powerful words. At the same time, what exactly *is* the 'Christian Gospel'? Again like Tillich, Robinson proceeds to fill in the meaning, much of which is hu-

manistic morality and humanistic caring for one's fellows. The bishop writes:
> Thus, not infrequently, as I watch or listen to a broadcast discussion between a Christian and a humanist, I catch myself realizing that most of my sympathies are on the humanist's side. This is not the least because my faith or commitment is in doubt. . . . (p. 8.)

Indeed, the good bishop does not doubt his faith because in the minds of some critical readers there is still doubt as to exactly *what is* the content of the bishop's faith.

K. WHAT DOES GOD-TALK TALK ITSELF INTO?

God-talk often talks itself into contradictions, especially when it attempts to become more than a verbal ritual. Many believers have thought it to be very bad to get caught in theological contradictions. But to the contrary, this exposé of contradictions is necessary if theology is to improve itself, that is, is to develop daring and bold conjectures containing content. Naturalism, too, as well as doctrines of the Absolute and other metaphysical conceptual schemes – all have contradictions. The more important metaphysics is not the one that demonstrates itself in verbal gymnastics. Rather, it is the one that is willing to admit openly its contradictions and ambiguities and to try to overcome them with 'inspired' new conjectures that are not mere syntheses of so-called thesis and antithesis.

What God-talk will talk itself into is nothing that I could predict. The issue of what the 'real essence of Christianity is' is asked by people who are bound to the word 'Christian'. What, it must be asked, is so important about determining what the essence of Christianity is? What problem is being solved? Does the question itself presuppose that one already has in mind what he thinks is the essence of Christianity?

It is clear that the word 'Christianity' has for many people accumulated a great assortment of values which they do not wish to lose. But also under the heading of 'Christianity' are other things which they regard as unworthy of commitment. Many who reject

Christianity do so because they identify it with the unworthy elements, whereas others identify it with the worthy elements. Who is right? The question has no intellectual importance. Are there not some worthy and unworthy elements under the heading of 'Buddhism'? Which is 'true Buddhism'? If we select only the worthy elements under the heading of 'Buddhism' and call this 'true Buddhism', would we subscribe to it? If not, then could we justify not subscribing to such worthy elements? If we do subscribe, are we therefore Buddhists?

I suspect that often when especially Christians speak of 'the Faith', they have in mind *a selection of worthy elements.* Whether belief in a transcendent deity is one of those elements worthy of our belief is a question with epistemological, metaphysical, moral, emotional dimensions. And that is why it is no easy question. It would be useful to ask theologians and professing believers in God to tell us what God would have to be like in order for him to require that humans believe in him. Strange as it may seem, theists have not talked at length about this and I suggest that such God talk might uncover some interesting and perhaps shocking statements.

A good therapist will not simply reinforce the ramblings of his client. Nor will he be content with the mere repetition of short answers. Rather, he will stimulate the client to talk in depth about new and diverse topics with a view toward 'insight'. Similarly, fruitful questions may stimulate and probe theists to *experiment with God-talk in diverse areas and on new topics.* We may expect 'insight' if our questions are penetrating and *if the believer is still willing to talk about God.*

L. WHO ARE THE OPPONENTS OF GOD-TALK?

It is a curious fact that both mystics and positivists are the opponents of God-talk. Neither of them believes that theology has a legitimate place. In fact, quite a number of pious believers seem to be suspicious of theology. One reason for this is that theology is expected to formulate itself into some kind of cognitively respectable statements, which is something that both positivists and mystics claim is impossible. Or, to be more exact, theology is expected to formulate itself cognitively and respectably and to *keep on doing so*. The apostle's creed, while ancient, is not a good theological treatise. Of great ritual and emotive worth, it has some vague cognitive value in the sense that it marks off a few boundaries beyond which certain theological statements are not permitted to go. But the boundaries are like the Rio Grande River in its shifting from time to time.

A scientific theory of conjecture is more legitimate if it has a wealth of content as well as a coherence or self-consistency. By 'wealth of content' is meant 'degree of testability'. That is, the testable theory does not hide under a bushel, so to speak, but boldly asserts itself in many directions. It makes articulate claims that can be pinned down. The point of pinning them down is to make falsification – if it ever comes – easily recognizable. A claim that is vaguely compatible with every conceivable state of affairs is useless in testing a scientific hypothesis because the claim says little to begin with. It is like the words of the fence-stradling politician who talks a lot but says nothing. It is ritual behavior, perhaps, but little more.

I hope I have exposed what my motive has been in calling for more God-talk. Let each theological statement be set forth, not simply to repeat prior theological statements, but to develop and throw light on the old creeds and formulae. Let theology seek to explain, and then explain more. *This is the theological parallel to empirical experiments.* If theology cannot suggest empirical experiments, it can nevertheless make statements that have a bearing on areas in which empirical testings do take place. Even *if* theology is regarded as only 'myth' (in the sense of untestable but suggestive and fruitful visions), its influence on more testable statements may be important. Of course, theology may in turn be influenced, which is the chance it will have to take.

I presuppose that all theological talk – or any other talk – will eventually run into its share of contradictions. For some believers, this is a frightful and threatening prospect, sufficiently threatening to make them demand a moratorium on theology. For others, however, stepped up God-talk is the challenge – and also the risk – of turning theology loose to wind its course where it will. The development of new theological problems, far from killing theology, can be an advance in creative metaphysical thinking.

Positivism, that bitter enemy of theology, would have damned up theology so that it could not even generate more *problems*.' Rarely keen and insightful as critics of theology, positivists sought to ignore it, deport it, and declare it unimportant (meaningless). Such anti-intellectualism has, fortunately, been exposed as an arrogant imposition on human curiosity. Positivism hated theology more than it loved the growth of knowledge.

Those who protest strongly the doing of theology protest too much. They arouse suspicion about their own 'metaphysical research program'. Are they perhaps asserting a quasi theology of their own, which they wish to spread far and wide as a standard paradigm, without its being thoroughly debated and cross-examined? We can perhaps learn from original Marxism, which attacked theology only to substitute its own gospel of the *Lebensmacht* and its own version of 'the meaning of history' (cf. Tucker, 1961). Indeed, Marx's attempt to define all rival views as 'ideology' is very much like the positivists' attempt to close off critical interchange and rational debate. It is a way of saying that all rival statements are 'meaningless', which is to say unworthy of listening to or reading. It was the fate of theology to have had both early Marxists and the positivists to refuse to debate with them. Fortunately, this short-circuit of rational inquiry has been located and corrected somewhat. We may hope that theologians will, in turn, resist the temptation to use the 'meaningless' argument in order to justify either failing to follow the arguments of their rivals or declining to engage them in critical debate. Any paradigm shift that comes about ought to be through rigorous and open interchange and not through ignoring rival schemes.

From two camps an attempt to keep theology out of critical debate has developed. One group would give theology a special license to say what it will without challenge – a kind of diplomatic immunity in academic circles. The other group would simply refuse to look at things through the theological framework. I have in various places already criticized this first group, which is one reason that the present chapters devote extra space for opposing the second group. The scholastic who refused to look through Galileo's telescope is the forerunner of those today who refuse to let themselves experiment with looking at things through theological conjectures. They do not realize that the telescope and microscope are not simply devices for obtaining a 'pure experience' of reality. Like some of the mystics, they think that somehow without conjectures, theories, and hypotheses they can just 'see' with pristine purity what is real. The telescope is no different from a theory in one crucial sense: it is a new way of 'seeing'. But the major point of this chapter has been that there are countless ways of 'seeing', which is why *critical* experience – i.e., *criticized* experience – becomes imperative in the quest for knowledge, whether of God or gravitational fields. C. S. Pierce's fallibilism strikes the claims of mysticism, science, and theology alike.

The-Meaning-of-Life Question

A. MORE THAN COGNITIVE MEANING

Many religious spokesmen insist that only religious faith can give the answer to the question of the meaning of life. Writing a chapter in a book entitled *The Meaning of Life In Five Great Religions* (1965), the Hindu philosopher and religious teacher, P. Nagaraja Rao, states, 'The Indian genius has largely given its life to two interests: one in finding the meaning and the purpose of life and secondly in outlining an elaborate moral and spiritual discipline for realizing the ideal' (p. 25). Psychotherapists report that in recent years a major concern of their clients is that of 'meaning'. Addressing the Conference on Psychological and Psychotherapeutic Means of Behavior Control, Dr. Perry London claims that psychotherapists will be called on increasingly to deal with the problem of 'the achievement of meaning and value in life'. 'We have', he says, 'moved from the modest hope of living without fear to the grand need for existential purpose. . . .' (1973: 10–13).[1]

Philosophy in the twentieth century seems to have been preoccupied with such terms as 'meaning', 'meaningless', 'meaningful', and 'meaninglessness'. In previous chapters I have in one way or another been dealing with the question of the *cognitive meaning* of statements. But it is clear that philosophers, theologians, therapists, and others have in mind something more than cognitive meaning alone when they concern themselves with the meaning-of-life

---

1. This quoted statement is all the more important in light of London's own position of behaviorism.

question. Without the cognitive strands and dimensions, *human* life could never be for the featherless cerebral animal who walks upright (physically at least). But, as the atheist and analytic philosopher Antony Flew has written, 'to insist only that philosophy is not everything, that there are and ought to be other things in life, is realistic, robust, and altogether unexceptionable' (1971:484).

There is some justification in the criticism that linguistic analysts spend a disproportionate amount of time talking about the grading of oranges and the game rules of cricket, when they ought to be using their talents to speak of meaningful living and dying, of decision and guilt, and of other questions which existentialists and the various traditional religions have devoted themselves to. However, in recent years even analytic philosophers – including some of those of the linguistic school – have felt it important to begin speaking and writing on these questions.

In this chapter I wish to utilize some of the approach of linguistic analysis to bring a workable measure of clarity to the question of the meaning of life.[2] My task will be primarily to show that when various people have used such phrases as 'the meaning of life', 'meaningful existence', and their opposites, they have often said a number of different things. Yet they have also believed that they were saying something profoundly important and even crucial to their lives. The following will not be an attempt to reduce what has been said to one common theme. It is more important first to listen to what various representative groups have actually said and are saying.

B. MEANING THROUGH A COSMIC GOAL

The Jewish, Muslim, and Christian religions in particular often teach their adherents to believe that the universe as a whole serves a purpose or a scheme of transcendent purposes. Often when they say

---

2. For some very useful articles on the 'meaning of life' or a 'meaningful life', see Kurt Bair (1966), H. J. Blackham (1963), Delwin Brown (1971), Ilham Dilman (1965; 1968), Paul Edwards (1967), Anthony Flew (1963), Ronald W. Hepburn (1963; 1967), Kai Nielsen (1964), Philip Thody (1961), and John Wisdom (1954; 1965). Freud examines the 'way an object-loss becomes an ego-loss . . . ' (cf. Ricoeur, 1970: 216ff.).

that the universe or the world has 'meaning', they define this 'meaning' as simply serving the divine purpose or goal.[3] That is, the universe is not self-explained but is explained *teleologically*. That is, it is believed to be moving in a direction toward a goal which has been more or less predetermined by the Creator.

When existentialists like Albert Camus and Jean-Paul Sartre say that the world is 'absurd', they have in mind to deny this teleological meaning. Apparently because they grew up in a culture influenced greatly by the Jewish and Christian view of things, these men came to *expect* the world to be 'going somewhere', to be aiming at a target, to be directional rather than aimless. But not being able to accept the thesis that in fact the universe is directional, they express their disappointment in the language of despair and agonizing grief.

What Camus and Sartre recommend, after recovering from their disillusionment, is that human beings *give their own meaning* to the world. What they have in mind is (at least) to encourage others to accept the great and profound disappointment without falling into emotional and moral paralysis. In *The Myth of Sisyphus* (1955) Camus argues that while life itself as a whole is going nowhere, nevertheless our human life can be meaningful in the sense of being challenging in itself (cf. Alexander and Adlerstein, 1959: 279). The theme of resolution and courage is very predominate in existentialism.

Some writers have held to a kind of transcendent realm of Value and Ideal rather than God. And they have sometimes believed that the universe does in some way harmonize with the Ideal realm. This is what they mean when they say that the world has meaning. Bertrand Russell (1872-1969), however, recommends a kind of cool and calm stoical resignation to what he regards as the fact that this 'harmony' exists only in the imagination. Meaningfulness for

---

3. 'For the Muslim, the meaning of life is defined in terms of submission to the will of God and serving as his deputy on earth. To serve as a deputy is "so to order his acts and his life as to realize in his human community the ideals which God has made known in his revelation".' (C. Douglas Jay, 'From Encounter to Community', 1965, p. 154).
'The meaning of life can be understood only in the context of the Giver of life and his purposes for creation. . . . A Book which is the supreme rule for faith and life, as it is the unquestioned self-revelation of God, given through Muhammad, His Prophet – this is Islamic Scripture.' (M. Rasjidi, 'Islam', 1965, p. 138).

Russell, then, is found in part in the cathedral of ideas and thoughts which men and women build over the years, although he warns that these majestic intellectual structures will, too, someday sink into oblivion (1957: 48f.). Yet stoic resignation is not the sole ingredient of meaningfulness for Russell. Like some of the ancient Greek dramatists, he calls for outgoing courage. But because courage does not grow spontaneously, Russell makes a plea for a social and intellectual environment that will *en*-courage individuals to face up to the fact that the universe seems to be indifferent to human values (1954: 207f.; cf. Wood, 1956: 237).

> *The world rolls round forever like a mill;*
> *It grinds out death and life and good and ill;*
> *It has no purpose, heart or mind or will.*
> (Thomson, *The City of Dreadful Night*)

In his later years, Russell explains in his autobiography that three overwhelmingly strong passions had governed his life: (a) the search for knowledge, (b) the longing for love, and (c) pity or compassion for his fellow humans in their hours of suffering. He found considerable meaning (satisfaction and fulfillment) in these passions. He explains: 'This has been my life. I have found it worth living and would gladly live it again if the chance were offered me,' (1969, I: 3f.) The poet James Thomson captures some of Russell's feeling:

> *In all eternity I had one chance,*
> *One few years' term of gracious human life:*
> *The splendors of the intellect's advance,*
> *The sweetness of the home with babes and wife.*
> (Thomson, *The City of Dreadful Night*)

But great numbers of people have confessed that they could *not* go on living if they should come to believe that the universe is without purpose beyond itself. They could not bear to live if they thought human purposes will eventually be lost in the cosmic dust. They have come to expect cosmic significance for their lives, and now they deny being able to go on living if this expectation is not met. Paul the Apostle goes so far as to say that if the Christians' hope fails to reach into eternity and beyond this finite existence, then Christians 'are of all people most miserable' (1 Cor. 15:19).

As a matter of fact, some people have *not* been able to live a bearable and generally satisfying life without believing that the universe as a whole fulfills some transcendent goal or Ideal. That is one reason they have been converted to certain forms of religion – Catholic, Protestant, Muslim, or whatever. On the other hand, some people, having once believed in a cosmic purpose but later in life coming to reject this hypothesis as an unwarranted assumption, nevertheless manage to adjust and find meaning (i.e. fulfillment and satisfaction) in their lives.

Numerous religious traditions have insisted not only that without a cosmic goal or plan, human life is 'meaningless' and 'empty', but also that *their religion alone* can provide the cosmic goal as well as the procedures and means for attaining it or for living in harmony with it. It is sometimes difficult to know which is the chicken and which is the egg. That is, did the vacuum first exist for these religions to fill; or did the religions first condition people through various programs to expect life to be empty without the cosmic goal?

C. MEANING THROUGH FINITE SOURCES OF ENJOYMENT

So, we come quite naturally to a second meaning of 'meaning in life'. Often when people say that they no longer find life meaningful, they are saying that they do not find *fulfillment, enjoyment, satisfaction, or pleasure* in what they are doing or in some major aspect of their life style. (Cf. Sam Keen, 1971: 88. Other important uses of the term 'meaning' appear in this interview.) Often friends and therapists help them to do so practical a thing as find a job that is more interesting to them, or find new friends, or whatever it takes to bring some *joy* into their lives. It seems important for the therapist, minister, or priest to know (a) when a client is worried about a cosmological or grand teleological question, and (b) when he is in trouble because he cannot find new specific sources and avenues of enjoyment.

It seems also important to see clearly that a person can have genuine intellectual problems which must be solved to some degree if he is to enjoy living. If his childhood frame of reference comes apart, then he may need assistance in reconstructing a new frame of reference that is more sensitive to empirical data and rules of logic. Some therapists, because of their own intellectual superficiality, have unwisely ignored the intellectual dimension of therapy. The intellectual world is a uniquely human environment which people must learn to live and cope with. The therapist is himself practicing 'avoidance behavior' when he pretends that this environment (or 'third world', as philosopher Karl Popper calls it) does not exist as a cultural reality.

D. MEANING THROUGH BELONGING TO A SIGNIFICANT GROUP

Very often when people say that life (for them at least) is meaningless they are saying that they do not *belong* to what they think is important to belong to. Now, what this 'something' is will vary from person to person, and the sensitive therapist will patiently discover what this 'something' is from his client's expressions and behavior, rather than hastily pre-judge. (Compare the automobile mechanic who superconfidently tells you what is wrong with your car before he has observed carefully. He is like a physician who thinks that all patients are alike in every way.)

You may not think it important to be on the committee in charge of planning social events for the community, school, club, etc. But Mr. Smith may regard it as terribly important to *him*. And if he finds himself no longer on the committee for some reason, he may soon be found saying that life has no meaning. *He* may not even be aware of what brought about these somber words from his lips. You as therapist or friend, however, may help him search for and find the cause. You may then help him find 'meaning' again by helping him get back on the committee or persuading him to take on membership in some other group of importance to him. Most people seem to need to belong to something, and mass movements will probably take advantage of this need if nothing else can meet it.

Tell a professional philosopher that he is fired, that he can no longer find work as a philosopher, and that he is no longer respected among his peers. If he believes you, then he is likely to suffer considerable meaninglessness, which in part simply *means* that he does not *belong* any more to what he thought it important to belong to. He has been removed from his 'significant context' and from 'significant others'.

Of course, if a person in trouble thinks that he absolutely *must* belong to some cosmic movement of grand and eternal dimensions, then a therapist will be able to help him only by convincing him either that he does in fact belong or that it is not, after all, important to belong to such a cosmic movement. Practically speaking, this second alternative may entail either the method of implosion (i.e., helping him to confront the emotional and intellectual consequences of disbelief in a cosmic movement) or the method of substitution (i.e., helping him to find other groups and activities which become at least as important to him as the cosmic movement).

A Pomo Indian once said to an anthropologist: 'What is man? A man is nothing. Without his family he is of less importance than that bug crossing the trail, of less importance than spittle or turds.' (Quoted in Cohen, 1968: 17.) Words have meaning only in grammatical and syntactical contexts. Humans have 'meaning' only in a social and cultural context. Words belong to a linguistic setting and people must feel that they share in a communal reality, for often the community *is* the 'meaning' of their lives, or is at least a considerable portion of this 'meaning'.

A practical problem for 'patients' and criminals is often that of finding a constructive group, community, or set of socially responsive values to share in. Most people tend to gravitate toward membership in some group; and if they cannot gain entrance, they may be found using the word 'meaningless' to refer either to the group itself or to their own lives on the outside. It may at times be useful to explore psychoanalytically why a person insists on belonging to this group rather than another. But it should be no great mystery – although it sometimes is to client and therapist alike – that a client finds life meaningless if he is excluded from the group significant to him.

E. MEANING THROUGH RECOGNITION

Group membership and recognition coming from others (e.g., wife peers, gods, saints, etc.) are similar phenomena, but it is perhaps worthwhile to focus a bit on *recognition*. (Ordinary language analysis begins to reveal that *the* one and only solution to the meaning – or meaninglessness – of life does not exist.) People have sometimes used the word 'meaningless' to designate the fact that they are not recognized in some respect in which they had strongly anticipated such recognition. Often the therapist helps – as does a friend – by himself recognizing the individual in certain respects. Freud, Skinner, Carl Rogers, and others who talk of the ingredients of therapy are very careful to emphasize that the therapist often functions as a 'recognizing audience'. The client's claim to happiness, to be listened to, to be given some consideration, to be seen as talented or responsible, etc. – all these need to be recognized; and the therapist may often be one of the most significant persons to recognize these claims and to recognize them as justified in some sense and to some degree. Almost everyone seems to expect some recognition.

Of course, in doing this preliminary spade work of finding out what people sometimes mean when they say that life does (or does not) have meaning, the ordinary language philosopher will tend to postpone or ignore certain kinds of judgments. He will not try to replace the psychotherapists. He merely provides them with some of the benefits of his research. They may find it useful in their work with their clients. As an analytic philosopher, one is neither recommending nor condemning greater social recognition, belonging to more groups, believing in a cosmic purpose, etc. He is simply calling attention to the fact that there are matters which often turn out to be of very powerful concern to some people. To understand more explicitly what these concerns are is often useful in helping people to 'come to terms with them' in a more rational way. So, let us continue.

F. MEANING THROUGH SATISFACTION OF STRONG EXPECTATIONS

It even seems true that very often the word 'meaninglessness' simply designates a certain strong expectation that has not been fulfilled. This is often one of the greatest sources of utter despair. Men and women set their hearts on something and seem often totally helpless either to satisfy their yearning or to break away from its enslavement. There are times when mere relief from having a desire or longing would seem to be heaven itself. But it is as if some expectations are carved into our very brains and yet are doomed to lead to neither joyous fulfillment nor peaceful extinction. If only Beth could be free of the sustained passion to be with Kevin, who has divorced her and married another woman. She does not ask to have him as her husband again. She wants only to be relieved of the agony of *wanting* to have him again. It is in such a state as Beth's that people often say in despair that life is no longer meaningful.

> Ah Love! could you and I with Him conspire
> To grasp this sorry Scheme of Things entire,
>   Would not we shatter it to bits – and then
>   Remold it nearer to the Heart's Desire!
>   (Omar Khayyam, *Rubaiyat, XCIX* [Edward Fitzgerald, trans.])

A million things can bring on the utterance of 'meaninglessness'. An effective therapist will locate as quickly as possible both the high expectation pattern and the low fulfillment. Sometimes a person is very reluctant to acknowledge clearly his very high expectation, for in a primordial moment of insight he may already have seemed to himself to be silly, absurd, weak, greedy, arrogant, or unrealistic for having this expectation.

It may turn out that much of the contemporary talk of meaninglessness in one's life is the result of so simple a matter as deceptive advertisement. Through commercials, songs, pictures, etc. people are often led to expect certain peak experiences or efficient performances from this or that manufactured article or machine. There is little doubt that much advertisement is in excess of performance. Hence, people feel cheated, disappointed, and even enraged. If this rage is not come to terms with, the individual could easily begin to reveal symptoms of depression – slight or intense. And this state of depression is very often designated as 'meaninglessness'. Therapists may discover that they must train themselves and their clients to come to terms realistically with the false promises and deceit of advertisers. Otherwise 'meaningless' might in some cases continue without relief. At least this is a hypothesis worth pursuing in an age of the over-promise.

G. MEANING THROUGH A SENSE OF CONTROL AND PERSONAL WHOLENESS

Related to this notion of high expectations is the notion of completeness and control. Many people who do not expect to live after death do nevertheless expect to complete certain things in life.[4] The nineteenth century English philosopher John Stuart Mill writes:

> It is not, naturally or generally, the happy who are the most anxious either for a prolongation of the present life or for a life hereafter: it is those who never seem to be happy. They who have had their happiness can bear to part with existence, but it is hard to die without having [truly] lived (1958: 78; the word in brackets is mine).

Quite often the phrase 'a meaningful life' seems to designate a life lived in which the individual believes that he has a certain amount of control over his circumstances, or at least over his response to them. He is more or less content if the conditions under which he lives do not rob him of his sense of effectiveness. He is pleased or satisfied with his own actions and reactions. Like an artist, he feels

---

4. 'The nonreligious subjects [in a study of certain male college students] expressed concern that their lives might end without their having accomplished anything of importance' (Alexander and Adlerstein, 1959: 279).

that while life's conditions may cause him to work in this or that way, nevertheless he shares in the process and is not an alien spectator to what is going on. He feels that the relationship between himself and his situation manifests a certain completion and wholeness. He sees a pattern and is more or less content with it.

For example, an automobile factory worker may find himself saying that his work is more meaningful now that he has some control in planning the production process. He may come to understand the production pattern (rationale) better and perhaps to appreciate it more, especially if he sees that he not only helps to structure it, but also helps to complete it. It all 'means something' to him now, whereas previously it was 'just a job'. His life is thus called meaningful, or at least a bit more meaningful.

Of course, what is completeness and a sense of control to one person may be frustration and great discontentment to others. In short, what is a meaningful life for one, might be a meaningless life for another.

H. MEANING THROUGH A SENSE OF AESTHETIC COMPLETENESS

We might pursue more fully the theme of 'patterns' and 'coherence'. This is admittedly a difficult theme to disentangle. Nevertheless, many writers and speakers do seem to use the word 'meaningful' to designate what they take to be a certain pattern or coherence in either their own lives or in some broader whole (from the tribe to the cosmos). Even though the universe (or whatever) may not be expected to 'go' anywhere, some people nevertheless believe that there is some pattern to it all. Things 'add up to something', like a profound painting.

Or if it is simply one's own life, then it may reveal a kind of coherence or pattern in itself. Hence, a meaningless or unexplained event in one's life takes on 'meaning' when it is seen as an element of a pattern or a coherent picture. This may be more of a logical or aesthetic pattern than something teleological or directional. It is like a musical score in which each part has its 'place' in the scheme of things.

Spinoza's (1632–1677) 'intellectual love of God' (or Nature) may be a kind of enjoyment, appreciation, or even admiration of the world as a whole. One's own life is thought to gain meaning by being located in the grand and total Scheme. One 'finds himself' and thus has no desperate need to 'prove himself'. Some phenomenologists seem to use the term 'meaningfulness' to characterize a kind of pre-moral 'appreciation of Being' or 'respect for essences' (cf. Johann, 1966: 30).

Some people find meaning in the world in the sense of appreciation of it *as it is*. Others have appreciation for what it may *become for human purposes* and ends. (The ordinary language philosopher may choose to argue with either of these two attitudes. But his preliminary job is to bring them to light, to explicate them, including the apparent conflict between them.)

I. MEANING THROUGH ORIENTATION

We cannot make sense of a phrase unless we are enlightened by its context. In itself alone a phrase does not *mean* anything. A person's life tends to lose meaning if his environment (vocational, recreational, religious, or whatever) becomes disordered beyond a certain point. He can no longer 'read it'. It is meaningless to him, and soon his life may be designated as meaningless unless he finds an ordered environment again. Where nature sometimes fails to provide this order, culture must supply it. Man the cultural species usually needs an order of his own collective making if he is to avoid a serious personal disorientation, which is sometimes called 'meaninglessness'.

Rapid changes in his immediate or remote environment may cause an individual to complain that he does not know what is going on. Industrial, technological, institutional, or theoretical charges may evoke the confession of 'meaninglessness'. A pious Roman Catholic who believes in the tight unity of his Church may come to suffer meaninglessness if the unity seems to be threatened. He may say, 'I don't know what it all means. I don't know what to believe any more. Nothing makes sense. Nothing significant stands out against the background of confusion.'

J. MEANING THROUGH SERVICE TO OTHERS

Most people seem to have been raised to say that a person's life enjoys very little meaning if he is concerned for his own happiness *alone*. This implicit definition (or ingredient) of 'meaningfulness' here is found to include some measure of love or caring for at least *some* others. Often counselors, clergymen, and friends have advised a person to look beyond his own problem to those of others in order to help them, thereby gaining meaning for his own life (cf. Mark 8:35). Of course, his problems increase if he finds himself simply 'doing' for others regardless of whether *what* is done is *genuinely helpful* to them. If a person is not actually helping us, we may tend to resent his making his own life meaningful at our personal expense. We do not say that he is unselfish but rather that he is a busybody. If we can make our charge against him stick, then we reduce the probabilities that he will feel his life to be meaningful in this respect until he learns to be helpful in more realistic ways. Indeed, sometimes an overpowering sense of 'meaninglessness' is nothing more than the realization that one's efforts have in actuality done little to help others. Sometimes, to be 'meaningful' is to have one's efforts count for something in terms of giving realistic help to others.

K. CONCLUSION

In conclusion, I hope I have shown that the phrase 'meaningful life' means a number of things. In many cases, although not in all, we could substitute the phrase 'a happy life'. But this would still not be a sufficient substitution. In most cases the term 'meaningful' adds that this happiness must also be a part of some wider context which is regarded as highly significant. In some cases a person's life is declared 'meaningful' even if the individual himself does not gain much happiness. But he must *contribute* to the happiness of others or contribute to a context that is thought to be wider and more significant than himself. If the wider context is judged to be of great worth, then one's own life is defined as 'meaningful' when it participates in or contributes to this context.

One interesting insight that seems to spin off from a more intensified ordinary language analysis of 'the meaning of life' and 'the meaningful life' is that what is taken to be highly significant may vary enormously from group to group, person to person, and time to time. No pastor or counselor could go about his business with profound skill unless he had some awareness of this measure of relativity as to what is declared to be significant. A woman marries a man and says that life now has meaning. She has children and asserts that life now has meaning (for her, at least). Another woman has children and says later that her life was quite meaningful *until* the kids came. Another woman gets a divorce and tells you later that life is more meaningful for her, now that she is single. So it would seem to be rather naïve to ask in general about 'the meaning of life'. Meaning for whom? When? In what sense? Under what conditions? Ordinary language analysis seems to make it *more possible to ask our questions more definitely and pointedly*, thus increasing the possibility of finding useable and practical answers.

When religious leaders speak confidently of 'the meaning of life', they sometimes seem oblivious to the overwhelming diversity among peoples and individuals regarding what they themselves count as meaningful in their own lives. And if one group simply *stipulates* what is meaningful for all groups, there is nothing to prevent each group from stipulating its own definition for everyone else. I have argued against conceptual or epistemological relativism, but I am less confident in arguing against relativism with regard to meaningfulness that is more than cognitive. To be sure, some people wish their fellow humans to be more uniform in their value preferences, but this lust for greater uniformity is itself no less a value preference than is the lust for diversity.

Bibliography

Aaronson, Bernard (1974), 'The experience of the body and transcendence', in: John Y. Fenton, ed., *Theology and Body*. Philadelphia, Westminster Press.
Alexander, Irving E., and Adlerstein, Arthur M. (1959), 'Death and religion', in: Herman Feifel, ed., *The Meaning of Death*. New York, McGraw-Hill Book Co.
Alland, Alexander, Jr. (1972), *The Human Imperative*. New York, Columbia University Press.
Allen, Joseph (1974), 'A theological approach to moral rights', *The Journal of Religious Ethics*, 2(1).

Bair, Kurt (1966), 'The meaning of life'. Inaugural Lecture at Canberra University College.
  Published in: Morris Weitz, ed., *Twentieth Century Philosophy: The Analytic Tradition*, 1966, pp. 361–379. New York, Free Press.
Barnhart, J. E. (1972), *The Billy Graham Religion*. Philadelphia, Pilgrim Press, United Church Press.
  English ed.: Oxford, England, Mobrays, 1974.
  German ed.: *Die Billy Graham Story*. München, Claudius Verlag, 1973.
—— (1975), *Religion and the Challenge of Philosophy*. Totowa, N.J., Littlefield, Adams and Co.
——(1976), 'Egoism and altruism', *Southwestern Journal of Philosophy*, 7(1).
Barnhart, Mary Ann (1976), 'Religion and society: A comparison of selected works of Emile Durkheim and Max Weber'. Unpublished M.A. Thesis, North Texas State University, Denton, Texas.
Barth, Karl (1960), *Kirchliche Dogmatik,* Band IV/1. Zürich, E.V.Z. Verlag.
—— (1956), *Church Dogmatics*, Vol. II/1; III/1; III/4. Trans. T. H. L. Parker *et al.* Edinburgh, T. T. Clark.

Becker, Carl L. (1932), *The Heavenly City of the Eighteenth-Century Philosophers*. New Haven, Conn., Yale University Press.
Bellah, Robert N. (1967), 'Civil religion in America', *Daedalus*, 96(1): 1ff.
—— (1970), *Beyond Belief. Essays on Religion in a Post-traditional World*. New York, Harper & Row.
—— (1974), *Emile Durkheim on Morality and Society*. Chicago, University of Chicago Press.
Berger, Peter L., and Luckmann, Thomas (1966), *The Social Construction of Reality: A Treatise on the Sociology of Knowledge*. Garden City, N.Y., Doubleday & Co. ('Anchor Books').
Bergson, Henri (1956), *The Two Sources of Morality and Religion* [*Les deux sources de la morale et de la religion*]. Garden City, N.Y., Doubleday & Co.
Berkouwer, G. C. (1956), *The Triumph of Grace in the Theology of Karl Barth: An Introduction and Critical Appraisal*. Trans. Harry R. Boer. Grand Rapids, Eerdmans.
Blackham, H. J. (1963), 'The pointlessness of it all', pp. 105-127, in: H. J. Blackham, ed., *Objections to Humanism*. New York, J. B. Lippincott & Co.
Bradley, F. H. (1955), *Appearance and Reality: A Metaphysical Essay*. 9th Impression. New York, Oxford University Press. First published in 1893.
Brightman, E. S. (1940), *A Philosophy of Religion*. Englewood Cliffs, N.J., Prentice-Hall Inc.
——(1958), *Person and Reality: An Introduction to Metaphysics* [Posthumously]. Edited by Peter Anthony Bertocci, in collaboration with Janette Newhall and Robert Sheffield Brightman. New York, Ronald Press.
Brown, Delwin (1971), 'Process philosophy and the question of life's meaning', *Religious Studies*, 7(1): 13-25.
Buren, Paul van (1963), *The Secular Meaning of the Gospel*. London, S.C.M.
—— (1972), *The Edges of Languages. An Essay in the Logic of a Religion*. New York, Macmillan.

Campbell, James L. (1971), *The Language of Religion*. New York, Bruce Publ. Co.

Camus, Albert (1955), *The Myth of Sisyphus* [*Le mythe de Sisyphe* - 1943]. Trans. Justin O'Brien. London, Hamish Hamilton.
Carnell, E. J. (1960a), *The Kingdom of Love and the Pride of Life*. Grand Rapids, Eerdmans.
—— (1960b), *The Theology of Reinhold Niebuhr*. Rev. ed. Grand Rapids, Eerdmans.
Chalmers, A. C., and Irving, John A., eds. (1965), *The Meaning of Life in Five Great Religions*. Philadelphia, Westminster Press.
See also under: Jay; Rao; Rasjidi.
Church and State, 28: 1 (January 1975).
Claiborne, Robert (1974), *God or Beast*. New York, W. W. Norton.
Clark, Gordon (1961), *Religion, Reason and Revelation*. Philadelphia, Presbyterian and Reformed Publ. Co.
—— (1963), *Karl Barth's Theological Method*. Philadelphia, Presbyterian and Reformed Publ. Co.
Cohen, Jack J. (1959), *The Case for Religious Naturalism*. New York, The Reconstructionist Press.
Cohen, Yehudi A., ed. (1968), *Man in Adaptation: The Cultural Present*. Chicago, Aldine Publ. Co.

DeHaan, M. R. (1951), *The Chemistry of the Blood*. Grand Rapids, Zondervan.
Deutsch, Steven E., and Howard, John, eds. (1970), *Where it's at: Radical Perspectives in Sociology*. New York, Harper & Row.
DeWolf, L. Harold (1949), *The Revolt against Reason*. New York, Harper Brothers.
—— (1957), *The Case for Theology in Liberal Perspective*. Philadelphia, Westminster Press.
Dilman, Ilham (1965), 'Life and meaning', *Philosophy*, 40(4): 320-333.
—— (1968), 'Professor Hepburn on meaning in life', *Religious Studies*, 3(2): 547-554.
Diamond, Malcolm (1974), *Contemporary Philosophy and Religious Thought: An Introduction to the Philosophy of Religion*. New York, McGraw-Hill Book Co.
Drijvers, H. J. W. (1973), 'Theory formation in science of religion and the study of the history of religions', pp. 57-78 in: H. J. W. Drijvers and Th. P. van Baaren, eds., *Religion, Culture and Methodology*. The Hague and Paris, Mouton Publishers ('Religion and Reason', Vol. 8).

Eccles, J. C. (1973), 'Cultural evolution versus biological evolution', *Zygon*, 8(3-4).
Edwards, Paul (1967), 'Why', Vol. VIII, pp. 296-302 in: Paul Edwards, ed., *Encyclopedia of Philosophy*, 8 vols. New York, Macmillan and Free Press.
At the end of Edwards article is a useful bibliography on 'the super-ultimate why-questions'.
Ellis, Albert A. (1968), *Is Objectivism a Religion?* New York, Lyle Stuart.
Evans-Pritchard, E. E. (1937), *Witchcraft, Oracles and Magic among the Azande.* Oxford University Press.

Ferré, Nels F. S. (1966), *The Living God of Nowhere and Nothing.* London, Epworth Press.
Feuerbach, Ludwig (1957), *The Essence of Christianity.* Trans. George Eliot. New York, Harper Torchbook. First published as *Das Wesen des Christenthums.* Leipzig, Otto Wigand, 1843.
Fisher, Esther Omar (1974), *Divorce - The New Freedom.* New York, Harper & Row.
Flew, Antony (1963), 'Tolstoy and the meaning of life', *Ethics*, 73(2): 110-118.
—— (1971), *An Introduction to Western Philosophy.* Indianapolis, Ind., Bobbs Merill Co.
Flint, Cort R., and Staff of *Quote*, eds. (1966), *The Quotable Billy Graham.* Anderson, S. C., Droke House.
Freud, Sigmund (1943), *The Future of an Illusion* [*Die Zukunft einer Illusion* - 1927]. Trans. W. D. Robson-Scott. London, Hogarth Press.

Gaustad, E. S. (1973), *Dissent in American Religion.* Chicago, University of Chicago Press.
Geertz, Clifford (1968), *Islam Observed.* New Haven, Conn., Yale University Press.
—— (1973), *The Interpretation of Culture: Selected Essays.* New York, Basic Books.
Gennep, Arnold van (1960), *The Rites of Passage.* Trans. M. B. Vizedam and G. L. Caffee. With an Introduction by Solon T. Kimball. Chicago, University of Chicago Press; London, Routledge & Kegan Paul.
Originally published in French: *Les rites de passage: Etude systématique des rites.* Paris, Emile Nourry, 1909. Reprinted with an Author's Addendum: Paris et La Haye, Mouton, 1969.

Gill, Jerry H., ed. (1968), *Philosophy Today,* Vol. 1. New York, Macmillan.
—— (1969), *Philosophy Today*, Vol. 2. New York, Macmillan.
—— (1970), *Philosophy Today*, Vol. 3. New York, Macmillan.
—— (1974) *Christian Empiricism.* Grand Rapids, Eerdmans. This book contains several articles, most of which by Ian Ramsey, see below.
Goodenough, Ward E. (1974), 'Toward an anthropologically useful definition of religion', in: Allan W. Eister, ed., *Changing Perspectives in the Scientific Study of Religion.* New York, John Wiley & Sons.
Goody, J. (1961), 'Religion and ritual: The definitial problem', *British Journal of Sociology*, 12: 142-164.
Graber, Glenn C. (1974), 'A critical bibliography of recent discussions of religious ethics by philosophers', *The Journal of Religious Ethics*, 2(2).
Graham, Billy (1966), *World Aflame.* New York, Pocket Book Inc. First published by Doubleday & Co., New York, in 1965.

Hammond, Phillip E. (1974), 'Religious pluralism and Durkheim's integration thesis', in: Allan W. Eister, ed., *Changing Perspectives in the Scientific Study of Religion.* New York, John Wiley & Sons.
Harris, M. (1968), *The Rise of Anthropological Theory: A History of Theories of Culture.* New York and London, Routledge & Kegan Paul.
Hensel, Martin (1734), *The Restored Mosaic System of the World.*
Hepburn, Ronald W. (1963), 'A critique of humanist theology', pp. 29-54, in H. J. Blackham, ed., *Objections to Humanism.* New York, J. B. Lippincott & Co.
—— (1967), 'Questions about the meaning of life', *Religious Studies*, 1(2): 125-140.
Hick, John H., ed. (1964), *Faith and the Philosophers.* New York, St. Martin's Press.
—— (1968), *Evil and the God of Love.* Glasgow and London, Fontana Books. First published by Macmillan, London, in 1966.
—— (1973), *Philosophy of Religion*, 2nd ed. Englewood Cliffs, N.J., Prentice-Hall Inc. First published in 1963.
Hocking, William E. (1912), *The Meaning of God in Human Experience: A Philosophic Study of Religion.* New Haven, Conn., Yale University Press.
Höffding, Harold (1906), *The Philosophy of Religion.* London, Macmillan. First published in 1901.

Horton, Robin (1960), 'A definition of "religion" and its uses', *Journal of the Royal Anthropological Institute*, 90: 201-226.
—— (1967), 'African traditional thought and Western science', *Africa*, 37: 50-71, 155-187.
Hudson, W. D. (1968), 'On two points against Wittgensteinian fideism', *Philosophy*, 43 (July 1968).
Huntsberry, Randy (1974), 'Secular education and its religion', *Journal of the American Academy of Religion*, 42(4).

Jay, C. Douglas (1965), 'From encounter to community', in: R. C. Chalmers and John Irving, eds., *The Meaning of Life in Five Great Religions*. Philadelphia, Westminster Press.
Johann, Robert O. (1966), 'Love and justice', in: Richard T. De George, ed., *Ethics and Society: Original Essays on Contemporary Moral Problems*. New York, Doubleday & Co. ('Anchor Books').

Keen, Sam (1971), 'Man and myth: A conversation with Joseph Campbell', *Psychology Today* (July 1971).
Kelley, Dean M. (1972), *Why Conservative Churches are Growing*. New York, Harper & Row.
Kierkegaard, Søren A. (1936), *Philosophical Fragments, or a Fragment of Philosophy*. Trans. David F. Swenson. Princeton, N.J., Princeton University Press.
—— (1938), *The Journals*. Trans. A. Dru. New York, Oxford University Press.
—— (1941), *Concluding Unscientific Postscript*. Trans. David F. Swenson. Princeton, N.J., Princeton University Press.
Koestler, Arthur (1952), 'The initiates', in: Richard Crossman, ed., *The God that failed*. New York, Bantam Books. Originally published in 1950, by Harper & Brothers, New York.
Kuhn, Thomas S. (1970), 'The structure of scientific revolutions', pp. 53-273 in: O. Neurath, R. Carnap and Ch. Morris, eds., *Foundations of the Unity of Science. Toward an International Encyclopedia of Unified Science*, Vol. 2. Chicago, The University of Chicago Press.

La Barre, Weston (1972), *The Ghost Dance: The Origins of Religions*. New York, Dell Publ. Comp. ('Delta Book'). First published in 1970, by Doubleday & Co., New York.

Ladner, Benjamin (1974), 'Why do ideas illuminate?', *American Academy of Religion*, 42(4).
Lee, Dorothy (1959), 'Are basic needs ultimate?', in her *Freedom and Culture*. Englewood Cliffs, N.J., Prentice-Hall Inc. ('Spectrum Books').
Lindsay, R. B. (1963), *The Role of Science in Civilization*. New York, Harper & Row.
London, Perry (1969), *Behavior Control*. New York, Harper & Row.
—— (1973), 'The future of psychotherapy', *The Hastings Center Report*, 3(6): 10–13.
Lukes, Steven (1973), *Emile Durkheim: His Life and Work*. New York, Harper & Row.
MacIntyre, Alasdair (1964), 'Is understanding religion compatible with believing?', in: John H. Hick, ed., *Faith and the Philosophers*. New York, St. Martin's Press.
—— (1966), *A Short History of Ethics*. New York, Macmillan.
—— (1967), *Secularization and Moral Change*. London, Oxford University Press.
MacIntyre, A., and Flew, A., eds. (1955), *New Essays in Philosophical Theology*. New York, Macmillan.
Malcolm, Norman (1963), 'Anselm's ontological arguments', in his *Knowledge and Certainty: Essays and Lectures*. Englewood Cliffs, N.J., Prentice-Hall Inc.
Marty, Martin E. (1967), 'Should Christianity be secularized', pp. 38–53 in: Robert M. Hutchins and Mortimer J. Adler, eds., *The Great Ideas Today, 1967*. Chicago, Encyclopedia Britannica Inc.
McMurrin, Sterling M. (1965), *The Theological Foundations of the Mormon Religion*. Salt Lake City, University of Utah Press.
Mead, George Herbert (1934), 'The social origins of the self', in his *Mind, Self and Society*. Chicago, University of Chicago Press.
Mead, Sidney E. (1954), 'Abraham Lincoln's last best hope of earth: The American dream of destiny and democracy', *Church History*, 23: 3ff.
—— (1967), 'The nation with the soul of a church', *Church History*, 36: 262ff.
Medawar, Peter (1974), 'Hypothesis and imagination', in: Paul A. Schilpp, ed., *The Philosophy of Karl Popper*, 2 vols. La Salle, Ill., Open Court Publ. Co.
Michaelsen, Robert (1970), 'Is the public school religious or secular', in: Elwyn A. Smith, ed., *The Religion of the Republic*. Philadelphia, Fortress Press.

Mill, John Stuart (1958), *Nature and the Utility of Religion. Two Essays.* New York, Liberal Arts Press. First published in 18 .
Mitchell, Basil (1973), *The Justification of Religious Belief.* New York, Seabury Press.
Moore, John Morrison (1938), *Theories of Religious Experience, with Special Reference to James, Otto, and Bergson.* New York, Round Table Press.
Mosse, George L. (1964), *The Crisis of German Ideology.* New York, Grosset & Dunlap ('Universal Library').
Mowrer, O. Hobart (1967), 'Civilization and its malcontents', *Psychology Today*, 1(5): 49–51.

Nettler, Gynn (1970), *Explanations.* New York, McGraw-Hill Book Co.
Nielsen, Kai (1964), 'Linguistic philosophy and the "Meaning of life"', *Cross Currents*, 14(3): 313–334.
—— (1971), *Contemporary Critiques of Religion.* New York, Herder & Herder.
Nilsson, Martin P. (1954), *Religion as Man's Protest against the Meaninglessness of Events.* Lund, Sweden, G. W. K. Gleerup Publishers.
Nisbet, Robert A. (1974), *The Sociology of Emile Durkheim.* New York, Oxford University Press.

Oates, Wayne (1973), *The Psychology of Religion.* Waco, Texas, Word Books.

Philips, D. Z. (1965), *The Concept of Prayer.* London, Routledge & Kegan Paul.
—— (1970), *Death and Immortality.* London, Macmillan.
Piker, Steven (1972), 'The problem of consistency in Thai religion', *Journal for the Scientific Study of Religion*, 2(3).
Popper, Sir Karl R. (1968), *The Logic of Scientific Discovery*, 2nd ed. New York, Harper & Row ('Harper Torchbooks').
—— (1972), *Objective Knowledge: An Evolutionary Approach.* New York, Oxford University Press.
—— (1974a), 'Autobiography', and
—— (1974b), 'Replies to my critics',
  in: Paul A. Schlipp, ed. *The Philosophy of Karl Popper*, 2 vols. La Sall, Ill., Open Court Publ. Co.

Price, H. H. (1972), *Essays in the Philosophy of Religion*. New York, Oxford University Press. This book of essays is a revision of the Sacrum Lectures, delivered in Oxford in 1971.

Pruyser, Paul W. (1974), 'Problems in the psychological study of religious unbelief', pp. 185-200 in: Allan W. Eister, ed., *Changing Perspectives in the Scientific Study of Religion*. New York, John Wiley & Sons.

Ramm, Bernard (1954), *The Christian View of Science and Scripture*. Grand Rapids, Eerdmans.

—— (1961), *Special Revelation and the Word of God*. Grand Rapids, Eerdmans.

Ramsey, Ian (1974a), 'Christian Education';

—— (1974b), 'Discernment, commitment and cosmic disclosure';

—— (1974c), 'Intellectual crisis', and

—— (1974d), 'The intellectual crisis of British Christianity, II', in: Jerry H. Gill, ed., *Christian Empiricism*. Grand Rapids, Eerdmans.

Rao, P. Nagaraja (1965), 'Hinduism', in R. C. Chalmers and John A. Irving, eds., *The Meaning of Life in Five Great Religions*. Philadelphia, Westminster Press.

Rasjidi, M. (1965), 'Islam', in R. C. Chalmers and John A. Irving, eds., *The Meaning of Life in Five Great Religions*. Philadelphia, Westminster Press.

Ricoeur, Paul (1970), *Freud and Philosophy: An Essay on Interpretation*. Trans. Denis Savage. New Haven, Conn., Yale University Press.

Ridderbos, N. H. (1957), *Is there a Conflict between Genesis 1 and Natural Science?* Grand Rapids, Eerdmans.

Rimmer, Robert (1936), *The Harmony of Science and Scripture*, 3rd ed. Grand Rapids, Eerdmans.

Robinson, John A. T. (1963), *Honest to God*. London, SCM Press; Philadelphia, Westminster Press.

Rumscheidt, H. Martin (1972), *Revelation and Theology: An Analysis of the Barth-Harnack Correspondence of 1923*. New York, Cambridge University Press.

Ruo Wang, Bao (Jean Pasqualini), and Chelminski, Rudolph (1973), *Prisoner of Mao*. New York, Coward, McCann & Geoghegan Inc.

Russell, Bertrand (1954), *Human Society in Ethics and Politics*. London, George Allen & Unwin, Ltd.

Russell, Bertrand—*(cont.)*
—— (1957), 'A Free man's worship', in *Mysticism and Logic*. New York, Doubleday & Co. ('Anchor Books').
—— (1969-70), *The Autobiography of Bertrand Russell*, 3 vols. New York, Bantam Books. These volumes were originally published by George Allen & Unwin, Ltd. London.

Schleiermacher, Friedrich (1928), *The Christian Faith* [*Der christliche Glaube nach den Grundsätzen der evangelischen Kirche*]. Edinburgh, T. & T. Clark.
Skinner, B. F. (1953), *Science and Human Behavior*. New York, The Free Press.
—— (1962), *Walden Two*. New York, Macmillan. First published in 1948.
—— (1974), *About Behaviorism*. New York, Albert A. Knopf.
Smart, Ninian (1974), 'The intellectual crisis of British Christianity, I', in: Jerry H. Gill, ed., *Christian Empiricism*. Grand Rapids, Eerdmans.
Smith, Elwyn A., ed. (1970), *The Religion of the Republic. Is there an American Religion?* Philadelphia, Fortress Press.
See also under: Michaelsen (1970).
Spiro, Melford E. (1965), 'Religion: Problems of definition and explanation', pp. 85-126 in: Michael Banton, ed., *Anthropological Approaches to the Study of Religion*. London, Tavistock Publications.
Stace, Walter T. (1952), *Time and Eternity*. Princeton, N.J., Princeton University Press.
Stove, D. (1970), 'Hume, probability and induction', pp. 212-232 in: Jerry H. Gill, ed., *Philosophy Today*, Vol. 3. New York, Macmillan. This article apeared originally in *The Philosophical Review* (April 1965).
Streiker, Lowell D., and Strober, Gerald D. (1972), *Religion and the New Majority*. New York, Association Press.

Thody, Philip (1961), *Albert Camus, 1913-1960*. London, Hamish Hamilton. 2nd ed. 1964.
Tillich, Paul (1952), *Systematic Theology*, Vol. I. Chicago, University of Chicago Press.
—— (1961), 'Reply to interpretation and criticism', in: Charles W. Kegly and Robert W. Bretall, eds., *The Theology of Paul Tillich*. New York, Macmillan.
Tucker, Robert (1961), *Philosophy and Myth in Karl Marx*. New York, Cambridge University Press.

Vink, A. J. (1973), 'Religious ethology: Some methodological remarks', pp. 137-158 in: Th. P. van Baaren and H. J. W. Drijvers, eds., *Religion, Culture and Methodology*. The Hague and Paris, Mouton Publishers ('Religion and Reason', Vol. 8).

Wallace, Anthony (1966), *Religion: An Anthropological View*. New York, Random House.

Wallwork, Ernest (1972), *Durkheim: Morality and Milieu*. Cambridge, Harvard University Press.

Warnock, G. J. (1966), *English Philosophy since 1900*, 2nd ed. New York, Oxford University Press ('Galaxy Book'). First published in 1958.

Weil, Andrew (1972), *The Natural Mind: A New Way of Looking at Drugs and the Higher Consciousness*. Boston, Houghton Mifflin.

Wisdom, John (1954), 'What is there in horse racing', *The Listener* (June 1954).

—— (1965), 'On asking the meanings of life', pp. 38-42 in his *Paradox and Discovery*. Berkeley, University of California Press.

White, A. D. (1960), *A History of the Warfare of Science with Theology in Christendom*, 2 vols. New York, Dover Publications.

White, Leslie A. (1949), *The Science of Culture*. New York, Farrar, Straus & Giroux. Reprinted in 1969.

Wood, Alan (1956), *Bertrand Russell: The Passionate Skeptic*. New York, Simon & Schuster.

Wuthnow, Robert, and Glock, Charles Y. (1974), 'The shifting focus of faith. A survey report: God in the gut', *Psychology Today*, 8(6).

Yeates, John W. (1975), 'Religiosity and the public school', *Church and State*, 28(1).

Yinger, J. Milton (1970), *The Scientific Study of Religion*. New York, Macmillan.

Index of Names

Aaronson, B., 84, 85
Abraham, 18, 45, 70, 154
Adam, 88
Alexander, I. E., 185, 192n.
Alland, A., Jr., 51
Allen, J., 43, 46–48
Anselm, St., 93
Ardrey, R., 51
Aristotle, 96
Augustine, St., 103

Baillie, J., 94
Bair, K., 184n.
Barnhart, J. E., 38, 61
Barnhart, M. A., 52
Barth, K., 5, 9, 94–96, 129, 161, 162
Becker, C. L., 36
Bellah, R. N., 65, 67, 114
Berger, P. L., 53, 81
Bergson, H., 49
Berkeley, G., 162
Berkouwer, G. C., 94, 95
Blackham, H. J., 184n.
Blanshard, B., 19
Boer, H. R., 95n.
Bradley, F. H., 173
Brightman, E. S., 3, 4, 96, 126
Bronowski, J., 3

Brown, D., 184n.
Bunyan, J., 33
Buren, P. van, 129, 167, 168

Campbell, J. L., 112
Camus, A., 185
Carnell, E. J., 19
Chalmers, A. C., 3
Christ, 6, 25, 37, 39, 91, 175
Claiborne, R., 51
Clark, G., 1, 5
Cohen, J. J., 1
Cohen, Y. A., 189
Copernicus, N., 15, 161, 163–165

Dart, R., 51
DeHaan, M. R., 163
Descartes, R., 76
Deutsch, S. E., 148
Dewolf, L. H., 19
Dilman, I., 184n.
Diamond, M., 174, 175
Dodd, C. H., 117
Drijvers, H. J. W., 3
Durkheim, E., 38, 112, 113

Eccles, J. C., 52
Edwards, P., 184n.

Index of Names

Elijah, 17
Ellis, A. A., 14
Evans-Pritchard, E. E., 125

Farmer, H. H., 94
Farrar, F. W., 94
Ferre, N. F. S., 87, 91–93, 107, 108, 122
Feuerbach, L., 3, 6, 81, 85
Fisher, E. O., 137
Flew, A., VII, 117, 118, 184n.
Flint, C. R., 137
Freud, S., 3, 6, 9, 184n., 190

Gaustad, E. S., 69
Gautama (The Buddha), 9
Geertz, C., 2, 4, 34, 80, 81
Gennep, A. van, 36
Gluck, C. Y., 84
Goodenough, W. E., 1
Goody, J., 1
Graber, G. C., 54–57, 59
Graham, W., 38, 40, 96, 107, 108, 137, 163–165

Hammond, P. E., 41, 43
Harris, M., 34
Hegel, G. W. F., 85n., 152
Hensel, M., 164
Hepburn, R. W., 184n.
Hick, J. H., 108, 111, 112, 117–124, 132, 132n., 143
Hocking, W. E., 8
Höffding, H., 1
Horton, R., 1, 26n., 28
Hosea, 27
Howard, J., 148
Hudson, W. D., 112
Hume, D., Chapter 10

Huntsberry, R., 65
Husserl, E., VII, VIII

Irving, J. A., 3

James, W., 16, 152
Jay, C. D., 185
Jefferson, T., 70, 71n.
Joan of Arc, 80
Johann, R. O., 194

Kant, I., 59, 112, 123, 152
Kaufmann, W., 19
Keen, S., 187
Kelley, D. M., 38, 139
Khayyam, O., 191
Kierkegaard, S. A., 16–19, 23–27, 55, 58, 93, 104
Koestler, A., 107, 108, 148
Kuhn, T. S., 138

La Barre, W., 3, 6
Ladner, B., 73
Lawrence, D. H., 60
Lee, D., 100
Lenin, V. I., 37
Lincoln, A., 70
Lindsay, R. B., 3
London, P., 33, 183
Lorenz, K., 39, 51
Lukes, S., 112
Luther, M., 163, 164

MacIntyre, A., VII, 43, 44, 69, 71, 72, 117
Malcolm, N., 92, 93, 97, 98
Malinowski, B., 9
Marty, M. E., 72
McMurrin, S. M., 127

Index of Names

Mead, G. H., 29, 55
Mead, S. E., 46, 67
Medawar, P., 145
Michaelsen, R., 72
Mill, J. S., 39, 96, 192
Mitchell, B., 111, 142
Moore, J. M., 7
Morris, D., 51
Mosse, G. L., 37n.
Mowrer, O. H., 53
Muhammad, 8, 9, 93, 185n.

Nettler, G., 149n.
Newrath, O., 155
Newton, I., 15, 161, 164, 165
Nielsen, K., 111, 112, 116, 184n.
Nilsson, M. P., 32
Nisbet, R. A., 38

Oates, W., 9
Oedipus, 89
Otto, R., 8

Paul, St., 84, 86, 134, 186
Perls, F., 33
Pearson, K., 145
Peirce, C. S., 181
Philips, D. Z., 112, 115
Piker, S., 22
Plantinga, A., 131, 132
Plato, 45, 47, 48, 76, 86, 150
Popper, K. R., vii, 18, 24, 106, 123, 130, 141–144, 147, 148, 150–154, 158, 168, 173
Price, H. H., 119
Pruyser, P. W., 17
Pythagoras, 77

Quine, W. V., 168

Ramm, B., 133, 135
Ramsey, I., 167, 168
Rand, A., 14, 58, 59
Rao, P. N., 183
Rasjidi, M., 185n.
Reichenbach, H., 143
Ricoeur, P., 184n.
Ridderbos, N. H., 135
Rimmer, R., 133
Roberts, O., 170
Robinson, J. A., 85, 176, 177
Rogers, C., 174, 190
Roosevelt, F. D., 37
Rousseau, J., 59, 70n.
Rumscheidt, H. M., 162
Ruo Wang, B., 102
Russell, B., 59, 60, 77, 123, 155, 185, 186

Sankara, 6
Sartre, J. P., 152, 185
Schleiermacher, F., 8, 9
Skinner, B. F., 34, 77, 78, 95, 190
Smart, N., 161, 168, 174, 175
Smith, E. A., 46, 67
Smith, J., 65
Socrates, 48, 76
Spencer, H., 58
Spinoza, B., 143, 152, 193
Spiro, M. E., 1
Stace, W. T., 19–21
Stampfl, T., 33
Stove, D., 141n.
Streiker, L. D., 40

Theresa, St., 8, 83, 89
Thody, P., 184n.
Thomas, St., 160
Thompson, J., 186

Index of Names

Tillich, P., 8–10, 85, 99, 143, 175–177
Timar, 89
Tucker, R., 180

Vink, A. J., 34

Wallace, A., 1
Wallwork, E., 112
Warnock, G. J., 125
Weber, M., 113
Weil, A., 81
Wesley, J., 163, 164

Whewell, P., 146
White, A. D., 52, 163, 164
Whitehead, A. N., 165
Wieman, H. N., 165
Williams, R., 65
Wisdom, J., 184n.
Wittgenstein, L., 77, 112, 173
Wood, A., 185
Wuthnow, R., 84

Yeates, J. W., 38
Yinger, J. M., 9, 111
Young, B., 65

Subject Index

Absolute, the, 85, 87
Agnosticism, 16, 17, 157
Anthropology of religion, 113, 114
Arminianism, 92
Atheism, 72, 111

Baptists, 65, 71, 136, 137, 138
Behavioral theology, 172
Being, 175, 194
Believers, VII, VIII, 17n.
Bible, riot over, 38
Body, the human, 85, 86
    St. Paul's view of, 86
Buddhism, 2, 5, 10, 22, 23, 69, 119, 178

Calvinism, 1, 5, 45, 47, 93
Capitalism, 14
Certainty, feeling of, 76
Christ (God), inside the body, 84, 85
Christianity, 10, 33, 44, 50, 72, 98, 99, 102–109, 149, 160, 175–178, 184, 186
Conjectures, 154, 155, 157, 158, 181
Contradiction, 19–24, 28, 29, 31, 125–139 (Chap. 9), 145
Conversion, religious and moral, 53–56, 133

Culture, 51, 52, 81–83, 100, 102
Cosmology, St. Paul's, 86

Darwinism, 88
Death, 9
Death of God theology, 175
Desire, 50, 51, 57, 94–97, 100, 101, 106, 108, 109, 191, 192
Disillusionment, on cosmic goal, 185
Dogmatism, degrees of, 132, 133, 146, 147
Doubt, 146, 147, 157

Egoism, 60, 61
Empirical testing, 17–19, 24–28, 111, 146, 150–152, 157–159, 179–181
Emotivism, 43
Eschatological verification, 14, 111, 112, 117–124, 143
'Essence' of Christianity, 177
'Essence' of religion, VII, 4
Ethics. *See* Morality and religion
Evangelicalism, 5, 6, 87, 133–138, 163–165
Extending theological statements, 163–165
Evolution, 64, 88, 164, 165

Subject Index

Faith, 107, 108, 154
Fallibilism, 181
Falsification, 17, 26, 111–124 (Chap. 8), 129, 130, 135, 141–155 (Chap. 10, esp. 147), 157–159
Feelings, 78–81
Finitude, concern over, 6–11, 15, 31, 32, 35, 91–109 (Chap. 7)
Form criticism, 134
Freedom, 82
Functionalism, 71, 113
Fundamentalism, 2, 163

Gambling, religious, 120
Gestalt therapy, 33
God, in outer space, 85
God-talk, 116, 135, 169, 181
Guilt, infinite, 92, 93, 98, 106–109

Heaven, 96, 97, 107, 118, 119
Hell, 121, 122, 132
Hinduism, 6, 149, 183
Holiness Christians, 99
Humanism, 2, 3n, 9, 65, 68, 175, 186
Hybris, 98, 106
Hypocratic oath, 50
Hypocrisy, 28, 29
Hypothetical imperative, 58

Imagination, 107, 108, 155
Implosion, 33, 189
Induction, problem of, 141–155 (Chap. 10)
 problem for theism, 123, 124, 141–155 (Chap. 10), 158
Internal criticism, 126–130
Is/Ought, 58
Islam (Muslim), 5, 10, 84, 93, 149, 185n.

Jehovah's Witnesses, 37
Judaism, 5, 184

Knowing, 88, 89
Knowledge, mystics claim to, 88, 89
 prereflective, 73, 83

Language, 114
 of Scripture, 133–135
Lawgiver, heavenly, 47
Liberalism, 5, 6, 65
Linguistic philosophy, 173, 174
Lord of the Flies, 151

Magic, 10, 11
Marxism, 2, 14, 36, 37, 102, 103, 107, 108, 149, 155, 180
Meaning, VII, VIII, 114–116
 in art and dance, 159, 160
 through belonging, 188–190
 cosmic, 184–187
 crisis in, 183
 as enjoyment, 187, 188
 of life, 183–196 (Chap. 12)
 in mathematics and music, 160
 no one meaning, 196
 through orientation, 194
 through recognition, 190, 191
 through satisfaction of expectations, 191, 192
 and sense of aesthetic wholeness, 193, 194
 through sense of control, 192, 193
 through service, 195
 in theology, 157–181 (Chap. 11)
 and work, 192–194
Mennonites, 63
Metaphysics, VII, 43, 161, 162, 167, 168, 178–181

Subject Index

Might makes right, 47
Mormonism, 65, 68, 69, 126–129
Moral conventionalism, 44–53
Moral transcendence, 46–53
Morality and God, 46, 47, 54, 55, 57
Morality, motivation for, 57–59
Morality and religion, 42, 43–61 (Chap. 4)
Mysticism, 75–89 (Chap. 6), 96, 97, 173, 178, 179, 181
   behavioristic view of, 77–87
   ineffability of, 77–81
   and the inner world, 78–81

Naturalism, 36, 55, 56, 84, 85, 94, 96, 98, 103–108, 111, 114, 120, 168, 169, 176, 186
Nazis, 37, 71, 72
Neutral epistemology, myth of, 63, 64
Neo-Orthodoxy, 6
Neo-Wittgensteinians, VII, 112–117, 165
Nichtige, das, 95–97

Objective reference, 167
Objectivity, 16–18, 63–73 (Chap. 5, esp. 66), 87
Oneness, sense of, 75, 82, 183
Original sin (conflict), 95
Ontological argument, 97, 98, 142, 152, 153

Paradox, 19
Perfect Being, 92, 93, 98
Perfection, 96, 97, 106, 107
Phenomenology, VII, VIII, 4, 43, 173
Physicist, 169
Pluralistic universe, 152
Polygyny, 68, 69

Pomo Indian, on family, 189
Positivism, VII, VIII, 43, 154, 155, 164, 173, 178–180
Prediction, 147, 159
Purgatory, 119, 122
Prudence, 47, 48, 58

Quakers, 8n., 63

Rational, two meanings of, 151, 152
Rationality, 15–17
Realized eschatology, 117
Relativism,
   conceptual, 111–155 (Chaps. 8–10, esp. 112–117)
   epistemological, 125, 126, 137–139, 144
   ethical, 43–53, 114
   religious, 100, 101
Religion,
   cause of meaninglessness, 187
   cognitive dimension, 13–29 (Chap. 2), 91, 141–155 (Chap. 10, esp. 149)
   definition of, 1–11 (Chap. 1)
   dimensions of, 11
   as divisive, 38–40
   education, 63–73 (Chap. 5)
   emotional dimension of, 31–42 (Chap. 3)
   exclusiveness of, 5, 6
   the ideal, 4, 5, 8
   moral dimension of, 42, 43–61 (Chap. 4)
   preliminary definition of, 13
   response definition of, 13–29 (Chap. 2), 136
   rising expectations of, 99–104, 106–109

Subject Index

Religion (*continued*)
  in state schools, 63–73 (Chap. 5)
  three kinds of definitions of, 6, 12
Religion of the Republic, 37, 40–42, 46, 53, 63–73 (Chap. 5)
Religious liberty, 40, 41
Rising expectations of religion, 99–104, 106–109
Rituals, 32, 34, 37, 80, 112, 115, 135, 160, 166, 167
Roman Catholics, 23, 68, 121, 194
Romantic passion, 56
Russian Revolution, 36, 37

Salvation, 14, 100–102, 104, 114, 148
Science, 3, 15, 26, 26n., 27, 28, 111, 135, 145, 148, 149, 158
Science and religion, 148, 149
Scientific 'method', 146
Scripture, authority of, 134–138
  language of, 133–135
Secularity, 46, 71, 72
Significant others, 55, 56
Socialism, 14
Society, as protector and creator, 53, 54
Sociology of religion, 113, 114
Southern Baptists and divorce, 136–139
Spiritual laws, 170
Statements, theological, 160, 161
Stimuli, 83, 84
Stoicism, 185, 186
Supernatural beings, 1, 2, 158
Supernaturalism, 1, 2, 178
'Symbolic realism', 114, 115, 175, 176

Theism, 168, 169
Theological system, 166
  as cultural reality, 165, 167
  change in, 161
  transitional, 175–177
Theology and morality, 43, 44
Theory, as cultural reality, 165–167
Tragedy, ultimate, 104, 105
Trance, 76
Transcendent Lawgiver, 46, 47
Transcendent values, 185
Transforming one 'language game' into another, 171, 172
Transitional theology, 175–177
Translating from one 'language game' to another, 169–173
Trinity, 162

Unitarians, 39, 65
United States Supreme Court, 41, 42, 45, 68, 69
Universalism, 31, 94, 132, 132n.
Utilitarianism, 58

Value and values, 2, 3, 175
Verificationism, 26, 111–124 (Chap. 8), 141, 164
Vienna Circle. *See* positivism; verificationism
Volkish movement, 37

Wheaton College, 133
Witches, John Wesley's view on, 163
Wittgenstein, VII

Zeus-like God, 176

Religion and Reason

Method and Theory in the Study and Interpretation of Religion

1. *Category Formation and the History of Religions*
   by Robert D. Baird. 1971, XII + 178 pages. ISBN: 90-279-6889-6
2. *Western Religion*
   A Country by Country Sociological Inquiry
   by Hans Mol (editor). 1972, 642 pages. ISBN: 90-279-7004-1

3 + 4. *Classical Approaches to the Study of Religion*
   Aims, Methods and Theories of Research
   by Jacques Waardenburg
   Vol. 1: Introduction and Anthology. 1973, XIV + 742 pages
   Vol. 2: Bibliography. 1974, VIII + 332 pages
   ISBN: 90-279-7226-8/90-279-7971-5

5. *Religion as Anxiety and Tranquillity*
   An Essay in Comparative Phenomenology of the Spirit
   by J. G. Arapura. 1972, VIII + 146 pages. ISBN: 90-279-7180-3
6. *The Cardinal Meaning*
   Essays in Comparative Hermeneutics: Buddhism and Christianity
   by Michael Pye & Robert Morgan (editors). 1973, 204 pages
   ISBN: 90-279-7728-1
7. *Logique et Religion*
   L'Atomisme logique de L. Wittgenstein et la possibilité des propositions religieuses. Including 'Logic and Religion', a shortened and adapted English version of the text
   by Jacques Poulain. 1973, 228 pages. ISBN: 90-279-7284-2
8. *Religion, Culture and Methodology*
   Papers of the Groningen Working-group for the Study of Fundamental Problems and Methods of Science of Religion
   by Th. van Baaren & H. J. W. Drijvers (editors). 1973, 172 pages
   ISBN: 90-279-7249-4
9. *Religion in Primitive Cultures*
   A Study in Ethnophilosophy
   by Wilhelm Dupré. 1975, X + 356 pages. ISBN: 90-279-7531-0
10. *Christologies and Cultures*
    Toward a Typology of Religious Worldviews
    by George Rupp. 1974, XIV + 270 pages. ISBN: 90-279-7641-4

FUNDERBURG LIBRARY
MANCHESTER COLLEGE

200.1
B266s